D1546728

The Poems of Lincoln Kirstein

An Eakins Press Book

The Poems of Lincoln Kirstein

ATHENEUM / NEW YORK

Author's Note

This book of fragments is neither documentation nor autobiog-
raphy. With the exception of well-known public figures, whose
deeds are now matters of history, all characters (and not the least
those speaking in the first person) are contrived composites, drawn
more from imagination than actual experience. Any similarity in
the use of names or physical attributes of people living or dead
is accidental.

For their work in the preparation of this book the author wishes
especially to thank Harry Ford, Edward Mendelson, Jane Emerson,
Edward Bigelow, Robert Cornfield, Leslie Katz, and Ballet Society.

Designed by Howard I. Gralla
Composed in Monotype Gill Sans by Michael & Winifred Bixler
Paper by Mohawk Paper Mills
Printed and bound by Halliday Lithograph

LCC 86–073016
ISBN 0–689–11923–2

Foreword   Once, I hoped to be a professional portrait-painter, but had no gift. I never aimed "to be a poet." I liked to write verse; this was always play with no pretension. Whatever counts for "sensibility," or sensitivity to personal emotion, did not occupy me. I was attached to history in its passage and as I passed through it. Failing as dramatist or screen-writer, light-verse served instead, with its game enhanced by rhythm, rhyme and metric. It's only fair to thank my masters, although all debts are obvious.

Two to whom I most often turn are Gerard Manley Hopkins and Rudyard Kipling, for sound and sense. I love to read masses of poetry; most of it is of no use when I come to type. As for a borrowed frame for current events I owe most to Valery Larbaud, Cavafy and John Betjeman. I have strived most to imitate Heinrich Heine and Gavin Ewart. Poets in the past that mean most to me are, (in translation), Horace, Martial and Juvenal; then Pope, Byron and Hardy. As for the present, Pound, Eliot and Auden.

L.K.
January 1, 1987

Poems of a Patriot

Rhymes of a Pfc.

World War I

Stateside

Germany

Poems of a Patriot 1955–1985

Ballads: Urban & Suburban

FOR GAVIN EWART

Odi profanum vulgus et arceo;
favete linguis: carmina non prius
audita Musarum sacerdos
virginibus puerisque canto.

Hate profane vulgar and ward off;
favour with tongues: songs not before
heard of the Muses the priest
to virgins and boys I sing.

Horace: Odes: III I (*trans.*: G. E.)

Urban

Sunny Jim

Busy, busy: 6 A.M.,—and so,—on:
    Olympia De Luxe Dinerette.
Patsy's in by 5; Steve and Spike since dawn.
    Ten regulars by 7, all set,
        crowding their cabin.

The usual: orange-juice: "One large Oh-Jay,"
    pressed fresh, squeezed outa no can;
solid vitamins, one last witching way
    rich orchards solace wan urban man.
        Sun-Kist. Delicious.

Spiros, Stavros; they're cousins,—(Spike & Steve);
    their greasy-spoon; maybe not too clean,—
(clean enough), tho' the food's first-rate, so we've
    made it ours. Greek-American cuisine;
        one waiter: Sunny Jim.

Spread flat, daily news fogs its blurred fable.
    Coffee, fresh-brewed, sizzling eggs on fry. Meanwhile,
threading tight tables, Jim's quite able
    to wigwag menus by thumb or smile
        to Patsy's hot kitchen.

No new news. Same old shit. Murder, rape. War.
    We'd best read Jim's sunburned pelt,
bronzed skull, shaved neck, while outside, trucks roar,
    sirens scream. Fire! Fire! Inside, we've felt
        Jim's easeful presence.

Animal aura, cool amidst flurries,—
    Smokey Bear in clean jeans. Former cowboy?
Sand-hog? Lumber-jack? Past him, Patsy scurries
    fast, her full tray. Goosey fingers annoy:
        "Jim! Keep your paws off!"

Jim who? What's his story? Stone-deaf, stone-dumb,
    blanked at birth, stern genetics have won
with no sorrow. He's serene, just stays mum
    on sums terrene or lunar. Save one:
        strong carnal ardor.

On our way to pay, thump his hunky back.
　　Charged ergs and dynes might skim off on us.
We break fast on his hush, his soundless lack
　　of noisy voicing: snarl, bark, snit, fuss,—
　　　　his seamless quiet.

Distilling bluff health, sap pulped from fresh fruit,
　　Jim's daemons beg not nor churlishly boast.
He dishes side-orders of silence, mute
　　modest feastlets: Oh-Jay, whole-grain toast.
　　　　Eggs, sunny-side. Up.

Pavilions

Mr. I. Solomon, the cloak-and-suit merchant
　　pets his ulcerated colon
hospitalized towards surgery. Not urgent.
　　Gambles, has lots to go on.
Eighty-three,—heart? Scarred, yes. Cardiac strain.
　　Despite the year's peak heat,
primed for what's promised as peril and pain;—
　　these he shall meet.

Thirteenth floor of a semi-private pavilion,—
　　TV, broth, air-conditioned bed,
estimates his estate, near six million,
　　(before taxes), and not dead
yet. Junior partners bivouac in the hall;
　　he sniffs sullen waiting.
Limp, clutched dahlias adorn their forced daily call,
　　hoping, hating

his arrant survival, snide flouting of fate.
　　His pulse ticks from spite. Oh why can't
his crack surgeons proceed? Damn it! Operate!
　　Then three sons can plan, their old plant
in dire disrepair. Too long they've been bossed
　　by a despot's frail gut.
Business bad. They know he knows what they've lost.
　　God! Let 'em cut!

Years, long years, heirs dreamed of the day he would die,—
　　he, alone, who created it,
their famed trade-name. He only could sell or buy;
　　years, the years he's dictated it.
His marketing, old-fashioned. They'll move in,
　　snap it all up-to-date,—
fresh patterns, smarter style. But,—when to begin?
　　Coöperate,

you old fool! Old . . . Fool? At dusk, he's half-willing,
　　then greed chills a misanthrope.
A pride of partners poised for the killing
　　won't smother haggard filial hope
verging on murder. Pinch-fist appetite
　　stifles their vigil's yawn.
Patience, men! He consents by purblind drugged night;
　　reneges at dawn.

His surgeons assess this appalling old goat,
　　in escrow their pliant skill;
tho' all real risk of amendment's remote,
　　diagnostic norms of life-span should kill.
No reprieve. Tensile suave eager fingers
　　itch for the classic slice.
Say the word! On pursed lips a faint *No* lingers.
　　Go slides on ice.

I. Solomon, die! Actuarially, you're through.
　　All factors concur, unendowed
by debts paid. The thrice twisted tripes of a Jew
　　sue off-chances for sorely proud
flesh. A prophet of risk wagers he'll win,—
　　so: "O.K. Operate . . . "
Enter lawyers, on cue to comfort his kin.
　　Internes palpate

his taut tum. They shave its plump pot in no haste.
　　Youths stroke grizzled hatchments of age
judging their mean office as something near waste,
　　scant craft even at their stage
of hacking cadavers. Strict on Seven
　　whet the scalpel's trim rite.

A spine's supine trance,—impervious heaven,—
        grant a fair fight!

Heirs figure their futures as due dividend;
        black-bordered for tomorrow's *Times*:
"In Memory of Father, Founder & Friend
        We Close Friday." Dollars, dimes
thrown away but well-spent. Rest in peace,
        Israel Solomon.
A pine box rough-planed, awaits no promised release.
        He may hang on . . .

He hangs on. All guaranteed auguries fail.
        Survivance confounds aghast eyes.
Sigmoid flexed, twin stout lungs Inhale. They exhale
        breath for blood; immortal surprise.
On cross-stitched scar-tissue this soul shall erect
        more sanguine pavilions
to succor sinners born and unborn. Project
        six, cool millions.

Buttons

This 50-ish frump, rat's-nest brittle hair
        frittered by stress;
scalp daily raked to amend one last damsel flare
        of auburn tress,
dredges her glazed phiz for a lost lass whose vestal stare
        frays on loneliness.

Her sphere is her father's,— PAPA,—long-gone,
        ever admired,
by whom all males must be scaled,—each sinning son,—
        most, those desired.
Her trifling joys, false fear, few friends; ungraced, alone
        and little required,—

save a good-address, port-wine, a change of frocks,
    PAPA's old comb;
his twin decanters secured by locks:
    limbo, but *home*,
immune from storm, rapine, turmoil. Delight shocks
    misery's monochrome.

Dangles, near her steel-door, the elevator;
    it's midget cell
manned. She'd only dwell where a strong operator
    obeyed her bell.
Rash intruder, beware! Ruffian, sex-fiend, predator:
    JOE stands sentinel.

JOSÉ, elevator-boy, dear handy-man,—
    feline; polite;
26, 4 kids; East-Harlem Porto-Rican.
    JOE's on, all-night.
August heat; outa-whack a vintage electric-fan.
    Her room is "a sight."

So is she. A stained torn crimson kimono
    loops spongy waist.
JOSÉ sighs: "*Pobra vieja*! Mahn! She no-for-Joe!"
    Furtive distaste
fixes her fan; (nothing wrong). JOE's manners won't show
    flirtation or haste.

His breast brags brilliant brass gleaming vibrant sexiness
    which she should shun.
Button-up! She x-rays a bronze chest in undress
    tanned by hot sun,—
Kitten eye-lashes, moustache. Ah, dare she caress
    1 button, undone?

Men. Animals all. All naughty-boys, (darlings, too),
    which includes JOE,
cute, sweaty, soft-spoken,—and one of the few
    exceptions, so
she twists a brass-button on a macho tabu
    cocoa mulatto.

Faultless in faith to a fierce ghostly Father,
       now deceived; dead,—
she fondles JOE's bobble. Buttons, he's found a bother,
       opts for, instead
quick zippers which oft-times may foul, tho' they're rather
       faster to shed.

Contact! She did it! Hey, JOE! You'd better look-out!
       Gorged veins surge in
loins where forbearance pumps up despair.
       Dirty-dreams merge in
fever. JOE merits reproof. And it's not fair.
       A mature virgin

screams: "Take your *hands* off! You beast!" Love's capsized ache.
       Raw nightmares haunt
glimmers of rape. He's refused: ("Fer Chrize-sake,
       whadja she *want?*")
Want? She wants you, JOE. She might say: "JOE, let's make
       woo, JOE!" But she can't.

JOSÉ, maleness mocked, fast flees past her chained-door.
       Ill-starred urchin,
stammers unluck: "JOE; he's sorreee. *Pardon, por favor . . .* "
       Hurt, masculine,
he shambles adieu to a starved bankrupt whore
       of a might-have-been.

Buz. Buzz. Buzzzz. Buttons below. Some furious son,
       relentlessly,
insists to be served. 4 floors in crossed unison
       buzzzz loud, off-key.
JOE, maybe lost, hopes his job isn't gone;
       begs landlord's mercy.

She, safe & sound, locked tight, hears his gates slam.
       Her hair aswirl
drains DADDY's decanters. Soon, she won't give a damn.
       Unkind furies curl
in her mirror,—PAPA, JOE; honor: "Oh, my! Am
       I *that* sorta girl?"

Gender Bender

"I'd be, simply, ME. But, who am I?" prays one MAX
    who'll end wed, in a Lesbian Commune.
His Pilgrim's Progress of drastic drama lacks
naught of this world's welter; in its weird way, smacks
    of black-magic: a guy, pruned to a goon.

Male, or female? Simple. After-all, Sex is Fact.
After,—all . . . To commence, what's exactly exact?

Maxy just hit 17,—randy, rangey, but lost;
    over-well-read, apparently burly.
Crams confusion compounded. Whatever the cost
trails trauma to where, on a Pacific Coast,
    amazons "play-house," more gaunt than girly.

Mazeltov! First-born of MARTHA and MORTIMER KOHN,—
proclaimed, maimed, disclaimed by his very-own,

but adored by BELLE, a smart junior sister.
    MAX, none of your run of Bar-Mitzvah'd boys,
master of math, chess, acrostics, ev'ry brain-twister,
(tho' sullen at *schul*),—agnostic, resister.
    No boy-friends. Girls? Oh yes. All of 'em *goys.*

Hence, we may at-once with full-confidence say,
MAX was *not,* in the last sense of a word: gay.

Glum, morose, sad,—a saturnine soul, since what
    his taste favors is female. He dreads *men,*—
one man most, his G-d fearing sire whose tribes rough-cut
quivering skin; who damps all endearment but
    awe of 1 god; his Commandments. Those 10.

"If there's a god, Pop,—how come Pharaoh? Hitler? See!
No god exists. If one does, show him to *ME!*"

Lithe & limber the lash while sister BELLE cries:
    "Pop! Stop it! Don't whip him!" Hard on his hide
the lank flail of ELOHIM. Pop's strap satisfies
ADONAI. As for Momma, G-d knows she tries
    to be fair. At floggings, stands to 1 side.

Muses MAX: "Am I wrong, or just sick in the head?
Can one live with one's folks who wish me dead?

"Am I smarter or plain dumber than others?
    Why mayn't I date Sue Smythe or Christine Jones?
Why's the sole cooking *kosher*, 1 kitchen,—my mother's?
If G-d's so great why Evil ever smothers
    most Good?" Arid brooding breeds in bruised bones.

Archetypes of atavistic legates of Zion,—
of SPINOZA, MARX, FREUD, EINSTEIN: MAX, a true scion,—

proscribed. G-d's antique norms abnormal in him.
    "If He cared, I'd be cured." Intuition
sets Reason to rest. Feel my way. Sense is whim.
In the locker-room of a YMHA gym:
    SHAITAN's kabbalist apparition!

Good-grass is got for less than 10 silver-dollars:
speed, crack, smack, unshackle Talmudic scholars.

"From depths have I cried. Now am I *high*. By free-will
    an Other I'll be. G-d! Grant me a sign!"
Neurotic Nirvana; skag and speed will distill
G-d's awful intent until it must fulfill
    a shorn, self-offered lamb; prone, on His shrine.

"BELLE,—you're too young. Mind-blowing's not yet for you."
His secrets are shared. Spared, she'll tell on him, too.

For Good or Ill he's betrayed. Envy's scary;
    blood-rivalries harry siblings to hell.
Pop clobbers his hop-head; "Dope-fiend! You fucking fairy,
you're no more my son. Now get-out, or marry!"
    Gets, out. No adieux from MOMMA or BELLE.

Sister's saved. Brother's banished from Heaven
on his own to starve, steal or get really even.

MAX's maleness malign,—how may he outwit it?
    A conjured re-birth? a G-d damned fraud.

Genesis; genetics. Where's He who hath writ it,
who made me this mess. How could Goodness permit it?
    Yet a Girl may emerge, by the Grace of G-d.

Physick's retrieval, a transvestite swap;
laser-beams' ray or fine surgery's lop?

Pop-science xeroxes computer-results:
    cardiac-bypass, transplants like spare-parts;
stand-by kidneys, silicone implants. MAX consults
expert cranks of chemo-therapic cults,
    gimmicks bionic,—for no mere faint-hearts.

Hormones, the big-help. Estrogen, by degrees
bolsters lipid tissue: cheeks, hips. Mammaries.

Minors are wards, thank G-d, of a sane welfare-state,
    snatched from quacks by compassionate cover:
"This case is not clear," prudent medics dictate:
"His spectrum wants balance in masculine weight,—
    some surrogate spouse or normal lover."

"But, DOC! That's just it! I never will marry!"
Small choice. Marriage, or a monastery.

Golden Gates ope on "concerned" foster-homes.
    12 self-widowed wives vote, bidding MAX in
where gender's vain rainbow pales to monochromes.
Their novice, given-head by rogue chromosomes
    is hired by a dozen dizzy women.

Brutal males banned, babes here are brought still to breast.
MAX gains hearth-and-home, a baby-sitting paid guest.

Diagnosis, prognosis; mania wills its Way
    tho' defused at first by rejection.
Maverick patients endure irritating delay,
but sage consultations only postpone the day
    for maximal genital resection.

Hard by, a moist wimp of dear disposition
consents to MAX's piteous proposition.

Thus with a groom-proxy, MAX is finally heading
    towards slicing by supercilious surgeons.
MAXINE, kid! Hi! BELLE flies West for the wedding.
Cropped bride and moist groom eschew ritual bedding.
    BELLE, as an aspirant Saphist, burgeons.

Scar-tissue indurates Super-ego and Id.
G-d shed His Peace on MAXINE's ballsy bid.

Palms

"Shouldna lef' my latch off . . . ," but Mercy! She did;
    later wonders, she'd no idea where he coulda hid.
Ran out, for one second. He musta slip up a back stair.
    Lets herself back, in. He's there. Just standing there!

Loft-space. Nice silk-screened drapes, north-light.
    An artist, she lives alone; always it's been alright.
He lurches into her room; stops, staggering still;
    hard to tell when a man's mad or physically ill.

"Whatzit you *want?*" Could be some sorta weirdo joke.
    He strops a bare razor, smiles. Requests a smoke.
Luckies. Well, here they are. Cold steel in his thick paw
    gleams. Stubby clubbed thumbs, mean grey stubbly jaw.

Her skylight's neatly repaired. Twin polymer palms
    in squat pots once graced a choir's Palm Sunday psalms.
Vacuumed weekly, Good Friday's sacramental booty,
    lustral souvenirs salvaged here for beauty's duty.

"Nice pad you got," he blurts. "'Cept them Christless plants.
    Plastic! Eccch!" Whets his blade on seat of torn pants
to improve two Christlessly ugly shapes, synthetic, insincere.
    Her soul seeks solace in nausea. He fixes to shear

fraudulent frond from each spongy phony frond.
      Plunging towards shock she taps catatonic despond.
'Don't frustrate or reject me,' states his stern stance.
      Briskly slashes palmettes and numbs her mute trance.

'What next? Will he simplify me?' throbs her emetic fright:
      'Is my left-hand too long? I only paint with my right.'
Waits. "How about,—a drink?" "Yup . . . Thanks." Mania's drained him dry.
      Bolting her spilled gin, he dooms her not, at once, to die.

"You're a cool chick," flaying her tattered neoprene tree.
      "You're . . . not so bad . . . yourself." More gin. Christ, save me.
He will. Her move. She moves. Another drink. He gulps, gags badly.
      She, aching, respite from God knows what, squints sadly.

"Doan wanna hurt you or nothin'." (Doubt not his health,—
      ever!) "I know I needa shave . . . " Let us share the wealth
'till now unjustly divided. His spare sententious sword
      reassigns what is unrighteously granted. Such is His Word

as given,—to rectify all grievous vile hideous shapes:
      "Them putrid palms! Jeest! An' you sewed them nice drapes.
How-come this plastic crap?" Mayhem is masculine.
      Erase error, or die. The Truth, only, is genuine.

Five fingers fist a steelshod threat; its glint. Its flick.
      He may mean what he says. He loves beauty. He's sick.
(Once palms were scattered like hers here I hack.)
      Crops one last stricken spray. His hand lets drop, slack.

(Why folks keep killing each other? Where will it all end?
      Make Love, not War. This babe here; she might be a friend.
Alleluia! Palm-branches hailed that first Eastertide.
      He who faltered, stumbled, ever be my guide.)

Failure can win. Weakness wreaks strength. Death succumbs.
      Doomsday's postponed. Fury leaks from unbloodied thumbs.
Lust lights a cigarette. The foul weed her breath redeems.
      A blue haze censes the nightmare she's dreamed she dreams.

Lucky! She, he, inhale luck. Thanks, Lord, so much.
    Where do we go from here? Her swift kick in his stuffed crotch?
No. He's quite harmless. Maybe,—he didna mean a thing
    so, he and she, hosannas may, in their way, sing.

Alleluia. He, rising or risen, palm or plastic, truth or lie,—
    should one mind what miracle next transpires? Two try
for love to surge and purge. What she and he actually did
    was be careless about getting her, his, or their, kid.

Bum & Banker

Flesh-&-Blood play for pennies
    coin chucked by one-&-all.
Skin-&-bones in tatters
    sprawl on a park's stone wall.
Rock its bed, filth its rags;
    lips sigh no sense or sound.
Scare-crow claw, sightless stare
    in bankruptcy abound.

Anxious, we may query:
    Cash,—what's the going-rates?
Across the street an answer
    in traffic irks, but waits.
Red-lights gleam green for him;
    he spots the mendicant
whose bones budge not a jot,
    nor famished, plead a want.

Its double deals on Wall Street
    bull-markets make him glad.
Rage bull's-eyed on beggary
    on bad days drive him mad.
The Big-Board's slump at noon,
    its test of pitch-&-toss,
bloats his risks. Win-or-lose,
    the-bottom-line is loss.

Weak balance in soft-selling
        won't lessen strain-&-stress.
Glaring at the derelict
        he curses unsuccess.
Augury betrayed him;
        now shrewd prestigious scores
mock a con-man's conscience
        the usury of whores.

This sleep-walking broker
        strides across his street;
relentless, stalks a prey:
        two sibling deadbeats meet.
Fiasco kindles frenzy;
        he tugs at his billfold,
yanking crushed crisp paper
        still bankable for gold.

Bones bagged on a parapet
        grab from their trance to snare
yield of frantic lotteries
        let slip as ruin's share.
Claws clutch god-sent handouts;
        paws clench clean tidy bills
as if arrears in payment
        its gross default fulfills.

Transaction consummated
        seals luck without a word,
countersigned in ciphers
        clinch an insane absurd.
No bonus gratitude,
        no overdraft of thanks;
forfeit and foreclosure,
        blame solid savings-banks.

Minus-or-plus, the banker
        earned opulent shortfall.
Plus-or-minus nets its naught,
        a bum upon a wall.

False Alarm

Flesh also is heir
    to this finale,—
matter of wear and tear.
    Shall he
just stare at his stool, brown-black, bloody?
    Costive, sharp minor-pain,
ill-omened data, or should he
    call Doctor at once,—or, then again
wait?
    No. Make up your mind, for already
it may be too-late.

Rocked, shaken, shocked, tense,—
    (could be false-alarm).
Still, scanning plain evidence
    no harm
in ringing that office. Fearsome Nurse
    couldn't be cooler. Voice
sanguine, sour, cruel. So now he feels worse
    and prays not to know, tho' has he the choice?
Sure.
    Flushed down the drain, what remains? Steady:
his temperature.

Impatient patient;
    the waiting-room wait.
Dread. Dolor. Life-banishment.
    Curt fate
lurks on-call, clad as a nurse with a card:
    Your name, date, address, phones
to file "New," before "Old" or "Discard."
    Back-numbers, tattered overtones,—
LIFE,
    TIME, WORLD-REPORT, print-outs of evil.
Chaos. Crime. The knife.

"Well? Whatsa matter?"
    "You, Doc, tell me."
Outside, streets chatter, wheels clatter.
    "Let's see."
Diagnostic disdain. We will show
    by dry lip or damp skin,
pallid, unsound, how we're programmed to go.
    No hero, the male mannequin.
Hell
    is ill-health, my doctor, the devil
who wills me unwell.

He leers: "Spread your cheeks."
    Split old butt, slackened hams:
clinical, finical peeks.
    Doc damns
hunks exposed for partition or freezing.
    Time's level reduction,
mincemeat for chopper, nor easing
    an adamant septic obstruction.
My
    trussed torso stripped raw of armor or grit
may still mollify

atrocious answers.
    His sardonic boast:
"Hemorrhoids just ain't cancers."
    A ghost
reclaimed, resurrected, ungrateful,
    nude, faltering, forlorn
endures his jocose, sneering, hateful
    omniscence. Yet we've won! We're reborn!
Why?
    Perhaps to challenge Doc with more wit
the next time I die.

Grifter

"Not by bread alone . . . " Bucky knows well one needs more
    than subsistence sheer.
Some shameless untamed bare-faced shyster ancestor,—
    bold buccaneer

repossesses his loins. Shy lad struts the sly man,
    pirate updated.
Of cozenage, craft, chicane the brash veteran,
    activated

by high-hopes, toss-ups, sure-fire. Cute but hare-brained, Buck
    navigates on nerve;
sleight-of-hand sets its sights by the devil's-own luck.
    Firm muscles swerve

where no mind curves a course. Trumped-up truth is sincere,
    a blunt conscience numb;
free-booter, free-loader, engineers to steer clear
    by rule of thumb

from shallow lee shoals. Buck's genteel knavery
    plights fancy's surplus,—
pots o'gold, magic-carpets. His glib, savory
    spiel could wreck us.

Buck just checks-in. Buttering slim fingers with greed
    he's been to the banks.
Granite vaults rarely honor the criminal breed
    of madcap cranks.

Daft? Maybe not. Deviant, romantic, artist,—
    even gifted.
Now, he'll option "*Charmaine*." If salvaged, the smartest
    graft yet grifted.

Launched in bootleg Twenties for a Perth Amboy duke
    on luxury lines,
drydocked forty years, her discovery a fluke
    which Buck defines

as pure destiny's due. Why won't brokers agree
    to blank-check his dreams?
He can't con the cash, and as for mean chinchy me,
    perish such schemes.

"But, look! We've shook out the bugs!" June to September
    cruise Long Island Sound,—
off-shore casino, boatel. Then from November,—
    merry-go-round,—

year around: Tampa, the Keys, on to Bimini Bay,—
    (Treasure Island crew,—
ex-Marines) past the dumb Coast Guard, (fast getaway!)
    All could come true,

if dense churlish investors lent more than their ears.
    Buck might launch "*Charmaine*"
on thrilling flash-bulb send-offs from derelict piers
    and cheap champagne,

breasting past tall Manhattan, a viable wreck,
    the bones of a boat
hosting seaborne fiestas, a whore-house on spec,—
    if it can float.

Sail on, "*Charmaine*." Slick glossy brochures estimate
    minimal repairs:
new screws, plumbing, pumps, turbines. Then each bold messmate
    can cop fair shares

of rum, fun, gold doubloons from post-menopause trips,
    rich widows shanghaied;
hunky hustlers, roulette,—cunning plausible gyps,
    Buck, the tour-guide,

chef, confidante, steward; artless juggler of books.
    He'll steer nip-and-tuck,
yet, counting coin squirreled by tax-shelter crooks,
    can one grudge Buck?

His credo: caprice. His charter: "I'm free as the breeze.
    Great gods smooth my sea."

They well may,—rogue, huckster, thief, quick-silver Hermes,
    spry Mercury.

But sticky nights fall, jobs flop, tricks fail. Bucky's sad.
    The god hides its face.
Will brave fortune now fade? Neither wise nor quite mad,
    Buck ducks disgrace,

to bounce back on slim gimmicks the shoreside of jail.
    He'll raise treasure-ships,
lend-lease blue-films to Ghana, peyote by mail,
    cut-rate hot-tips.

He inflames grey days with rococo promotions
    and festoons routine.
Thus, in time of small art, stale verse, filthy oceans,
    Buck decks the scene.

Micky's Dick

New York Post, February 27, 1985:

Dear Abby:
    I'm writing in reference to "On Fire,"
the woman who punched her neighbor (41) in the
mouth after learning that she had seduced her 15-
year-old son. Then the tramp said, "He's no boy,
he's a man; and with a little practice he'll be as good
as his father." Meanwhile, the assaulter went to her
priest, who advised her to apologize and offer to pay
for repairing her bridgework, etc. etc. . . .

I.

Neighbors in a mid-town, low-income tower,
    both strangers, Mary Wood to Anna Stone:
Mary on the 16th floor; four floors lower,
    Annie, a registered-nurse, lived alone.

Sales-person in a small boutique, Ms. Wood,
    divorced; her son, Michael, (disturbed; fifteen);
Anne, widowed, forty, but still looking-good
    pursued a calm effectual routine.

Neighbors by chance a mere three weeks, they then
    best-friends became. Lone women all need one
as sanctioned offset to the yoke of men
    of whom Mary owns three; Annie, just now, none.

Mary counts Ed, the husband who has quit her,
    Micky, their son; a current boy-friend,—Harry.
Ed's good as dead. Mick, the child grown bitter,
    wonders why his mother cared to marry.

On blank weekends, shut-ins from city frost,—
    beer, snacks, intimate girl-talk best-friends share.
Harry, his TV on, bids Mick: "Get lost!"
    Mike lacks the luck of tender-loving-care.

Along comes June, vacations in the air.
    Mary gets two weeks, Harry, his own two.
But wait; can they abandon Micky there
    alone? Kind of a lousy thing to do. . . .

But wait. As guardian who better than
    best-friend and registered-nurse, Annie Stone?
With her, the kid, not yet an adult can
    be cared for by a perfect chaperone.

II.

School's out! Mick's loose. An urban vacation
    brings fun to freedom. Experience starts.
The urgent pulse of sudden maturation
    boasts broad expansion of his private parts.

June nights steam sweat. Slow, soapy showers
    drench warm to rinse him clean and very cool.
His random strokes fuse prepotent powers
    to firmly exercise a supple tool.

The tube engorged stiffens its spongy tissue,
    brain and blood in tense connection
releasing dense matter of dire issue
    in a semi-permanent erection.

Cold-shower turned off, Micky's in the pink;
    cucumber-cool muscle fires him firm and fresh.
But, something's sorta funny. His damn dink,—
    bone-hard, proud, obstinate in arrant flesh.

Minutes pass slow. An hour. This ain't joking!
    A stubborn rod abides, stern, fierce and hot.
Unlike aftermaths of prior stroking
    limpness as a result this now is not.

Caught at it, Mick's mom warned him (so often!):
    "You keep this up, your palms will sprout thick hair.
Brains turn to butter!" Should it not soften,
    will it drop off to leave him nothing there?

A moral problem? No. Then it's not sin?
    No. Mild satyriasis; nothing worse,
if treated simply by good medicine.
    By whom better than a registered-nurse?

Anne's through her job; the duty's 8 till 4.
    After shopping for Micky's evening-meal
she hears him whimper through his bathroom-door.
    He needs her help. Her help is their big deal.

III.

Mary and Harry enjoy a great vacation,
    two weeks in Florida, not quite enough.
Back one night sooner than expectation
    catch Mike on Annie, blissful in the buff.

Mary's shock, fury, outrage! Can she name it?
    Harry, all smiles, finds Mike in splendid shape.
She, beside herself, can only blame it
    on that bitch, Annie. *Statutory rape!*

Laws label Michael an hapless minor,
    though youth's compulsion cancels any law.
But Mary socks Anne a smashing shiner
    and shatters bridgework in her lower jaw.

Annie sues in feckless litigation.
    Mary begs pardon from her parish-priest.
Father O'Rourke withholds mitigation;
    raw indignation moves him not the least:

"My daughter, listen. Where here lies the sin?
    Of you three, who sustains a lasting hurt?
Tax we Dame Nature when her claims begin?"
    (Mick taught and tempted by a real expert.)

"You dwell in sin, unmarried to your man.
    Kindless, you savaged her, your best-of-friends.
You chose her, Mick's appropriate guardian.
    Now, my daughter, you must make full amends."

Amends? Cash? Dental-fees plus legal cost?
    Harry's good-sense cuts all that crap. And so,
Mike splits from the 16th floor. Little lost,
    slips to the 12th, four floors below.

Look, Ma! I'm Dancing!
for Frank Ohman

Stage-struck as a girl, Doreen's a pudgy old bag,
    ex-hoofer, veteran chorine,
yearning to goose or grope tall, short, young or any-old, men.
    At forty, she's had it, slow to go, can't quit the scene,
        still aching for dressing-room noise,
        one-night-stands, divine chorus-boys.
        Bud, her darling, dares destiny's choice:
Baseball? No. Tap? No. Classic-ballet! He's put down, a fag.

She twirled on 'till she managed to manacle Joe,—
    engineer with a curt career
ran off his rails. Stroke. Bud, the kid, a spry sprig at ten,
    (Joe's sole sprout), faced two further fathers to fear,
      a brace of brutes she would find fun.
      Half-orphaned, a sly foster-son
      sniffed two horny males he must shun,—
Doreen, his ideal; dancing, his dream: tip-top, tappy-toe.

Ray, (Dad No. 2) falls on two brats at life's school. Their play,
    "Doctor,"—a game. Nymphet next door,
under her porch peeps at privately publicized parts.
    Ray paddles the pair. She weeps pints. Bud's butt stays sore
      a week from the caning he caught.
      Ray cools off but Buddy stays hot
      for babes and ballet. Doreen's forgot
kids grow, up. He's sweet, but no child jives it like Ray.

Ray's old jeep spills his skull on a skid. Enter Roy,
    her third. He growls : "No *man* can DANCE!"
Bud hides his vice with athletic stealth. Performing Arts,
    ball-game or ballet, blaze on skilled elegance.
      Doreen's fire melts Roy by degrees,
      down-draining him plumb to his lees,—
      a wino. So-long, Roy. Now she's
scared she's been deserted since a Good Lord inserts Buddy Boy

in an army. He's drafted. No call to sham queer.
    Dances! Despite Inspections, sweats
through rifle-range, K.P., shit-details. His secret P.T.,
    (Physical-Training) is *barre*-work (by night). Gets
      iron ankles, steel thews, rubber heels.
      After each clandestine stint feels
      great! To brothers-in-arms reveals
his strange aim. Some blink but absolve a straight musketeer.

Discharged, grown, up. Doreen still needs men. "Son, I'm so weak!"
    Yup. Joe, Ray, Roy. Gone. So here's Bud.
And so BIG! Hooked on early habit they agree to agree:
    twin-beds, hot-plate, tiny john; lease signed in blood.

Room-mates? Sorta. Clamped to one purse,
TV-package-dinners; a lot worse,
close-contact's calamitous curse:
nag. Peck. Fuss. Home-sweet-home, crowded, comfortless. Bleak.

For life long lost she still lusts: twirly-whirl, tippy-tap.
Classic-ballet holds Buddy tight
tempering tendons 10-fold, the Dance his supernal state;
Doreen, nightmare and nurse. A classmates' delight
he hurls girls with his easy slick
firm potent toss, no simple trick,—
sky-high. Mother says she feels sick:
"I'm *not* jealous, Bud, only not very well . . . " Pure, crap,

sprung from "Cellular-Science," a "spiritual-aid,"
emetic, distasteful diet:
bean-curd, liquid-protein, glucose. Is she room-mate,
mistress or wife? Name it. Buddy won't buy it.
So she swoons to fix him by fright.
Outraged, he strides into wet night,
back by dawn, drenched. "Oh Christ, alright,
Mom. You win . . . " Until next time, tomorrow, waylaid

by drastic pretense. Her heart? Her what? God, alone, knows.
"Don't leave me alone . . . " Her big-act.
Alone? Joe, Ray, Roy. Bud. Sighs, sobs, suicide-hints.
Bud, with Doctor (aside), attends to fierce fact:
"Son, that woman's strong as a horse.
You two sorta need a divorce."
Glutton desire minds no remorse.
Boy, you choose. Your guts, her greed. Your balls, her need. Who owes

what to whom? Mirrors blaze evidence: "I'm so *right!*"
beams a changeling unchained. His glass
a dance-doubling lens, glares sovereign truth. Yon pert prince,
a dancer adroit, romps. It's all come to pass.
His virtuosic tradition,
hours locked to 5th-position
are served by selfless submission.
Swift metrical motion ignites footlight and spotlight.

Dance promotes counterpoint. *Grand-jetés* float him free
    of flat floors. He banks on his *barre*,
his turn-out is trim. Suave *pliés* launch sky-rocket jumps.
    His prance is the pounce of a twinkle-toed star.
        High-style, finesse, genial charm,
        nice smile, nimble limb, strong forearm
        dim any shy partner's alarm.
Ballerinas fly and glide, hoisted by mastery.

Stern practice whittled his sprints. Perfection's a thirst;
    good dancers fuse fire in girt loins,
duets their true test. As cavalier, grace deals him trumps.
    Conscious craft is uncoiled as he crisply coins
        speed from space. This victor, apt, proud,
        pleases both Press and the Big-Crowd.
        Applause! Curtain-calls! Cheers! Bud's wowed
his world,—elastic, electric. Very well rehearsed.

Skater

"Artist"? Perhaps. Second-bested by "art"
    does he rate,—
dare-devil or dancer? No paltry thing
    to skate
loping low on stiff ice chilled black to wing
    by bland elegance.
Gimlet-spins blur the crest clean of his swing,
    kissing-cousin to dance. But,—does he "dance"?

Fleet of feet, he packs all the knack it needs
    a gymnast
to bond honed blades to bone, full-tilt to chase
    a fast
florid script, blue-steel streaking keen to trace
    scrawls stroked on scarred frost.
Swiftness whips crisp tracks on curved space,—
    its surface cross-hatched, not carved nor embossed.

The handicap: man-made ice, its cut rut.
    He's bemused,—
this waltzing serene,—is it art, craft or sport?
    Unused
to idle distinctions which only thwart
    adequate answers.
Careering big rinks, he still skims short
    of the ambit, the grandeur of dancers.

None to blame. One more headlong in motion
    than slack thought,
drifting on doubt with no solemn illusion,
    he's sought
transcendence, an old willful delusion.
    Launched on nonchalance
perfection darts past expert execution,—
    a free range, no restraint in performance.

A sculptured resilience is dancing;
    clamped to skates
slick surfaces crimp him. Glossy flooring
    dictates
stubborn over-glazed slicing, a boring
    metric repeated:
cramped contrasts,—glide, twist, slide, the same soaring.
    Easy on ice, skaters seem cheated.

Yet with dapper fierce startling finales
    the skater
hears arenas roaring his champion name.
    Later,
who'll rank a show greater, art, craft or game?
    A charmer enchants
by wit, poise, hazard conquered. Thus fame
    crowns his stunts,—strength or style. Dance or no dance.

Suburban

Bar & Grille

Well, they'll meet,—
at the plea of paid counsel on neutral ground,—
   "Ye Olde Ship's Lantern Bar & Grille."
She arrives, late as usual. There he's slouched, looming,
confident, stonily passive, mute, fuming;
   furious, with no fund of good-will.

Can any
brief shabby fix, humane or legal, be found?
   She acts as if they're still married,
nor will he trouble to rise. She smiles, at the least.
His scowl assigns her a seat to no fine feast;
   a fist-fight, with every blow parried.

The first round:
quick liquor. Martini or bloody-mary?
   Now no pleasant cordial nor heart-warming cocktail
for this night it's no banquet that they shall enjoy.
It's who packs the punch to recapture their boy.
   His ploy, muscle; her's smooth blackmail.

Keeping it
close as she can to their customary:
   "Martoolies?" she coyly implores.
"Bloody-maries!" Ice-cube eyes: "This is *my* dinner!"
She feints; holds fire: "Why, Bill. You *do* look thinner,"
   sparring, side-stepping, paying old scores.

Dalliance
cuts no ice. He tears at the tattered menu.
   Waitress waits, a blank referee.
"Onion-soup. Sauerbraten." Pause. "Chocolate parfait."
"And the lady?" "*Same.*" This round, his, all the way.
   Slow start. Any bets? We'll wait and see.

"How's Billy?"
Man! His flesh and blood in the coils of this shrew!
   In steams onion-soup. Cheese, or not?
He snaps "No cheese." "And the lady?" She lisps: "Cheese, please."
O.K. Cheese. Waitress scorns two bruisers who freeze,
   chilling toothsome broth she's brought in, hot,—

which gets them
nowhere. She ducks. Now can his footwork trip hers?
        "Billy's *fine* . . . He sends you . . . his love . . . "
Oh, he does, does he. Socko! Her cool may yet melt
him. "Billy's just fine." A foul, below the belt.
        His gut? No, his heart, inches above.

        "That young man's
gotta grow up! He's wasting his time. What's worse,
        you're turning him into a case!"
"I am not." "Oh yes you are!" Soup is nutritious
if gastric-juice flows. Bile, gall, distill vicious
        gas. One might catch ptomaine in this place.

        "Listen, Bill.
He's only thirteen. Give the poor child a chance.
        He's a very sensitive kid.
Let him develop his own personality."
Aw, doan try an' pull that ole crap on me,—
        slugs hard on a missed rabbit-punch bid.

        Bread and salt,
both eschewed; an end to savory romance.
        Famished, both aim at swift slaughter.
His high hopes for an heir are welter-weight lofty;
he'll maul his cub tough from bones of a softy.
        A manchild's his due, no dim daughter.

        This killer
bludgeons the breath of the she once his good wife,
        now fed up to her ears with him.
"Shut your mouth! Billy's *mine*. I came here to be *nice!*"
From her womb summons metal which won't suffice.
        She stalls, to haul him out on a limb,

        there lop him
off. Will he let her? The story of their life,
        two blunt lives, embroiling a son
ripe for expert objective attention,
incipient trauma too serious to mention
        and the bills haven't even begun.

Their waitress
can't help listening as two voices grate shrill,
    duet of a cannibal pair:
how can people in public carry on this way?
Tepid beef, gelid sauce; twin thawing parfaits.
    Seething, frost-bitten, they sit. And stare.

    Deadlocks can't
last. Something's gotta give. Caught-short, she feels ill.
    Empty, a tummy turns. She's sick.
She flees. Knockout. Surprised by such evident haste
he sniffs cold broken orts. To eliminate waste
    cleans his plates, then hers. Lick upon lick.

Western

Suburb of suburbs, Haugatuck here; leached its land,—
        late-fossil stage,
a "young" nation's archaic era; on every hand
        arthritic age.
"Colonial" relics; ecological signs read
        THE SCOTTS LIVE HERE
in a barn rehashed as a ranch-house for settlers whose dry seed
        stocks this frontier.

THE SCOTTS: Burton, Shirley, twin daughters;—a no-neck thing.
        Both girls quite bright,
Mary's engaged, Beth's at Bryn Mawr, but for the least sibling,—
        young Burt's not right.
Past the age of consent, soiled, hebephrenic, plump, bald,—
        bruin forlorn.
Conception, gestation normal, yet maturity mauled
        Burt Scott's first-born.

They've hired Great Doctors, world-famed specialists. The whole lot
        guessed as they could
but traced neither gene, germ or moral. What's been misbegot
        plods a parched wood.

Forest preëmpted: ragweed, poison-ivy, black birch;
        stripped top-soil base.
Its harvest,—cut-worm, gypsy-moth. Crows shadow his search.
        Out-patient case.

Burt Jr. mushes towards town, post-office, liquor-store,—
        pan-handling troll
howling hit-tunes and commercials from current folklore,
        his daily stroll.
Bull-dozers sheared thorn and vine; murdered skunks, moles, raccoons,
        woodchucks, rabbits
exiled from their roosts; those left, scared by pied-piper tunes,—
        Burt's bad habits,

his slobber, his slump. At "Lunch Box" he'll spy five cow-hands;
        cosmetic tan,
worn blue-jeans, smug, clean. Placid delinquents swill standard-brands.
        Shun Caliban.
(Why can't they corral him at home; hog-tie mental-ills?
        He's pissed his pants.)
Kids claim their café, quaff no-cal, cokes. Jovial juveniles
        blank Burt's advance.

This outlaw begs of his betters one comfortless word;
        he'd join their tribe,—
sheriffs who, on maverick or moron, ride a hard herd.
        Burt's brought his bribe,
beats them all to the draw. Here's a skunk, his kill, a stiff
        bull-dozers slew,
flushed from a freshly flayed field, his earnest of skill. Its whiff
        blots the air blue.

Burt, punch-drunk outlaw, a Bronc-Busting Villain, now ropes
        his "Last-Chance" Bar;
slings a furry hunk on its slab. The Lone Ranger lopes
        up! Good Guys star!
Sheriff, a Hero, our postman, makes his posse's arrest,
        a steer's lassoed.
Bad Guy Bites The Dust. Cowboys, Indians play Wild West:
        suburban mood.

Meanwhile, Back At The Ranch, where the Burt Scotts nullify
        noonday's nightmare,—
Junior's overdue. They guess an idiot's alibi,
        bored by despair.

D. O. A.

Dead-On-Arrival. Facts follow
    dogging dubious dawn.
        Nobody's guess,—so, through flat stodgy hours
        courage cowers.
We're solid, alive. He's hollow.
    Sleepless, I stuff his hulk with a yawn,
sampling flesh cooled for keeps; gape, cough. Swallow.

How did it all start to stop here?
    Haste makes waste. Why haste?
        Reckless, he swerved a cursory career,
        careless to steer
towards a rubber-sheet puddling guts. Fear
    stacks morgues, its savor a tart foretaste
of what's in store for statelier biers,—

our own. Shallow fellow; he drank.
    Loss? Life. Wear & tear.
        Ivy League alumni couldn't care less
        for his distress.
Heartless, behold him, breathless and thank
    God who, so far, hasn't plugged us where
snapped steering-wheels pin adults point-blank.

This sad sack I'd not really known,—
    no friend, by a mile.
        Sometimes we'd shy-off at gas-pump or drug-store.
        Old sophomore,
brass-buttoned, bow-tied, now skinned to his bone,
    modeling mens'-wear latest flash style;
lip, eyeball once wet, drained cold to dry stone.

Parkways at night. Sleet and iced rain.
    All are well-advised,
        bright luminoid script: SLIPPERY WHEN WET.
        He could read yet
sloshed, glum, bleary-eyed, overwork-strain,
    strong liquor aged smooth (as advertised),
drained a super de luxe lush scatterbrain.

Wind-shield wiper's trim tick-tock-tick.
    Half-shut underpass
        stubbed a glib gambler's bet. Bat outa hell,
        he drove quite well
sober; zonked,—zombie, lost lunatic.
    His Jaguar, its tiger-tanked gas,
(bragged double-page spreads), spikes a thunderbolt kick.

"Does anyone know," cops query,
    "who this wise-guy is?"
        I fill in two names, a blurry address;
        am billed witness.
Strangers in life, blood writes we might marry.
    Leaves no survivors he could claim his.
So what. Next dirty job: mop-up. Bury.

Clutter of wives, litter of kids
    through the post-war years:
        problems. Drugs. A.-A. Divorce. Who screwed who?
        Offspring withdrew.
Big, in public-relations. Then, the skids,—
    "brilliant" but "unstable." Success hears
it's lost a last fat account; no new bids.

While he was smug, swagger, street-smart and rude,
    we'd little to say,—
        supine,—ferments to a near cry of kin,—
        but genuine
his massacred marrow's mean plenitude:
    ten toes in two socks yanked on yesterday,
half-nylon, half-wool; half silly, half lewd.

His accounts written-off, dirt-cheap death,
   as oft sermonized.
      Hype, intrinsic to fame's nitty-gritty;
      more's the pity
he took small stock in big-bargains of breath.
   Corporate-image, gloss merchandised,
gone to grass. Grass? Man is as the Psalmist saith.

Gear-Shift
for Eric Holwerda

For oiled analogies, service-stations offer much;—
watch Eric, teenage tickler of the sticky clutch,
   a chassis-tuning sophist. His simple view
      pairs piston-slap, a cylinder's chipped block
      with fractured vertebrae or neural shock;
   gas as veinous blood; tendons, cam or screw.

Such jejune metaphors enchant junior scholars
shy of great data. Deftness deals him dollars.
   He makes more than teachers who confuse him,
      an epoch's drop-out. On duty night and day,
      his toil less labor than complacent play,—
   though now, plugged manifolds may less amuse him.

Constant or transient patients, giddy stock-car freaks
lug him their buggies,—odd jobs, brass-bound antiques,
   foreign, domestic, beat-up, in poor condition,
      imploring prognosis of conked connection,
      fast-flush, thrown-rod, hot-spot correction:
   cardiac murmur, infarcted ignition.

To heal these once made magic. Sleek metal fierce in grease
slaked stress in total transfer, steadfast past caprice,—
   combustion's alchemy a marvel. Its melding
      stung flame to rank perfume, health sublime in grime,
      luscious sweat rinsed clean of crankcase slime.
   Jalopies wooed the warrant of his welding.

He glows, a male live-wire magneto: poles, shaft, core.
His brawn frisks rust and rot; clip or shim restore
 tension to wan expansion, wide contraction.
  Knack bred cool cunning; supple grip on tools
  tantalized amateurs, among whom fools
 flock, lured as much, by chemical attraction.

Among whom, this Porsche, its lush, lurid gleam
a florid trophy. An hot-rod's stream-lined dream
 chugs up at dusk, braggart of bumptious sheen.
  Under gloss and glint, our expert taps the leak,—
  surging cross-fired voltage, rotors weak.
 Asthenic spark-plugs wound a singed machine.

"Man,—you got problems . . . " Nor shall these soon repair.
Grins Porsche: "Have I, ever . . . " Feckless, debonair,
 owner and ailing engine hard as nails,—
  flab at the center. Eric frisks for fever,
  palpates a skulking cankered lever,
 rods bent or broiled; valve cracked. Float-level fails.

Dogged by debt, a fraud would rid him of his wreck.
In hock to demons, spook or human, his breakneck
 flights floor-boarded freeways in rash gleeful haste.
  Eric pinpoints a circuit's taut, blocked relay;
  testing rear-end torque, driveline delay,—
 blood-pressure, spasm, stroke: high-speed's fatty waste.

Whence came this physic? Self-starter's knowledge,
piston and pump a truant student's college
 disowning his tribe's priggish expectation,
  this diplomat of bit, wrench, spanner
  drills special science to a medic's manner,
 disarming ergs' and amps' prim oscillation.

Now, stale mechanic serfdom fags him slack.
A Porsche's frittered havoc mocks its sullen lack
 of jounce. Day fades. Get lost; wiping off a smear,
  slams shut its hood: "Let's leave her 'till tomorrow."
  Boredom bids botched business borrow
 from shared malaise twin bottles of chilled beer.

Silence is sipped. A wastrel's toy is done for.
It's trifler, still willful, figures fast: "What fun for
    us to settle-down,—and run a spare-parts' shop."
        Eric could use a smart-ass wheeler-dealer.
        A rascal lubricates his fatuous feeler:
    "Boy! You take my bus! We'll count it towards a swap . . . "

Ripe plunder's surplus! Wheels, tanks, pumps: limbs, lungs, hearts.
Cannibals of junk gnaw on fragged butchered parts,
    scrap-metal salvaged from surfeit's trashy slag.
        Yet similes from Eric's tinkerings dim.
        His mind, a mechanism slurred, determines him.
    Tired steel can bend like lead; jaded routine's a drag.

Headstrong in scope, Eric's artless absolute
contrived a motor metric. Ball-bearing slid to suit
    frames more fragile than muscles' native recoil.
        Now, less beguiled, he brakes on thin conceit,
        steers off fond whimsy more fanciful than neat;
    Sight and sense spurt stronger stuff than gas or oil.

Batteries charge. Coils clear. His generator jolts
transforming void dynamics into sparking volts.
    Raw hot extra impulse converts to cool.
        Eric's romantic rigged hypotheses
        his gridlock splits. A gangway future frees.
    Shock absorbed, gears shift: "*I'm going back to school!*"

"Dear Abby"

My 16th birthday. I went through this alone.
Kids grow up fast. I didn't want it known.
I should have asked someone, like my own Dad.
They're divorced. Mom says his advice is bad.
She thinks I'm an angel. I let her down, she'd die.
I couldn't dream up what didn't sound like a lie.
If I told "Jerry," he'd pretend it wasn't true,
so I didn't tell him. I was scared what he'd do.

Tough luck. The doctor I went to knew his stuff.
In bed a week, "with a bad cold!" It's rough.
Jerry, (not his name), left, for the time being.
I guess he guessed. We wouldn't be seeing
each other. Things pass even when you're in pain.
It wasn't like we'd never see each other again.

Sometimes somethings seem really unreal:—
coincidence, how strange things happen. You feel
you're part of a plot, in it only to lose.
My 18th birthday. Door-bell rings. Could I refuse
to let him in? Jerry! He stands there, stock-still
like he never seen me before. He says: "Hi." I will
never forget: "Is your Mom in?" Like she's his *date!*
I said nothing. Sometime they just call it fate.

I played dumb. A one night-stand of course I knew
he and Mom had more than once. Now I see it's a few
more than one-nights. He and Mom! I'd sure try
not to think what happened. I couldn't laugh or cry.
I really didn't want to let Mom ever know
I knew Jerry before. It's like fate. Anyways, so
he says: "We're thinking of getting married." Like *that!*
It seemed just a joke. It's not. Jerry! That rat!

Can you imagine. I never imagined Mom dreamed
he's more than my teen-age boy-friend. He seemed
my age. He's older by maybe more than ten years.
Ten years younger than Mom. If she had any fears
about my being a virgin, she never said. After all
who's so pure before marriage? This was late Fall;
they thought of being married in early Spring.
I hoped time would take care of this whole thing.

A week before Easter I'm alone in the house.
Jerry kept his key. I didn't hear him. That louse
slips in. His two hands start to pull me down.
I said: "Cut it, Jerry, you great big clown;
who the hell you think you are?" Jerry's strong.
I got scared. I was expecting this all along.
I'm not weak. I can kick. He got it in the nuts.
This hurts a man; more sensitive than his guts.

He gets mad, pulls himself together. He said:
"You say one word to your Mom, I kill you dead."

Then I get mad. I had no time to be afraid.
Any reaction to his advances was quite delayed.
Not entirely unexpected way for Jerry to act,
but shocked me when what I expected was a fact.
I did some thinking. So what about his threat?
Would he kill me? I knew him pretty well. I bet
he wouldn't. But what's the next thing for me?
Him and Mom. If they did marry, where'd I be?

I said nothing. Let nature take its course:
But I had thoughts, some of them, rather coarse.
Like sharing Jerry with Mom. Maybe a normal thing
in a realistic way. Accept facts; try managing.
Jerry is still attractive. Mom is fond of me.
This sort of thinking was, of course, too free.

You can't help thinking more than just one way,
and take what fate brings. I spent a whole day
trying to figure this out. So that very night
I decided I would sit right down and write
that columnist on the New York POST,—what to do.
I thought her advice sensible. Actually I knew
someone she gave advice to as who to marry.
So here goes:
          "Dear Abby, I met this fellow named Jerry,
(not his real name), and he and my Mom. . . .

Team

Dad led his team: Grandma, Bob, Beth; their twins.
     "*Play Ball!*" His whole life,—
          but he's gone with his old-pro's know-how.
     Now, acting-captain, his wife
incurs gross violations,
out-of-bounds, off-limits violations,
          so his team's on the bench.
No one wins.

There's still a same race to be lost or won.
    A mother-in-law
        tries to tackle her team just on trust.
    Alas,—it's only Grandma,
never near scoring the same,
who couldn't quite learn the name of the game,
        with no nose for fair-play
nor much fun.

She lives near by, too darn close, with old Tex,
    her blind labrador.
        Bob and Beth both work their alternate shifts:
    his, eight P.M. until four
A.M.; hers nine A.M. to five.
Add one hour more, to and from, to drive,—
        when's there any time left,—
well, for sex?

Beth needs rest. Dozing by day, Bob does too.
    Their twins, a neat pair
        to be washed, fed, packed off on-time to school,—
    the heart of problems they share.
With Grandma's increased leisure
who can forbid her the fervent pleasure
        of these surprise visits,—
nor would you.

Surprise-visits,—the old team's new headache,
    Grandma's sole delight.
        Never warnings by phone; she'll just drop-by,—
    once the old-folks' rite or right.
With Dad, these were brief. He died.
She, brimming with love, quite unoccupied,
        arrives; stays the whole day.
Hard to take.

Also Tex, her labrador; blind, ill-bred.
    When Beth seeks some rest,
        Tex whines, snaps, whimpers at spectre or mouse,
    noisy, noisome, a pest.

Arsenic dosing his dish,
still on-hold, is Beth's criminal wish,
        but her kids love the beast,
so it's fed.

First time in months, Bob and Beth breathe alone,—
    the twins off with friends,—
        long-promised a fun-holiday.
    Grandma drops-by, with Tex, spends
the whole lost day, together,
Beth in fury, and glorious weather.
        Why, oh why couldn't she
at least, phone!

At home, shit hits the fan, later:
    "Bob, this is The End!
        She's your mother I know; you can't be blamed.
    I'm your wife,—I hope, your friend.
There's a chance we'll still make it.
Bob, I can't stand it. Bob, I can't take it.
        It's either she or me.
I hate her."

May one foretell or forgive Man made meek?
    Bob, a single son,
        chose a spouse of more supple mettle.
    Once she seemed the perfect one;
Beth was: "Just like my mother . . ."
When it transpired she was quite another,
        storms stirred. A weary girl
might soon freak.

Bob's split in two. The twins must inherit:
    "Beth, dear. Try. Be kind."
        Now it's no more a question of kindness;
    more urgent, a peace of mind.
Bob's brain-washed? No. He's afraid;
terror or error, his manhood's mislaid
        or lost. He's quick to grin
and bear it.

"It's her unannounced-visits,—is it not?
        Yet,—if we knew ahead,
                Grandma fears then we somehow must bother.
        And, yes; since Granddaddy's dead
she worries only for us.
If she'd call ahead, we'd only just fuss.
                She adores our old team."
So, they're bought.

Life jogs on. Time's left to play, but grows late.
        May penance or prayer,
                the stern sport of saints, help this team win?
        All standing-rules are unfair.
We need drastic devices,
uncommon common-sense; sacrifices.
                Bob and Beth may strike-out
on home-plate.

Billy-Boy

With both eyes open I've married again;
                took on Fred's son.
Trying to love the lad tho's he's a pain
                is not much fun.
He's not a "bad" boy,—a type for the times.
                A trial, too.
His problems, neurotic, not actual crimes.
                We'll see him through.

No question whether I want to or not.
                Fred adores Bill.
Always he worries where or when he ought
                to turn up. Still,
marriage to one man's enough. Now I find
                I've married two
reaching the point where I'm losing my mind.
                What can we do?

Billy's too thin for a child of fifteen.
        Wool sweaters won't work:
"Too jerky a *statement* for me to be seen
        in. I'm no jerk!"
No sleep. Dirty T-shirts. Cold fast-food trash.
        Wants his own car,
slams 'round on skate-boards. So far, no crash.
        He drinks,—that bar

open-all-night for rich under-age kids.
        His 6-speed bike,
cowboy in traffic, a killer on skids.
        I wonder like
I'm his own mother with him my real son.
        I can't blame Fred
but it's a nightmare when one day someone
        calls: "Billy's dead."

We're stay-at-home parents and we don't want
        to waste-time, spend
wee-hours down-town spots, fly any-old jaunt
        on chic week-ends,—
Aspen, Sun Valley. Not just the expense:
        Billy's a must.
Fred's basic genes, plus my own common-sense,
        parental-trust

can somehow count. Then so far, Billy's luck.
        We've faith in Youth;
I say it's character. Fred calls it pluck,
        but, as for Truth,
can we believe: "I'm just staying tonight
        at Jack's, (or John's)"?
Then staggers in bloody, weeping, a sight
        for winter dawns.

Or, as he swears, with Jo-Anne, in Old Lyme,
        (folks in Palm Springs);
or high-school dance, or "just a quiet time
        at John's" which rings

false. Or, preparing for chemistry-tests,
        (free-basing cocaine
in a locked lab?) Yes, we're a pair of pests,
        creeps, who complain:

"It's-for-your-own-good." We check at odd hours
        to catch him out.
Mutual rapport's not so hot. It sours
        should we risk doubt.
Can we require notes from Jo-Anne's father,
        or chaperone,
verify his lies? No. We'd far rather
        leave it alone.

Bill despises disease: cancer, strep-throat,
        slipped-disc, acne.
"Wimps *wish* to be sick!" His sole antidote:
        blunt bravery.
No looks before leaps; no whip, leash nor cage
        bless Bill to save
a skin from relish or rapture, the rage
        he's cursed to crave.

Pride prophesies teen-age tragedy,—
        Bill's rôle supreme:
Huck Finn, Hem, Superman, Dirty-Harry,
        Rambo, his dream!
Sweet, sly, shrewd, alibis slip easily.
        Everyone's charmed.
His threat or boast: "No one can mess with me!"
        And he wins, unharmed.

No lesson or license, operates fast;
        flies, without wings.
Smokes, sniffs, snorts, injects, absorbs, yet can last
        over-dosings.
Total-control, minus forethought or fear:
        "The world's my show."
Raw holes in patched jeans, a stud in his ear:
        "I know! *I KNOW!*"

Great gamblers don't lose by using their brain.
        What's next? A shrink?
My smarts and Fred's, all our answers in vain:
        Billy won't *think!*
It grows cold. Who can handle this better?
        The boy is lost.
I wish he'd wear a heavier sweater.
        Our fingers crossed.

Last Name First

He's a bland, manly boy,
his sponsor's pride-and-joy,
    "Mother's" staunch sweetheart,
    a good lad,—stubborn, smart,
although "Father's" not his dad;
this mother he's never had.
    A present plight brands him bastard upstart.

Now topping five-foot-ten,
straw-blond as born, but then
    ash-blond at seventeen;
    soft-mannered, fair-spoken, keen,
stumbles on what it's all about
finding too absurdly out
    whom is he not; whom he has never been.

Birth-certificates swear
no Why, but Who, When, Where
    a one gets truly born.
    Twin witnesses signed, sealed, sworn
attesting names writ not quite the same
as an heir's fair legal name
    who from a crib untimely may be torn.

Which happened once to Dick
whom foe and friend dub "Rick,"
    by "Dad" as "Richard's" known;
    "Ticky-Tavy" his "mother's" loan,
but with the local draft-board filed
crudely as "an un-named male child,"
    now, despite early pruning, rears full-grown.

From physical-exam
runs home: "Mom, Dad, who am
    I?" Why doubt? He always was
    the cute and single kin because
he's been well-kept as kith and kind.
Kinder if all had stayed as blind
    to blood-lines; verities, old rusty laws.

Legal he will not be;
sworn to steep secrecy
    eighteen dead years ago,
    next-door neighbors panicked to show
their plump prepotent pregnant child
some guileless stripling beguiled;
    a middle-class proscribed its embryo.

They shoved the brat next door,
paroled its dam, a "whore";
    shipped its sire "away."
    Shy foster-parents pay
a debt foreclosed by time,—
impotence their mortal crime,
    postponing futile future exposé.

Hence now a lurid scene
which never need have been,—
    a citizen accused
    by a boy misused:
"Who *is* my father?" Wrath's flame:
"Oh! You need a nobler name?"
    "No. My own." Long, lovingly disused.

Who am I. Who is he,
and what is he to me?
       A median man
       no less enfranchised than
some unfeigned sign pinned to his head,
begat on what foundling bed;
       no by-blow but got on a goodly plan.

Here fact juggles on air,—
a youngster hunched up where
       he munches on worry,—
       this oldster in no hurry
to adopt so rude a riddle
from chance plumb in the middle
       of bone-bare ghosts. A new-found guardian: me.

"Say,—your mother's alive,
scarcely past thirty-five,
       happily married.
       Would you now undo her, harried
by baseborn backlash doubly-crossed?"
Uncashed, uncashable cost.
       Better if such stay safely buried.

What loomed at first immense
explodes in common-sense.
       Who'll ever ask his name?
       It is all quite the same.
An heir who's self-betrayed
won't blame how he's been made;
       forgives a world its wisdom for his shame.

Blueberry Muffins

One hour from Manhattan there's a condominium neat;
Mitzi's in the kitchen slicing-up a gourmet treat.
Warmish June the weather so her menu's coolish cold:
cold-cuts, beet-&-carrot salad, plus a fancy Jello-mold.

Comes Saturday once a month her son drops by for lunch.
Today he phoned: "It's special." So luncheon's more than brunch.
Often Fred brings Tom along, his room-mate of many years.
"The boys," (both males past forty), she speaks of as "my dears."

Mitzi, an ex-math-teacher at Saint Mary's junior-high,
fears there isn't quite enough; she needs a store-bought pie.
Dad, a worldly long-haul trucker, but recently retired
is sometimes sorta puzzled by the manly son he's sired.

Dad drives Mitzi to the superette, to procure extra fare;
with fresh blueberry muffins, pie in no way can compare.
On their return sit Fred and Tom, speechless in the room;
blank, anaesthetic aura is suffused in deathly gloom.

Tommy always has a hug for Freddy's darling mother;
Dad takes Fred's pleasant chum as some sorta foster brother:
"If two guys choose to live like them, where's the f . . . g harm?"
He shoves muffins in the oven to serve them fresh and warm.

Fred bets: "Today,—they'll ask us. What can they have heard?
'Are you and Tom . . . ?' How will they say it? Christ, help with a word.
'Is Tom one? Are you one, too?' We've always been discreet . . ."
But, since there's no further problem, they pull up chairs to eat.

Mitzi muses: "It's a lack of cash, both boys are still unwed.
On visits I have noticed they just share a double bed.
I'm not narrow-minded. Any bad thoughts along this line
can certainly have little reference to any son of mine."

Dad knows this world: "So what. They really seem to care.
Mitzi's bothered by a bed. Far more than that they share.

Should they wish to bring it up, then it's O.K. by me."
Common-sense breeds wisdom; he's endured much silently.

Tom prays: "God help the ignorant, innocent and blind.
Older folks are vulnerable; to me, these have been good and kind.
When ghastly truth is out and Freddy's fate is aired,—
surely they'll not repudiate a love we all have shared."

Bless beet-&-carrot salad, cold-cuts, Jello-mold dessert.
Muffins abate avowals, but Fred feels he must blurt,—
"I gotta tell you! Tom and me . . ." Dad prompts a civil halt,
his gift of seemly grace: "Son, please just pass the salt."

Despairing, Fred is frantic: Will they never understand?
Damp eyes, dry throat, he grasps for Tommy's steady hand:
"Mom and Dad,—you've guessed I'm gay. Tom, here, isn't straight:
We're lovers!" Vows his Dad: "These muffins sure are great."

Fred pushes back his chair against the kitchen wall.
Guilt throttles stammered anguish, for he's not confessed it all.
Tears leak in flood; sobs shake a soul. An end to masquerades.
He's tongue-tied, so Tom affirms: "Fred's contracted AIDS."

Abysmal mortal stupor. Mom seeks sounds to let her speak:
"Tommy, do I hear you? Freddy's dead within a week?"
Scarcely an expert, Tom risks an amateur's grim score:
"No, Mitzi dear. A month, a year. Even, maybe,—more."

To Dad it's no big-deal, for Fred thus to turn out gay;
if that's the way he wants it, grown men have their say.
But this is deadly serious; he'd always thought Fred smart . . .
Syncope snarls an artery sustaining Mitzi's heart.

Tom commands the situation: to Dad: "Let's take a walk."
In sun outside,—salvation. Two men can try to talk.
Mitzi, a guardian-angel, breathes: "Fred, let's do dishes."
If beggars could be choosers, blueberries were wishes.

Fred's not touched a morsel: "It's not soon, Mom. Don't cry."
Three cool muffins chill a plate. He'll not starve. He'll die.

Stale bread warmed-up may be tomorrow's breakfast toast.
A triune jury, Mom, Dad, Tom, acquit their hapless ghost.

It's time to go. On Mitzi, Tom bestows a filial kiss.
A mystery. By, through, what,—has this all come to this?
Dad awards slow opulent embraces, a hug to one and all.
Arm in arm, two close friends, stride swiftly down the hall.

On The Sound

Sam Grossman, export-importer of marginal renown,
aetat three-score plus grizzled years, invades a coastal town
hight Eastport, seaside suburb, mini-vacation site
to filch time-out, day-off, mid-week, a dead routine's respite.

By Eastport on Long Island's Sound floats a marina fair.
Sleek hulls, blunt outboards, spanking sloops, ride for hire there.
Upon its salt-grained teakwood deck is docked a yare young man.
Randolph Reed Jr.'s epiderm toasts bronze-bright beach-plum tan.

Junior's no amateur. Twenty summers minus one
recap a fever-chart career intemperately begun.
Totaled three cars within twelve months; to accident is prone.
Currently uninsurable, released now on his own

recognizance. Probation. Hence, bargaining for bail
a rôle as master-mariner evades a jaunt in jail.
Grossman notes this hotshot; contracts him on the spot.
How Randy esteems Sammy is not so all-fired hot.

Junior's downy pelt and paw flaunt their velvet glow;
six-foot-one fosters fun in a bell-bottom, hip-hugger beau.
Grossman is no fashion-plate; skin is waxen dun;
its hirsute ventral area withers from want of sun.

Yet investing torpid tissue lurks a questing hectic strain;
weekly gross is writ as loss; adventure may be gain.
Caprice kicks custom. Inspired, he'll dare the deep.
Randy hauls his anchor up to gratify this creep.

Veiled sun's befogged. Wavelets lap. Wind? A foiled delight.
Sails flap. Speech lapses. They can't have shoved-off right.
Sensing frustrations of whatever sorry sort
smalltalk faking frankness is scarcely merry sport.

Junior's tentative faint grin, spry formula to please,
cozening contrivance, mocks shyness as a tease.
Arch flirtatious tricks adorn his feline boast.
More. A switch. An hireling crew converts to Grossman's host.

Gulls screech on high, careening. Soft cloudlets saunter slow.
Skimming a shoal of swifter skiffs Randy hails hallo.
Clansmen of his ilk salute, boy-breasted mermaids, too,
cap-à-pie in bra and slack, a privateer, unisex crew.

Sam, lamely apprehensive, stifles thin chagrin:
"Tell me, son,—about yourself . . ." Right-on! "How'll I begin?
Pop passed away some years ago. Mom's in real-estate."
He & she let him, the eldest child, always stay-out-late.

Grossman seethes faintly seasick: not nausea,—his sad-shape.
Marooned flotillas chide slack sail, stalled on a stale seascape.
Snob piracy snubs wizened oafs. Sam's pennon droops uncouth;
he's condemned to walk the plank of skull-and-boney youth.

Randy risks plain-dealing; his word may irk or work:
"I reckon, sir, I turn you off as an adolescent jerk."
Lips lock; he's gainsaid naught. Silence is a launch.
While skipper spins his saga, cargo pats its paunch.

"Near Inverness our hostel was kept by a dour Scot.
Northern-lights ignited; plaid comforted our cot.
Curfew missed, Jock locked us out, maugre pennies paid.
We nestled by a loch all night, me and a Bryn Mawr maid.

But, sir, you can't imagine! Back through shuttered streets,
chill above our twosome slant auroras streaked in sheets!"
Flares past Arcturus iced slim tongues in sherbet frosty air.
Lean pennants quivered firmaments of shimmering maidenhair.

At Nikko, daybreak dewdrops diamonded cypress trees.
Wood-giants had their toenails trimmed by loyal Japanese.
Rocks combed a braided waterfall. Fresh-lacquered scarlet floors
censed aromatic altars under samurai sycamores.

Alberta's uplands: free-lance, he campaigned forest-fires;
grizzly-bear and snowshoe-hare leapt stupendous pyres.
One enormous moose broke loose, antlers a blazing torch.
Randy's eyebrows sizzled in the savor of its scorch.

Sam scorns mild travelogue. No tropic virgin's breast?
No arrant confessional? Discretion,—test or jest?
This kid's history, demure, provocative,—a waste.
Disclaiming sin as arrogance, a liar vows he's chaste.

Yet subliminal compassion fumbles its guttered wick.
Randy's half-sorry for a sucker,—Sam on his furtive kick;
hung-up oldster, fortune's fool, squandered half a day,—
for forty silver dollars played the luckless stowaway.

Aimless drift daunts buccaneers spliced warily apart.
Confronting eyeballs mirror small comfort in each heart.
Rusty sunset strikes their sail. Moorings sway offshore where
low-tide ebbs on anchorage stranded shipmates share.

Weather-eyes quickened, whim as ballast weighs its cost.
Sam's scuttled wager founders, by an helmsman double-crossed.
Here's their landfall's wharf on stilts.
                                        With Randy's future gambles
callowness, nay, callousness may bungle shallow rambles.

Between the Wars

Taxi

Owns his own cab. Not that 2-ton ole Mack-truck.
    Ageless, balding, pushing 60,—
but swears he still has all the luck.

Trucks are for kids or young men. He's got him sense.
    Why knock his sef out afore his time?
Good doctor, great wife,—both Immense

when he took that recent stroke & nearly died.
    So, takes it easy. Bed by 9;
this hacking, simple. Just a joyride.

Nice guy. Wry smile. Easy does it. Hop right in.
    It's pleasant driving with this joe.
You like? He'll gab. If not, this spin

hurries no trouble. So, now; here,—let's talk.
    30-year man. In combat? Sure:
Artillery-Mules. Could they balk!

Would they! Did they! But allows them critturs war
    jus' one-way to shove guns up on
Salerno beach-head, down-coast far

as K-C-No. From Arkinsaw, he knew his mules;
    transferred to M.P.s at The Rhine.
Mules! In *Artillery?* Yup. No rules

to buck or abide by. Remembers, one-time:
    Frankfurt; big railroad bridge blocks us;
& Patton, Blood-&-Guts, or I'm

a liar! Him cussing, not loud. Not mean. Sad.
    Bridge: too low. We need them bridges.
Patton, sweating. It look bad.

Biggest gun you never saw. Bridge can't take it.
    Won't git thru. Gotta blow that bridge.
One expert knew how to make it.

Jus let air outa this fucking gun's fat tires,—
      half-out, one ole trucker's fool trick.
It squeeeezez under! Patton admires

this joe's smart savvy. Soldier, he says: cute trick.
      Says so hisef. Patton *say* that!
Moren one-way to skin a mule. We'll lick

them dumb krauts yet. Gun greases thru. Wars are over
      15 years. Joe still backs the Brass:
New Year's Eve. He's taken cover

in taxi-line; waits,—at the Mayflower Hotel.
      Ike's inside; some big-shot banquet,
inside. Joe knows his limo well,

a long, black job. Its driver played his radio
      too long; battery gone plumb-dead.
Ike comes out, climbs in. Damn car won't go.

Joe hauls his cab outa that long taxi-line;
      gooses the White House limousine.
Ike, from its rear, thumbs-up, waves V-Victory sign.

Joe still has all the luck. Few have such tricks to lend.
      War, peace, both won by nudges.
Thanks. Watch your step. Have a nice weekend.

Hustler

From the Deep-South:
                  "Fer nigras, doan care-none.
I lern meh erleh, nevah trus' a one.
Snow over Thule. Felt an enjin crack.
Sayfteh-system shot. Almos' blew mah stack.
Mah engineeh, a shif'less cullud man,
(wi' some whait-blood). He do a bes' he can.
No-gud enuf. He panick. 'Whar's ma chute?'
Man, if we ditch naow, it'd be a beaut. . . ."

2 motors flaring stoke their raucous joke;
twin fans reverse, suck up stiff acrid smoke.
Wild rampage of his all-thumbs engineer
fouling the shrouds and tackle of his gear.
Jerked the rip-cord, blunt inside the plane,
hysteria smothering cushioned insane
ballooning bubbles of raw muffling silk.

"Man! That nigra. He turn whait as milk!"

Routine disaster over Labrador,
good engines feathering, 3 outa 4,
flaming for minutes. Fried past any bet,
yet made it into Gander. Yup. No sweat.
Hairy. Scary. Though his canceled prayer
drained his confessional:
                              "I jus' doan care . . ."

Count, discount, his time clocked inside 3 years,
time-and-a-half to prove or disprove fears
he's hardly had the heart to tag. So now,—
where is he?
            In an air-corps, anyhow.

A rangy stud of 22, or -3
checks lonesome citizens professionally.
A feral night-hawk in his 2-tone shirt
leans at the bar; malignly sips the hurt
of his cropped wings. Acts wise, to let you think
he'll swap true-stories if you stand him drink.
His uniform's no-go in dawns of seedy peace;
silk-scarf's thin prink, trousers jack-knife crease,
a cut-rate dandy's sullen smiles caress
spoils of sham leisure in mean fancy-dress.

"Dumb haigh-school punks train cheapeh on the groun'.
Call 'em 'kay-dets.' It sorta make it soun'
fantastic. Oh, aneh fool kin lern him haow to fly
so long as he doan try it in a sky . . ."

Who does he think he is?
                              (Kinda laik to know,—
so long as you doan try an' tell meh so.)

Get him to bed. Lay him down hard and straight.
Test his brick belly. Weigh his perfect weight.
Go ahead. Do him. Trapped in his locked knot
he's holding onto everything he's got,
as if to make it matter.
                              Yet, to whom?

Bored, aimless, hapless, in a fetid room
first-times are wasted, over and over
for one bribed avid nerveless rover.

Luckless? No. Call it anarchy's design,
rough-weather, meager guess-work, spongy spine.
Grudged stingy auspices lurch, hit-or-miss,
a servile schedule's shallow armistice.
Spasmodic mainsprings sag. Disgruntled boys
juggle morosely with expensive toys.
Ingenious turbines in high languid speed
purr with an animal's complacent greed.
Scowling cub-tigers stir in winter-sleeps
dreaming fresh kill. They rouse, to play for keeps.

Sleep well, sergeant. It's what we've hired you to.
Our education's taken care of you.
Unheeded threats blare their stupendous taunt
of guessless menace as shall ever haunt
our hobbled hero's dubious enterprise.
No stringent crisis firms him otherwise.

Our skies are crammed with unexploded stars
colliding fainter than the furthest wars.

Hallowe'en

This stripling,—less son than mother's lover,
    his father's younger brother,
flirts with parents by those pet-names
    they reserve for intimate games.
Free he's been since first he nursed
    from most famed ills: hate, hunger, thirst.

A winsome pup, normal past all belief,
    clean of want, woe, need or grief;
let or hindrance none, for any
    might have crimped one of his many
talents. I.Q. percentage high.
    We've learned such true quotients seldom lie.

Amazing mom and dad, he scares even me.
    All Hallows Eve: mystery,—
witching-hours, ghosts. What devils
    haunt the season's noxious evils?
Three elders sup, a fourth,
    younger than sin, intrudes his worth.

Heir of time's heinous excess, wise as we,
    tries wines, smokes, quips pleasantly,
nor blinks at hints of ripened wrong.
    A grown-up's chum longs to belong
to our coherence. Let's go
    up to his well-lit studio.

Ho! What have we here? The frank pomp of death!
    Three bipeds catch on short breath.
Lo, on stained, mirror-polished floor
    a drastic dummy leaks fake gore:
corpse caparisoned in black,—
    Storm-Trooper, a dirk in his back.

Stone-dead kraut *Leutnant* in fine full fig,
    a butchered trick, one stuck pig.
Aghast at this gone gruesome sight,
    weirder than waxworks. The kid's real bright,
an artist in his own right.
    This brat hobgoblin mocks delight.

Up his steep stair to small bed-sitting room,
    cosy 'midst encircling gloom
tapers wink on a trimmed altar.
    Three full seconds, six eyes falter.
Dad's reaction? Mom's,—yes: mine?
    All genuflect before this shrine.

Praise we Saint Adolf! Many calcined Jews
    owe sanctity to thy views.
Hail,—Hitler! Praise this snotty kid;
    practical joking's not forbid.
Hitler, hail! Father, Mother,
    Bud's inheritance recover.

Creativity endowed his den.
    Bud's had help; none at first, then
mail-order houses cashed in,—
    trashed relics, all genuine:
swastikas, drear souvenirs,
    ensigns of torture's volunteers.

Side-arms,—a baleful era's rich dreck,—
    5 decades, long years to check
truth for sale, fabled renewals
    sold as a mad hero's furbished jewels.
Bud names Rommel as Robert E. Lee.
    Who's taught Bud Modern-History?

Führer's smoked icon, obdurate, smudged,
    by scholiasts timely rejudged,
now hails Hitler more clown than cruel.
    Bud's innocence worships a ghoul.
Who wants fact? Let's adore him
    who abridged much life, love and limb.

Lenient Gentiles, unobservant Jews
    shun logic lent to excuse
those equating mortal terror
    mostly as psychic error.
May smart old-timers help
    teethe a glib witless wolf-pack's whelp.

Mr. Clean

From Fort Lauderdale, Florida, I incarnate perfect-condition
     by super-conditioning. The prize, a beautiful-body.
I work on mine. It's my wholesome, mature, manly mission
     to make more perfect what is granted by God. He
lends me this gorgeous torso as luck, life and religion.

Behold my biceps, triceps, deltoids; these impeccable pecs.
     (Pecs?) Body-builders name king-size pectoral muscles.
We've sure know-how for maximum-development,—abdomens, necks,
     hoisting-weights. Press: snatch: jerk! No wrestling nor tussles
Contact-sports are Out! And, for Christ's sake, lay off the sex.

Diastatic-malt; bean-curd, figs, our fuel. I'm no carnivore.
     I don't drink. Peristalsis is chronometric but strong.
For pix in health-magazines millions of fans frankly adore
     well-oiled breast-plates of bronze. Was I wrong
acting-up, as I did, when joining the U.S. Army Air Corps?

Not Infantry, Navy, Marines. Not them. Should I waste
     supreme symmetry on dungy earth or dregs in the sea?
In fresh-air I breathe, inhale its clean hyaline taste,
     so air gets my lats (lateral obliques), and for free.
A patriot? No. I'm for me. This became plain when I faced

their needles and shots for tetanus, typhoid, yellow-fever.
     Would I let medic ghouls infect a pure blood-stream
with putrid germs sucked from sick cows? Never!
     Where were my Constitutional Rights? And, did I scream
when that Doc wished a slight tight phimosis to sever . . .

Steak! Diet disgusting. Raw, rare flesh, day on day.
     No greens organically grown; bloody beef meal on meal.
Digest? My sigmoid colon's flora just faded away.
     I lose weight. I can't sleep. So I start to feel
lousy. Depressed. Nor can I relax or just play

at dumb ball-games with any dumb meat-eating fellow,—
     nor would have Jesus, Mahatma Gandhi nor Lord Buddha.

I'm not vulgar or rude. No. I just wouldn't howl hello
    at every darn-fool, not one of whom understood a
sensitive person. Then some even swore I was yellow.

This lieutenant strolls up. I'm stationed quite decent, on-duty.
    I practice passive-resistance at rigid-attention.
He reams me out for no reason. My stance is *not* snooty.
    I'm no fag but suffer from mild-hypertension.
He's insulting. I smell his hate. He calls me a fruit. He

sights on my chin, but telegraphs a slow blow.
    I sock, in self-defense, his aquiline nose.
I'm no swish. Massive muscle is mine. I know
    where nerve-ends end. I'm up, on my toes.
He drops. Out,—his beak bent. Naturally. So

it's six-month the Stockade. Hard-labor, no less;
    time to learn self-control by keeping-the-peace.
My muscle-tone melts. By push-ups I pray. I guess
    it's dishonorable-discharge. The worst is, release
rests not on repentance. Yet I should confess

I mustn't sock guys,—even him, since also he's Thine,
    tho' it's Thy fault, Lord, too, who from Heaven above
shoved my fist in his face, since Thy power divine
    let me down, flat. So,—we're no longer in-love.
My pecs I still pet, tho' they're not Thine now. They're mine

to mould as I will. My will. My will's in deep-freeze.
    Ill-willed my bad-dreams, they congeal past midnight.
Sordid, unthinkable thoughts arouse me to tease
    filthy tempters whose tentacles coax and excite.
Push-ups are not prayers. Stiff, up from my knees

my loins lock. So,—shall I take to strong-drink;
    abandon bar-bells? Get me, God forbid,—laid?
Let myself,—go? Where? To hell. In its motherless stink
    rats gnaw my nuts. I'll pay. But who's to be paid?
The End, if ever I,—well,—start trying to think. . . .

Interview

for Peter Viereck

You've come to "interview" me. Your voice is lost.
    Your tribe? It's Tartar? Kalmuck? Kurd?
    A Mongol's mask, brow fuzzed with fur. Your word,—
    whinnied apology, in English, blurred.
Your throat's phlegm coughed, I'll count you double-crossed.

To Kiev's Grand Hotel, a slippery neutral-zone
    I've brought with me an honest pill,
    anti-biotic. So possibly it will
    help, should you risk strangers' cure or kill.
You grip my hand. You snatch the telephone.

Listen; detach it; lift framed prints off a wall
    depicting Dnieper under ice.
    Through frosty windows, Dnieper's wintry vise.
    My drug's no marvel but it may suffice.
I'll wait. You reconnoiter the entrance-hall.

Hostels in limbo screen wide eye and ear
    to monitor the guileless spy.
    Forbid is give-and-take. Wide ear, sly eye
    coerce ventriloquy. We testify,—
tense tourists both, to some expedient fear.

Thin ice cracks custom. In fraternal reach,
    goblets; vodka in a bottle.
    This elixir obliterates glottal
    cloture. Swallow briskly to unthrottle
trickles of riddles dammed by stifled speech.

What captious code is keyed? Dare we confess
    to make our valor worth a drink?
    Sympathy, empathy by wary wink.
    Two swindled agents teeter on the brink,
selling state-secrets neither may possess.

A pact is briefly honored. I remember
      the penalty in misplaced pluck:
      Canadian, half-Ukrainian: Canuck,
      an whole youth in Manitoba. Now stuck
here, for keeps, in Kiev's iron November.

Why did your father fetch so frail an heir,
      he, long-exiled, from this black-earth?
      Near Winnipeg, tall silos mocked his dearth
      of homeland; gave you life, lent him a berth.
He's dead, in Kiev. His black-soil's your snare.

Expert, you arraign me: "*Are The Rangers*
      Champions? How do The Dodgers do?"
      You mourn an Eden where a native grew.
      Hunger's a lonesome forfeit here where you
wither, starved friendless by cousin strangers.

I fail. My dull candor holds cheap such sport
      or banter, niggardly confess
      my supercilious absence of address.
      I've hurt your feelings by inept finesse.
You bid for aid but bought a blank report.

An innate sweetness tolerates the fault
      in this strained thin-skinned face-to-face.
      Your smile, the shadow of a sought embrace
      denies a moment's memory of place.
Dnieper chills any treaty. Here's a halt

on amity. What's the least worst of chance,
      home or haven? Dare one wonder?
      Sullen outside now, impending winter-thunder.
      Your lapsed passport's trivial blunder
mimics treason's harsh surly happenstance.

You've found your tongue. You thank me. So, fare well,
      yet linger. Is this thus ended?
      Reluctance smoulders, unbearably blended,
      a sad and stoic self. Here was intended
more of a share of secrets we could sell.

I risk no dangerous comparison,—
    politics, prevailing tension,
     our stiff censored utterance, nor mention
     the core of hurt corrupting a dimension
of brotherhood. This orphaned sorry son,

cursed prodigal, resumes his mask of Tartar.
    Alas, he'll assume I blame him
     for misery. Mute eloquence won't shame him
     with self-pity. What vast schisms name him:
"Hooligan"? Traitor? Felon, foe? No. Martyr.

Eisenstein
for Jay Leyda

Relicts of famous men
survive their fate and fame;
re-run careers over & over again.
Pupils, apprentices gather, one after another
to staff a working-partnership, wherein discover,
a new husband, teacher, lover and brother
under the graced auspice of a valid name:

Thus,—SERGEI EISENSTEIN,
slain fifteen years still breathes
in a two-room flat by Borodino Bridge,
stuck in an ant-heap bee-hive, just built, now falling apart,
holding relics of cinematic art
warmed in late October by brain and heart
of a diabetic widow. She bequeathes

to an apt succession
intention: sketch, plan, note,
folio on filed portfolio, labeled, neat,
garnered in an anonymous domestic modest shrine
crammed with memoirs and memories. Some of these are mine.
In the early-Thirties I loved Eisenstein,
tho' one I met then seems infinitely more remote

than her same *Sergei*, here,
grinning in snapshot's breath,—
poster, icon, puppet, ex-voto, dance-mask,—
souvenirs: Paris, Harlem, Tehuantepec, Leningrad,—
splinters from a True-Cross one needn't imagine sad
estimating their sum, influence he's since had.
Yet pondering a precocious death

it strains avid belief
in spans of fulsome life.
Let's wonder on great inexpendable
leveled by the odd hasty harvest of an urgent gift:
Mozart, Keats, Seurat,—specimens of what cosmic thrift?
But from such sterile metaphysic we'll shift
to a plenteous sequel with an ill wIfe

hoarding vital tokens,
boxed abounding, preserved
towards "State-Publication,"—6 volumes, and more.
Here, this very afternoon, official-committee will sit,
comprising 8 able experts, each of whom edit
their bit: scenario, photo-script, speech. It
looks like, ultimately, Sergei is well-served.

This is he surely owed.
Image, act, fact,—he made
firm for an age when much art's improvised decor.
He snatched stern changeless high-signs from a far or near past,
radiant once, then dimmed, forging each anew to last,
ephemeral "flickers" fired like bronze re-cast:
ice, shield, lance. Horse-hoof, skull. Stair, bridge. Barricade.

Lo,—here's his grandest plan
roughed-out in short-hand glee:
1st shooting-charts for "The Battle on the Ice":
chilled metal; snow-ballet: spear, sword, locked flexible defense,
cuirass, hauberk, helm, frame on frame, carved in cold snow, dense.
On black-ice a steel freeze, burnished magnificence,
stoic and statuesque: *ALEXSANDR NEVSKY!*

And,—peons chained in sun,
shaded, black; ponchos: white.
Aztec eyelids echoing obsidian,
carved in his camera: eyeball, nostril. Skin taut. Hot breath.
Stone skulls, heaped: bone-skull, sugar-skull; copper glossed sheath
of nerves. Lashed stallions pounding fresh flesh to death.
Two boys, half-buried. Alive. Their dumb-ox fright.

¡QUE VIVA MEJICO!
Murder. Catastrophe.
Months of work, miles of film, miserable. Waste.
His best, butchered by cheap crooks, like a meat-animal;
its stupendous uncut footage rotten, in cans. All
proposals drained to treacherous loss. To fall
on such bad-luck! What's left, to salvage. Or see. . . .

EISENSTEIN, in New York,—
morose, one nervous-wreck.
The film. Ruin. Facing: failure. A thing: worse.
Return to Moscow. What *They* would think. What *They* will say.
No thing brought back. Sergei, two lieutenants: ALEXANDROV, TISSÉ,
pack in my Ford to Brooklyn. All the way,—
mumbling one word, only one: *Tehuantepec.* . . .

That site: Tehuantepec;
what Mexico had cost.
Manhattan Bridge loomed like Borodinsky Most,—
to a Sand-Street speak-easy. Jumping. Loud sailors. Blue smoke.
One drunk, teddy-bear, crewcut gob cracks a shitty joke
at me, guide to three Bolshies; takes a poke
at Eisenstein. The American Navy lost.

Naval-tactics he knew:
ARMED CRUISER PATIOMKIN.
Witness: mutinous men at wormy chow:
tarpaulin hauled over cropped skulls, huddled; to be shot.
He panned down on animal-horror, its central rot.
In Sand Street, he gentles a gross infant whose hot
rotgut cools. Sailor melts into a sweet grin,

swears eternal-friendship.
Price? One more bathtub-gin.
Sergei Mikhailovitch strokes his Mohawk tuft;
sailor snores. Thru dawn-mist Manhattan, we roll back to bed
for 3 hours. At the dock, in his cabin, he then said:
"I'll see you soon." Soon. 30 years,—15, dead.
So, in Moscow, now,—I begin:

Pera Atasheva,
Kolya, Valya,—fast friends
to this me. We stoke our eternal-flame.
She deals-out sturgeon-aspic, crystallized cranberries; cake,
while we mine his bullion, each with some personal stake.
Phenomenal effort must she always make,—
all the more trying, since it all depends,—

injected insulin:
"Don't mention. Bloody-bore . . ."
Soon enough, eats a bit. Gets happy. Stays bright.
Tells stories. Asks for mine, half-invented as these must be.
It's been 30 years. Vanity augments memory,
though this speaks truth enough to foster-sons. Honestly, he
remains, a very reliable councilor.

By Stalin, with other
lesser fry, duly slain
in a clumsy plausible murder.
Pera Atasheva smiles. It happened like this. We nibble
on nougat. She pulls, from folders, some pen-and-ink scribble:
a vulture's beak: Ivan, Tzar. Terrible;
savage sketch for make-up. Cormorant disdain.

IVAN THE TERRIBLE!
Ivan Grosny, demon,
granite under coronation's pelting coins;
brocaded tarantula straddling insensate powers.
Hate absolute, menace infected,—totters, droops, devours
idiot princeling, black priests. Tall outrage towers,
stumbles, staggers: A Tzar: automaton.

Stalin sees his own mask
in a magic mirror,—
two of a three-part portrait; filmed in wartime,
day-to-day, produced on strategic schedules, pressing haste;
plot, takes, planned like a partisan campaign, and no waste,
yet all his vast wonted luxury, truth, taste,—
resplendent bull's-eye lens on terror.

To Kremlin summoned then
for urgent rush-screening.
Stalin fixed those faults as forced both their futures.
His supreme objections: *first*, Ivan was no tyrant, not
hysteric. No maniac. No bestial despot.
Key-scenes ordered promptly to be re-shot
corrupt the film's jugular meaning.

Eisenstein's "heart-attacks"?
(No history of "heart").
Four reels of Part III,—in cans. Dead, at his desk.
Post-mortem slices an healthy skull's young perfect brain.
Ashes for Novodevichi in November's rain
briefly support widow's pain, a hero slain.
By Krushchev "restored," now stands for Soviet-Art.

How long may thus he stand?
How long will this peace hold?
Today, hard to tell. Teams of "demonstrators"
line-up, past Borodino Bridge, hot red banners saying
in italic, enormous: CUBA SI! YANQUI NO! Playing
with fire. Mobs, facing our embassy, staying
far-side; policed traffic. Loud-speakers. We're told:

COME BACK TOMORROW AT
NOON. Kolya will explain:
Newsreels need more enthusiastic gangs.
Today, day-light was poor. Besides, *They* want the whole show BIGGER.
I'm not political. I just hope this hoax won't trigger
more trouble, so, while Valya broods, I figure
how to fly home on *any* neutral plane.

Then Pera asks me, flat:
"Are you our enemy?"
Am I? She loves me, sure. Surely, I love her.
Eisenstein dowers our chance movie-marriage. His bright-boys
fumble around with Chinese puppets, Balinese toys,—
excellent camera-men. Outside, noise,—
street-chants, sound-effects, rise: dialectically.

A wizard juggler
once told his tricks,—to me:
"PATIOMKIN"? The long-wharf; How did you
make The Mother, (on-cue) sob real tears for her dead sailor-child?
Easy. Mirrors set at sun, blinded a moujik's mild
eyes. Here, truth's tapped wet as tears. "We shot it, styled
on newsreels." Hiring no rehearsed actors, he

bribed instinct from habit.
TEN DAYS THAT SHOOK THE WORLD!—
still shake it. Us, on it. Watch Lenin's earthquake
as pedestrian warfare. His Winter-Palace attack:
ants, swarming across cobbles in demoniac
wild insectile raid, charged frames; shot-loaded track,—
action assayed, controlled, arrayed, then hurled

by epic flow of force,
polity as filmed act.
Eisenstein still lives his doubled lives, true as history.
Cineastes swear he stole from newsreels; his mystery
of mirror-metaphor. High mastery
invents symbol for finite fact.

U.N.
for Robert Craft

A city sleeps below
fifty-five storeys of office, bureaux.
One lone armed-guard in starched chinos, grey,—
hums passively, sighs, hums; wait for his new next day

when he'll be off-duty. Black waters six-hundred feet down
recalls another locale, Stockholm, clean canal-town
where he was born, raised, found a vocation. There & then
he volunteered for service in the U.N.

Service,—to worlds of men,
unbounded leagues past Stockholm, past Sweden,
past Europe, past print in books, on charts
into diagrams where it's felt loose parts
might bond, together, to manage politics fairly well
making hopeless peace possible. Better than probable hell.
Well-born, well-bred after a fading feudal fashion,
a guard serves without question and no passion.

And it's a good thing, too.
Leave ardor to those, floors below, who
play at power. He does as he can;
nobody is storming up here to harm a man
guarding air-conditioners which keep reasonably cool
air, subtracting irritation from statesman, patriot, fool.
This justifies idle watches in long alien night,
he waiting for an unaccustomed skyline to take sunlight.

On the 38th floor,
lit like noon, cables and typists explore
the Secretary-General's space,—
also a Swede, diplomat with his horsey face,
a quizzical thoroughbred. Abrupt pace of warmth and mind,
doing what he can do, is sworn to do. But can he bind
deals with simple Americans, furious French, fierce Russ,
Africans? Trying to do what's best for all of us

through this, his last, best,—hope.
Neither last nor best, but having to cope
with weak men, their machines,—what to do?
It beats me. More than half the time it beat him, too.
Half the time loved the game for itself: irresolute men
jumping like short-circuited beetles, on again,—off again.
Last? Best? At least a firm dream here below to make work
it all out a bit better, and this none may shirk,—

least of all, Hammarskjöld,
who takes it as an uncivil household
with him chief-janitor or tutor,
he, prime spark or fuse, at once shrewd slave, sly suitor
of naughty children. Some cretin, malformed or spoiled. Others
hiding precious hints; a few, almost amiable brothers.
Certainly no unworthy nor even senseless dream;
he sounding better than most with so fair a scheme,—

seeking always for tone
or style, his; maybe even his alone,
based on a considerate manner,
not boring or brazen; plain means for a planner,
very courtly correct. At root, perhaps, hasty or vain.
He wished to wield good-will as well-framed by what he sensed as sane.
Reasonable. If not, exactly what's rational, then?
Rationally, the inexact end of rational men.

He showed me his U.N.
once. He was always content when
he could show-off some new ornament,—
connoisseur's eye adorning his clean monument.
He liked good-pictures; taste of his time was his perfect-taste;
nothing outlandish. He borrowed work by Braque, Matisse. We faced
a latest acquisition. He nudged me in alone
so I might bump a huge slice of smooth dark stone.

The Meditation Room:
good-taste in liberal religious gloom.
Polished table-top. Altar? Maybe.
Hewn rock-natural hunk he wished everyone to see,
tougher than any hard terrestrial substance yet known,
irreducible super-charged basaltic meteor flown
from outer-space. Hauled here at reckless expense,
a private patron's benign extravagance.

This abstract, solid, thing,
indestructibly concrete, and should bring
all wicked bickerers, tribe or clan
to some dense potential in the soft monster: man.

Hammarskjöld, poet and priest, incarnates here this crass fact.
Here one meditates endlessly on the unsignable pact,
strength or weakness. Softness, shy resistant or spry weak.
As symbol, this slab reads merciless, blunt, bleak.

What our problems were, he
knew. He disdained to think we'd ever be
unwilling to try. He was my guide
to where a thin bronze plaque was meant to coincide
with the fate of another Scandinavian we ought
to, though few do,—remember: stubborn, peaceful Folke-Bernadotte.
Here was measured on an all but blank white-plastered wall,
plenty of room for plaques recalling us all.

Dag's half-smile, unhappy.
In the elevator, his kind, snappy
kidding of a tannish (Indian,
Uzbek, African?) girl. Her elevator-fan
buzzing coolness, clicking up fifty-five storeys where
a boy waits, on a patient guard-mount, unexpectantly there.
Sometimes Hammarskjöld drops by for a late call up here
lighting up long nights with good old Swedish cheer.

How very tired he was.
In his car, later, he invoked the laws
of modern-art,—music,—paint, verse
promising next year's Nobel Prize to St.-John Perse.
When everyone howled, disgusting shrieks frequently heard
he sought to sweeten them in his own ear by a well-wrought word,
how often succeeding? Now, he seemed musing in pain
and I feared I might never see him again.

Nor did I. When the news
spread through thick confusion, what could one choose
between versions? In Africa's night,
a plane humming, hunting a space, a right place
to set down. Fasten your seat-belts. Disturbance ahead,—
or fire. Leaden half-seconds before fans fail, systems run dead.
Dead, with his secretary, his Swedish guards. They all
have their full-names on bronze plaques in a bare hall.

Star, Bar & Stripe
for Charles Shannon

I.

Montgomery motel, "by dawn's early light." TV-trucks track in.
        Six o'clock,—
"so proudly hailed." Yup . . Let's eat. A cop's gizzard grin,
        redneck crock
croaks: "You-all, dam' Yankeh agitatohs . . ." A waitress, she's
        stiff as steel,
southerness, hatin' us: "Fray'd aigs? Sunneh-saide up?" Yes, please.
        Cautious meal.

Green-casqued State-Troopers stand-guard, on whose house or what home?
        Above the
Alabama State Capitol's high classic dome
        snappily
flaps Stars & Bars. Third Army's brass cools, colonels in jeeps.
        Clear skies wipe
gleaming dawn. Nowhere flown by these drear Ku Klux creeps
        star nor stripe.

Church-yard: marshaling area, (like Normandy, '44).
        We may boast,
marking time, invasion's finally launched. This means War!
        Well, almost.
Our big gang's reinforced, by sore locals all ignored,—
        this deep breach:
police guesstimate, ten, twelve? More. Thirty, thousands. A horde,
        (Omaha Beach).

What holds us back? Something wrong? Here they come, straight ahead!
        Flashing vest;
Selma boys slogged fifty miles corseleted in day-glo red
        six abreast.
Church-yard's full. Snail's pace first. Trot a bit. Now, run, man! Run!
        Three miles on
our team hand-in-hand, priest, nun, kids having fun. We've won!
        But file on.

Banners blow: M.I.T.; U.C.L.A.; YALE. It's slow,
                packed, fierce, strained,
trudging through centuries. For one glorious day? Who'll know
                what's been gained?
Who wins, white or black, slave or free? Hymn's full swell: "We shall
                overcome,
some day." Not today? No. Then when? Well,—still and all,
                shout: *"Freedom!"*

School-kids cram windows barred, salute this funny parade,
                jovial din.
We bid them join. They wave us: "We can't." It seems they're betrayed.
                They're locked in
by teachers outside. Teachers? Keepers, learned in old lores
                from white-folks
whose slogans scream: "Them priests, them nuns. They is whores!"
                Dirty jokes.

Their yell: "You doan live heah! This ain yoh faight!" Whose is it?
                We've no right.
Forget the whole deal after one day's thrilling visit.
                Not our fight . . .
So let them be as they've been. Why should we be involved?
                O'er that dome
floats their flag in habit and health. They've got this thing solved.
                Best go home.

"Mine eyes have seen the glory . . ." Ancient chant, battle-hymn,
                organ verse.
Hoist cute kids pickaback; from the kerb, ugly louts, grim;
                hear 'em curse:
"Them's yoh pappy's black bastids?" Cops, side-armed, just in case.
                Third Army,
wary troops hug side-streets, saving who's hooded face?
                'Tis of thee.

A long day. We're tired. Disperse us in peace. Day gets night.
                We are gone.
Who's won? Who's lost? Miles beyond,—black-boy, a woman, white,
                drive straight on.

Their car's hounded by hunters. Target: two sitting-ducks.
                    "Stop that car!"
Bull's-eye blast. You-all kin caount on ah ole Ku Klux:
                    civil war.

Civil state. States of grace. Misunited states of mind.
                    North again,
safe and sound, our selves saved. Same old self, deaf, dumb or blind,
                    in no pain.
There, waydown South stays dismayed at time's lag. We're aware
                    of somewhere
dawn drags, clocks stop, blood boils. Here, back-home, we try to care
                    or not care.

II.

"Magnificent distance,"—Washington, D.C.,—L'Enfant's scheme,—
                    architect
echoed Versailles' grandiose clear imperious dream,—
                    vast project,—
mudhole for years,—Brasilia, Canberra, New Delhi, the same.
                    Nonetheless,
war, peace, they stand, built stating each their politic claim
                    to impress.

Capitol Hill, "magnificent distance,"—six miles from that dome:
                    Arlington.
Here, Robert E. Lee, his wife (née Custis), kept home-sweet-home.
                    War's begun,
April, 1861. Civil War. Now Lee must decide
                    in one night,—
(veteran West Pointer; he'd hung John Brown), on which side
                    will he fight.

Doric colonnade, freeman's mansion, no single slave.
                    Lee shall choose
in agonized hours futures for whites, blacks, craven, brave.
                    All will lose.
Christian Virginian, aristocrat, his strategy's fate
                    petrified:
Lincoln vs. Northern Virginia,—Lee's sovereign state.
                    When Lee died

94

Arlington, Virginia, national boneyard became,—
                  fair estate,
headstones aligned. Here's a couple carved "Kennedy." Famed name,
                  recent date.
Last year, past Lincoln's column-clad fane, imperial seat,
                  marble throne,
I scanned bivouacked battalions, our immortal elite
                  stunned in stone.

In prayer Lee paced his portico, his sacred place.
                  He refused
Lincoln's offer of armies, clamped to earth, clan, class, race.
                  He confused
Virginia with set states of mind, staunch, stubborn, untamed
                  and ingrained.
Stern corps of stiff markers blur thousands, nameless or named.
                  Foreordained?

Magnificent distance: Washington, Lincoln and Lee;
                  Kennedy.
Marines halt, this graveyard's permanent burial-party.
                  O we see
to one side by noon's level light, what's final though fair.
                  Black and white
boys present-arms to a crate whose corpse serviced its share,
                  wrong or right.

One veteran black chose this site as his destined spot;
                  many could.
A mess-sergeant, World War II, loads a private plot
                  as he should.
Burial-detail; captain in dress-blues, shavetails proud
                  fire three blanks.
Over raw soil, fold, for a wife, Stars & Stripes, a shroud;
                  her mute thanks
gagged by grief, yet death doth endow what life hath him robbed;
                  seemly sight.
Three shots. Honors. Kennedys killed, half a world sobbed
                  half a night.

"Some day!" in clay we'll all lie with sergeant, Lincoln, Lee,
                  timelessly;

no need to march or muse, dream or doze. Sly enemy,—
        apathy.
Today, a delay. Selma to Montgomery: O say
        can you see
by what dawn's murky light who wins where? And this is a
        rich country.

Arlington, by shrapnel unscarred, hosts bones of the lost.
        History
congeals in cut script. Interred as spent dust, count the cost
        thriftlessly.
Magnificent distance; in victories won or failed,
        famous dates
adorn large design. Here, O what was so proudly hailed,
        half-thanked, waits.

Domes

I. M.: William F. Lynch, S.J.

I.

In awe of order, drawn nigh to wrought portals
    of Zion's late home,—
gilt-mosaic, good-taste of proud Hebrew mortals,
    high resonant dome,
one lays at the faldstool of Yaveh, our jealous god
    a weak caitiff's rage
at self, injustice: this world,—its scourge, its rod
    on fretful spent age.

He weeps. Shoulders shake. Tears moisten tense fingers.
    Neurosis or grief?
No. Terror of order. God's orders. Fright lingers
    in guilt's lame relief.
Unfocused sobs in loose order throb sadness.
    A mind starts to spin
on waste panic. Hysteria; not madness
    the state he is in.

So here comes the rabbi to bolster his pew;
    meaning well; nice man.
Pats a paw on shook shoulders: "Man, may I do
    for you what one can?"
Thanks. But is ours any mendable trouble?
    Tears? Sure,—mainly nerves
but pain leaks from that single or double
    sense which, when sound, serves

order. So rabbi notes he's not nuts, although
    nervous. Hence, in reply
risks his avid grief: "I'm married. Unhappy. So
    I've a mistress. I
love her. She,—me. My wife doesn't know. Must we tell?"
    Hates to hurt her. "D'you
think we should?" Woe melts on a comrade in hell
    kept by God, a Jew.

II.

I may cite Priest Gen-do in Nan-zen-ji's shrine
    to God-Goddess Mercy.
Helping Gen deck Kan-non with quince, plum-bud, rock-pine
    friends were made, barely.
Crushed stone, plush moss, clear stream, his paths raked,
    begs downtown each morn.
By hope unpossessed, all possessiveness slaked
    thanked his gods he'd been born.

Rabbi, hypertense theologian concedes:
    "Ah, yes. I can see
East and West create each their creeds, but . . ." He reads
    Kipling: "*Never the*
twain shall meet." "Their Buddha? That image; it's fat.
    Our life-style's dynamic.
He's passive. We can't then live like that
    since we're both manic

and depressed." Hey! Wild yelps! The pew, right ahead:
    a sincere drama:
loud, plump brat, spoiled on lox, chicken-fat, rye-bread,
    cushioned by momma.

Irving howls, throws a fit. *Frecheit!* Grab him. She spanks.
    He slaps her straight back.
Rabbi flies to succor the scene. His due thanks,—
    a Bronx boy's prompt whack.

In no-time, Irving, his permissive mother
    quit their holy place.
Rabbi recaps a loss which shrinks to small bother.
    We both feel we've lost face.

III.

I'd cited Kyoto, Japan,—miles, years gone.
    It's not simply Zen.
Zen? For us? No. Fair practice, yet scarcely one
    for quick Western men.
Gen-do grinned. Grace held no threat. Shut, lonely, strong,
    his stone lamp shone bright.
Its wick repaid need without greed. He's all wrong?
    For him it burned right,—
which one strained to explain, but a Lord God of Hosts
    in synagogue rich
warned us both: "Requite thine own Pentateuch ghosts!"
    Poor son of a bitch;

poor mistress; poor wife; poor us. Rabbi's sad, soft sigh:
    "An eye for an eye."
Blame smells sweeter than bless. What gods, blinding us, lie?
    Adore that old lie.
Lord-Lady Kan-non, thy mercy; Gen's firm chants,
    stone lantern's lean fire
glow in ease,—yet they fade, for some postulants
    hear another choir.

IV.

Islam's scimitar script, credo to behold,—
    our West may forget
marble marvels, pale tulip domes in clear gold:
    mosque, mihrab, minaret,—

iron prose of their prophet, Apostle of God;
    Buraq, his winged steed.
We recall how millions deem none of this odd,
    a norm for a need.

Nearby,—to that Furthest Rock, back, in free flight,
    far more than a myth,
spanning star-dome to hell and back in a night
    won Prophet the pith
of his proof. Five times a day, strangers in ranks
    share the muezzin's call.
For domes geometrics, all our earthly thanks
    for a Taj Mahal.

V.

Is one blind to lapis-blue, deaf to psalms sung?
    Ribbed vault frames stained-glass.
Lo, there on crossed oak a nailed corpse heavy hung:
    monad of the Mass:
this One, this Other, of God and Man, a son.
    In blood, wine and bread,—
fount, flow, source, ever three, yet always One:
    heart, belly and head.

Whatever's besought, wherever its shrine,—goddess or god,
    does not all depend
on when and where is first found seed in our sod
    however we end.
In a furnace of fact, singed by metaphor's flames,
    true gods never burn,
To Yaveh, Kan-non, Muhammad, Christ,—domed names
    towards order we turn.

Thus, three-quarters along our god-given span
    tired men can turn home
to supper set out for those jaded by man,—
    'neath any old dome,
shrine or sky. Wafer crackles its echoing crunch.
    Gods, in deeds, exist,
and, after all, many wean on one heavenly hunch,
    The Eucharist.

Rhymes of a Pfc. 1943–1980

FOR MARIANNE MOORE

> . . . They're
> fighting in deserts and caves, one by
> one, in battalions and squadrons;
> they're fighting that I
> may yet recover from the disease, My
> Self; some have it lightly; some will die. . . .

Marianne Moore: *In Distrust of Merits* (1944)

World War I

Fall In

My mother's brother hauled me to the big-boys' club,
    Where they swam nude, drank beer, shared secrecy.
Males young and old held mystic privilege.
    I was condemned to join their mystery.

These men were hairy on belly and groin;
    The boys were hairier at least than me,
No boy, no man, a neuter in-between,
    One hairless silly, neither he nor she.

In locker room my uncle stripped me raw.
    My shyness shivered at his shameless, bare,
Terrible body. Off he tore my drawers
    And shoved me naked to the brink of where

In a tiled cage they'd sunk their sacred pool,
    Clean as a toilet bowl, its water poison-green;
No mama near to save or cry "Forbear!"
    The taste of infamy is sweet chlorine.

I knew that death swam near but hated uncle more.
    If I were doomed, then uncle, he must pay.
I'd scream, I'd make a scene, or the extreme:
    I'd plummet to bottom, midget martyr play

Profoundly drowned, which simply took despair
    (Distinct from courage since it involved caprice),
Hold my breath to bursting waiting The End.
    In suicide is blackmail and release.

He tugged me out with terror, even awe.
    I felt my fright infect his grizzled chest;
Palpating this drowned rat to retch and drain,
    He knew I knew who'd flunked his foolish test.

Thus one bears fear in action, guilt in pride.
    I was his sister's son, yet still no male.
The spineless kin he'd vowed to make a man
    Confounded polity and saw him fail.

The rage of armies is the shame of boys;
    A hero's panic or a coward's whim
Is triggered by nerve or nervousness.
      We wish to sink. We do not choose to swim.

World War I

Du bist der Kaiser Wilhelm! Thy Huns shall rue our blame.
Dad teaches us to hate thee. It is a stirring game.
    On the back of a Cuban cigar box the scowl of Kaiser Bill
    Embossed upon its glossy lid evokes a ritual thrill.

On many a night, just before bed, we gravely open it.
Upon thine iron moustachios Dad, I, and my brother spit.
    Dad's parents both were German; so were Mama's too;
    His pair poor, her pair rich, pure types of German Jew.

Dad's folks came here from Prussia in 1848
With Karl Schurz and some exiles, and not one day too late.
    Dad sent me my first postcard—*Das Brandenburger Tor*—
    With guardsmen in spiked helmets—*Kronprinzens elite Korps*—

Whose officers when off parade mock tourists touring town,
And when they smell like German Jews, they knock my daddy down.
    Hence now we needs must trounce them with witchcraft and with gun
    Who skewer Belgian babies and rape old nuns for fun,

Which I learn from thrilling pamphlets cooked up by staunch George Creel,
Though it's sex more than compassion that I truly really feel.
    German spies spy *everywhere*. Ma swears our neighbor's Fräulein
    Signals from a Marblehead Beach her secret submarine-sign.

Karl Muck conducts the symphony; a steel svelte villain, he—
Ma says he's Wagner's bastard son ("Daddy, what's *bastardy?*")—
    Conducts "The Star Spangled Banner" in clearly treasonous style.
    Mother shrewdly decodes this, watching his back the while.

Our weather's *mighty peculiar:* clouds rarely rain; they *pour.*
Phenomenon caused by bombardment, in this our first World War.
    We save sticky peach pits, too, 'mongst other momentous tasks,
    Which by chemistry or alchemy are rendered for gas masks.

Our scout master, Harvard '17, enlists at the very first
Of Pershing's call for volunteers. Ah, that day is the worst
    When he takes leave of us, his lads, who pray he may not die;
    We partake of sarsaparilla and a splendid communal cry.

Joe, my father's office boy, whose acne spoils an angel face,
Turns up for Sunday supper in the guest of honor's place
    Scrubbed beet-red, immaculate, in manlike sailor-white.
    I'm ten years old. I love him dear. His uniform is Navy tight.

My pa is past an age to fight, but everyone else we know
Plays his irreplaceable part against an implacable foe
    Save Earl O'Toole, the janitor, mulatto with much progeny,
    My first preceptor in the lore of absolute necessity.

Earl shows me things and tells me things I'm not supposed to know,
But without my knowing or being shown, how'm I expected to grow?
    Curiosity kills no nine-lived cats. It's true. Can I ever repay
    Him for his grand advisements? He discovers a practical way.

In wars the rich are warm enough, the poor frequently cold.
Anthracite or bituminous fuel may not be bought or sold,
    Yet with a magic ticket got from he won't say where
    They hand me chunky bags of coal simply for standing there,

In a queue of wives in shawls with kids, gath'ring before the light,
Shuffling through steel-shovel forenoon deep into slip-ice night.
    I'm well aware of my tailor-made togs: reefer of Harris tweed
    Betrays an interloper's lack of legal material need.

But I'm Earl's apt apprentice and shall double for his dole,
And I'm O'Toole's accomplice who'll cotch him rationed coal.

An end to battles boiling peach pit, mustard gas, and blood.
Kaiser and Clown Prince in exile take turns at sawing wood.
    Scout Master's back at college. I'm sent away to school.
    Pondering all my prayers for him, I sorta feel a fool.

This World War turns out to be only the first World War,
A problem for teachers to tackle without making it seem a bore,
    But gleaming through forty-five winters I see by a coal-gas fire
    A tutor telling me better than my own shy tongue-tied sire:

His marbled mulatto eyeballs, half Irish, half African:
Earl, he demonstrates on me how is it you make a man.

A B C

War leaves some half-shot young men
Who wage it, get wounded, and then
Take long aimless walks through the night.

I learned this, if I recall right,
Somewhere between twelve and thirteen,
When, precociously keen,
My family all safely asleep,
I dreamed up appointments to keep,
Got up and got dressed in the dark
To walk down that broad strip of park
On Commonwealth Avenue,
Block after block through light dew.

Elms fanned above the wide mall
Giving scale to their big and my small;
Street names spelled an odd alphabet
Whose rubric I'll never forget:

Arlington, Berkeley, Clarendon,
Dartmouth, Exeter, Fairfield, on
Past Gloucester to Hereford, where
I picked up a well-deserved scare.

A trench-coated man tapped a cane—
Canadian ex-soldier in pain
Inhaled the dank airs of the night.
Like me, he couldn't sleep tight.

My prowls in a tom-kitten youth
Pursued some vague personal truth,
Though often my daddy warned me
Against living dangerously:
I was not to risk the fierce morn
Nor discover how or why I was born.

Yet here I was early, and met
A sleep-walking loony. You bet
He was bats: a classical case
Since he lacked a third of his face.
His folks owned that château and tree
This side Fairfield at Newbury.

I shadowed him mutely around,
Out of sight but not out of sound,
Though he was too far gone to care
For some curious kid staring there—
Shy me playing sly Sherlock Holmes,
Protecting the health of our homes
From a typical type of shell shock.
If only two fellows could talk.

But he was oblivious of me
Envious of maturity;
Me drawn, hot, aching and wild,
Half a man, to him, half a child—
Me plotting great war books on where
"Over the Top" 's "Over There,"
Though I'd been nowhere but here,
Damp in teen-age erotics of fear.

I stole strength from his adult shell shock
Past each alphabetical block.
A-B-C spells L-O-V-E:
Mayn't I magic his blindness to see?
I wasn't his dad nor his son;
My own epic had barely begun.
Hence I was content me to stalk
My wounded stag rock over rock:

Exeter, Dartmouth, Clarendon,
By Berkeley to Arlington,
While he led the perilous way
Past Arras, Bapaume, and Cambrai.

Stateside

Basic Training

Belvoir! What's war to someone who's never known war before?
       Our Civil War—
Splendid in springtime, a sprightly gift sent us from worlds away;
       Under rubbery clay,
Popping out of Virginia hills, coral-pink bushes bud; thrushes sing,
Stirring our fuzzy green fresh clean wildly promising
       Tender marvelous May.

Eighty years gone, more or less, all these roads ran to Bull Run,
       But now our fun
Apes a miniature shadow of such vast disaster to spot
       A few snapshots of what
We've come to suspect has little to do with wars we ever shall see
Fought on land or sea: tanks; planes. No horse cavalry,
       Minié ball, nor grapeshot.

Yet my civil war's nearer than that war over the blue:
       World War II,
Which means zero to me save for drab facts which inspire me to fear;
       I'm absurdly quite here
Trying hard to pretend our crack halfback lieutenant, Bill Beady Eye,
Risks a charge under raking cross fire to let fly
       Carbines and a thin cheer.

This weak dull pun on battles our schoolbook creates
       Between the States;
Where First Massachusetts and Third Tennessee pitched scarecrow tents,
       They've hewn stone monuments.
Better than Brady in albums, a leap towards historical fact
Is fooling with live ammunition, trying to re-enact
       Real warlike sentiments.

What sort of an officer's Bill Beady Eye? He's all right—
       By a damn sight
No West Point paladin, Stonewall, Stuart, or Lee. Full of zest,
       Does his beady-eyed best
To haul our poor amateur ranks up a knoll he insists we must take.
Victory! It's took. He awards us a ten-minute break.
       I relax with the rest

And try to recall Dick Hales, a boy I'd known since a child:
     Meek was, and mild.
His dad, a drunk, tossed him his cavalry saber; quit home for worse.
     Dick, a sissy of course,
Tacked the sword to his wall, whimpered for Mummy to come and be kissed;
Never won games nor a girl; to Canada crossed to enlist
     In their Royal Air Force.

Yesterday, in some clippings from home I chanced to have read
     Dick Hales is dead.
Slid his flakked plane sidewise low over Sussex to spare a girls' school;
     No trick for coward or fool.
He had the presence of heart or head to make his enormous bet.
Now is he hero, haloed and holy. His mummy can get
     Used to life being cruel.

Dick: what is left of you now, with my civil war please coincide.
     Kidding aside,
Accept sprig of apple or plum which pitiless April has brought,
     The meager tribute I've got;
First to fall among men I have known, always sure to get hit—
Or, after the fact, seems so—your crash links history a bit:
     Minié ball, flak, grapeshot.

Barracks

I couldn't swing a pass tonight and hitch to town; it doesn't mean
    I'm punished. Desk-sergeant fills his wretched quota early.
     Restricted to the post, frustrated, nervous, surly,
I'll cruise the enlisted-men's canteen.

Nothing doing. One ping-pong table busted; last week's *Time* and *Life*;
    Debris depicting a tattered still-life of sullen fun
     To fill a futile evening; time-off barely begun,
Back to barracks; write the little wife.

Steam overheats our barn. In the latrine's firm Lysol smell and taste,
    Radio blaring, one dumb Polack buffs his brilliant shoes
     Already shined; rub and snap mark time to grimy blues.
No choice endows us but puny waste.

Safe and sound *in vacuo*, this side of oceans which run to blood,
    We've no right to brood on boredom as disaster.
    Genuine adversity hurls its iron verdict faster;
We dabble idly in the rising flood

Of imminent change. Stiff in double layers down our hollow hall,
    Blank beds accuse each tardy, lost, or absent candidate
    Off whoring. Boxed in bed, the tossing wakers wait
Late tumblings-in, curse, or beer-born call—

Revenge on early sleepers. Wide eyed, resist all simple slumber.
    Self-pity's smothered tantrum disguised as dogged sorrow
    Postpones reveille until abrupt tomorrow
Indicts us for Name, Serial Number,

And Shipment Overseas. Bongo thunder, penny-scattered rain
    Caress mute victims whose feeble protest faints to snore or groan.
    Wifeless but warm in woolen, hugging skin and bone,
Nurse counterfeit despair as sterling pain.

Map & Compass

We city kids have quit the town
        In search of Mrs. Nature.
        We seek her nomenclature,
Abandoned since our Boy Scout youth
Which still proclaims poetic truth:
        How starry winkers prickle night
        Till frail pink dawn slams strong sunlight
On ground that's not macadam black but rock-rib green or brown.

The stay-at-homes fill featherbed;
        They lie there softly dozing,
        While here I am exposing
Extremity of toe and nose
To smashing sunup's crimson rose,
        A spectacle unseen for years;
        And as for song, my rousèd ears
Hear counter-tenor cockerel to raise me from the dead.

Bivouac's an ancient cossack hut
        Remaindered from a war
        That took its toll before
We knew a thing. Now they teach us
New techniques for the present fuss,
        Indoctrinating tenderfeet
        For hide-and-seek advance, retreat,
By drilling civil eye and ear to fortify the gut.

Here is my compass; here's a map
        With cryptic markings on it.
        For mystic marathon, it
Posits by curving contour plan
The progress for a partisan.
        We're not draftees, man. We are men,
        Range riders chasing the Cheyenne,
Or cop and robber, hot at heel of Jerry or of Jap.

I cannot spot magnetic north;
        My needle dances madly.
        I draw a sketch map badly.
To ask for help is worse than sin;
We're on our own from here on in—
        Coördinates a keyless code;
        I'll *never* hit that sunken road.
A bird-brain nitwit, spoiled at school, my fame shall be henceforth.

I call it quits to take a walk
        In mild June's wildwood weather.
        A rooster's of my feather,
Brass cackling in the forest park.
His master is a hermit dark
        Whose shack is stacked in tamarack.
        He bids me in to share a snack,
Corn pone, pot likker, turnip greens, and smooth didactic talk.

Here I admit to being lost.
        We agree, for he's lost too,
        Or hidden from common view
Of men at war; loves beast and bird,

Enjoys their noise, credits their word,
    No newspaper, nor radio;
    A neighbor store's where he can go
To get him food, drug, tobacco at no tremendous cost.

I put my compass in his hand.
    It makes precious little sense;
    Equally, we two are dense.
I spread my map upon his floor;
As far as sense goes, this makes more.
    He knows his terrain like no one
    And shows me what I should have done
By longitude or latitude. Armed with such contraband

I hit my sunken road, right smack
    On the button, way ahead
    Of wise guys who've only read
Compass and map as their textbook.
Hence I'll take me a longer look
    At Mrs. Nature's gazetteer,
    Hoping that through the wars I'll steer
No path a map or compass trick to take me off my track.

Cadets

I.

August and you two sting our salty eyes:
    A brisk couple, seasonably dressed,
Lean, virginal. Such pairing mystifies
    Even sophisticates; we are impressed.
    But what to call you? Must you be addressed
As officers? Cucumber-cool bearing
    Kindles a nimbus churlishly caressed
By our limp envy, nor are you caring
For any flat, basebred, furtive staring.

We are draftees, by lottery chosen;
    Protesting vaguely, we surrendered hands,
Heads, and hearts, reserving souls as frozen
    Against all terminal extreme commands.
    You volunteered. Despotic whole demands
Upon your sacred persons or honors
    Enhance a ducal air which here withstands
All error, disciplining you owners
Of feudal grace—its stewards and donors.

Under leathern vizard, immaculate shirt,
    Strict pants, bright boots, taut belt, firm pumiced chin—
Abstainers from vernaculars of dirt,
    Dapper braced greyhounds—your careers begin
    On us, a mongrel kind, since our coarse skin
Proclaims another breed, closer to earth.
    In our twin truce we've but one war to win,
Delaying measurement of common worth
And confident we share no common birth.

West Point made you; your granite mother,
    Cliff nestled and rock mantled, tinged your sight
Its armored glint. Each grey cloistered brother
    Disdains endearment, taking his delight
    In stern alliance for the handy fight;
Friends we may never be. Our slack buddies
    Console us all en masse. Cadets incite
Us to tricks past individual studies—
War's homework, boring before it bloodies.

II.

Second Lieutenants, your crisp commissions
    A fortnight granted, to Belvoir take you,
Subaltern instructors, where traditions
    Frame the tribal rites wherein we'll rake you
    With ready wit and rude, yet it shan't shake you,
Expert at hazing and inured to this.
    Foolish conceit to bet we'd ever break you:
Our duel initiates with an armistice—
Courage at odds with inverse cowardice

To prove us both professional. As when
    We play the game to build a Bailey Bridge:
No officers; noncoms, enlisted men,
    Choosing an ill-considered anchorage
    For both abutments. On a backdrop ridge
Stylish West Pointers overlook the scene,
    Amused, no doubt; vaunting their privilege
By nice withdrawal. Sidewise, watch them lean
Fancy, against a fence, as if to preen

Their eaglet plumage. Sodden in midstream
    The home team wrangles crisscross-bolted steel—
Two dozen raw ambitious paws. Blaspheme
    The martial law under whose mucky heel
    We flop hip-high in mud, and no appeal
To extra aid. A section slips an inch,
    One inch is all. Frail caryatids feel
Dead hefty tonnage slide, and it's a cinch
Our pipestem backbones won't support the pinch

Of backbreak lock. Buckling, we stoop to founder.
    Sharp yells and thrashing wavelets snap their lash
On drifters whose twelve spent shoulders flounder.
    Tendons splinter to a supple mishmash
    Of muscle. Our span, staggering to its splash,
Lurches. Disaster depends on metal.
    Two dive, with swift reliable panache:
Cadets hop in to calibrate their mettle,
Grasping that wrought-iron flower, the nettle,

Safety. So what? We'd have won without you
    And shall insist you were never needed
Though some quicksilver sleight-of-hand about you—
    Even had you never interceded
    On our behalf—claims you both stampeded
Towards realms above the silly stink of swank;
    Necessity herself you fair exceeded
In pure exuberance of valor's prank,
Though such fine manners we are slow to thank.

Later, with whisky-sodas at your club
    We bet you bask in congratulations—
Baptism by fire—and were we there we'd snub
    Your champion clique's cavalier citations—
    We, envious of luxury rations:
Good alcohol and praise. In warm showers
    We'll cherish bruise and welt. Niggard nations
Compete by pattern; pelts tell our story.
You saved our skins. We grudge you this glory.

Top Kick

So he me hates whilst me he awes. First Sergeant is a Thing apart.
A looming threat, a gloomy gus; a flatfoot with a felon's heart.

Our company commander's God—one real swell joe with little fuss—
But Sergeant guards his gates so well a lot of good God is to us.

At each request, Sarge steels himself; stares down my avid, servile look;
Refusal barks in stingy snarl. He justifies this by The Book.

More than mere bible is The Book. Its every sentence spells OBEY.
Nor rhyme. Nor reason. Logic reels. Order alone shall win the day.

Anxieties his sphincters rasp. His sole cosmology: CONTROL.
Control of what? Control for what? Control: the crux; control the GOAL.

Grim and apart in sullen wrath, compulsion prods him, ill at ease.
A furry tongue, a nasal twitch prognosticate some drear disease.

Now Sergeant learns he's losing weight; suspects that glob in rheumish eye.
Inspects his stool. Each night, in hell, dreads lest some virus urge he die.

Increasingly, feels he's unwell, yet dares not risk our medics' skill.
Instead, pumps hints from sly internes staffing a civil hospital.

These sniff his fright. They tease this fool. It's hepatitis (at the least).
Clap, cancer, syph, measles, polio unfit him both for man or beast.

Hence now he doubts his present post. He has pursued it near ten years,
Nor yet admits the slot he's got is what precipitates his tears.

The route he's come's a one-way road. It shall derail him in its rut.
An officer he'll never be. Enlisted guys all hate his gut.

"Then let them loathe me," sighs this soul. "Hatred implements my command;
Martial efficiency I serve. Mine is sheer order's iron hand."

But he's not iron. He's flesh; he's blood; and blood corrupts while flesh may rot,
So makes a pet of one stray cur to share the curse he's somehow caught.

Pup shuns the wretch, like new recruits who sniff his fetor yards away;
And when he makes a friend to Man, then That will be the Living Day.

(*Later, for him.*) Glimpse him morose, upon a pass, in our glad bar
Where men booze strict from gentle men, an hygienic rule for war.

Noncoms and kids who sip bad beer distinguish sane crocks from those mad.
Sergeant makes covert signals blink. Our lids wink: Man, he's got it, bad.

Tireless, obsessed, useful, possessed, with orders stuffed and love denied,
Worrying resentment's anarch bone, our top kick's ripe for suicide.

4F

He works on *Life*, deep down the masthead of the Lucemachine.
    There life works him over, noon to night;
Grinds out fifty weeks of cynical techniques:
    Current events; empiric, erudite.

At first sight, you'd think him out of school ten years;
    Harvard or Yale, not Lehigh nor Cornell.
Self-taught, he'll never rate as any graduate
    Of any place save personal hell.

Peddles fragrant charm, exudes a furtive worldly scent,
    Synthetic after-shave, part snuff, part tweed;
Sells his bogus stance serving main circumstance,
    That sly compliance mass media breed.

Tackles every assignment as if it almost mattered;
    Hot on it, roots to the mean essential;
Sucks up to older men who love to tell him when
    Asked, how Wall Street boosts our war potential.

Interviews the manufacturer of Jet Jumbo Jems,
    A smug thug jobber who's just switched his tools
From rhinestone fobs to deadlier nobs:
    Periscope parts for imitation jewels.

Might fill a back-book page with picture, caption, short text;
    Doodles absently his thin outline,
Brain half alive. Who has the right to survive,
    Cads or crooks? Whose war is this, theirs or mine?

Survive. So far, survived he has. Now, he needn't worry.
    Secure on *Life*, his draft board knows the tale:
Orphan since three; years of neglect; TB;
    Weak lungs still. Poor risk. How can he fail?

It's all true. He isn't strong; often, sleeps poorly.
    Nightmares toss him back on battles' borders.
Far from raw life yet tapping global strife,
    Hoards gobbets snatched from the secular orders.

To him war's a pictorial, framed in stunning snapshots:
    "*This Great Picture* . . ." What battles, ah what battles. . . .
Photogenic dead endow their double-spread.
    Typography accommodates death rattles.

Yet riddles lurk in this tense, lonesome pulsating person,
    Unguessed by his most ardent researcher:
He keeps sanctum like sin for sad gloatings in;
    A brownstone walkup leased to this shirker.

Bolts bathroom even against his once-a-week charlady,
     Its tiles papered with pix filched from *Life*'s files:
Eugene Smith on duty for photo-finish beauty,
     Snapped shots shot on red Pacific isles.

Enters the Head; font, throne, pit, purgatory, heaven:
     At eye-level sees men oversleeping—
Under shredded palms, Marines at work on Guam.
     Gnawing their gains, his loss, slumps. Weeping.

Gloria

If you doan mind, would you please Mind moving over, *please*.
Thank YOU. There's Plenty of room for All us girls. Jeez,
     hon, I'm Sorry; really. So how should *I* know. I thought
     we was All girls here, though now I see you are Not
but can take the Joke. What a Relief! For about One
second I was scared you'd Sock me; but honest, hon,
     you Do remind me of Someone I knew years ago:
     just your type although you yourself might'n think so—

I mean super-fishulee—crew cut, all your
Classs. It's that clean-cut Navy Look; it always sure
     beats Me, though I was Army, but it wasn't the Real me.
     I adore Navy. The Most. The U.S. Navy—
but what admiral would want me? I'm asking you, man:
does this Interest you? Oh, you, Stop! So . . . I can
     pro-ceed? Sometimes it's quite Hard to know who is honestly
     inerstid. Fred was the First I knew when he

Joins the Navy and such a Good Kid, naughty but nice,
wild And cute; wicked, he's just the kind you look Twice
     at, but he never got into no trouble Untillll
     he was in Service. Then, mann, did he get his Fillll!

This all Begins *Years* before, but let's Skip all that;
I was living in a little cold-water flat;
     I was being Alone, then. Fred, sometimes, spent the night;
     he was working Out of Town and doing All Right—

Sold National Advertising for some Large Concern,
not High Pay but he was just beginning to Learn.
     One day, we weren't even At War yet, he wanders in;
     "Gloria," he grins, "I dood it." He done it, En-
listed. I was Dumb-Founded. I gave him a big kiss;
We got Screamin. Imagine! In *Uniform* This
     One would look like sheer Mad heaven; simply cannot beat
     your Navy blue-and-gold or that old Navy neat-

Nessss. You All look ssoo Damn *clean*. Why does Army *never*
in spite of all them soapy showers look Ever
     clean? Fred done his first bootcamp bit way out at Great Lakes.
     Tough, but made it—WAIT! You're Leaving! Now, for Land sakes,
You need One More Beer. Now *please*. This one's on Meee. Now then . . .
I lost my apartment. Bitchy landlady, when
     I spend Weeks ripping plaster, Complete two-coat painting,
     and Entire interior Ree-Decorating—

The Back Room apple-green, trim in Black; the front, a brick wall
hung with a *Huge* baroque mirror. Sooo, after all
     this, she raise the Rent. She said I wasn't a good Bet.
     I paid on the Dot. I should be living there Yet.
But let's not talk about Meee. Fred's at Norfolk, now onnn.
I didn't hear One word for Weeks. I thought; he's G O N E
     and Shipped Out, but then, smack: in the middle of the Night
     a *telegram* phones. It's from Fred all right, all right.

"Come Norfolk At Once. *Difficulties.*" My Poor dear Fred.
I couldn't sleep a Wink, just lay Thinking, in bed
     And scared Green, and I mean for Himmm, not at all for Meee. . . .
     By mistake he'd written a Letter, you seee. . . .
To my Old addresss, since he hadn't my New Addressss—
Wrote on the envelope his *Own* address. I guesss
     That landlady Did it, but we'd never rightfully Know;
     it was opened by Errorr. I never saw it, though

Fred said it was Something Like as how he'd Met this Marrr-
velous mahogany-haired marine, some Gay Barrr,
    and went up In Smoke. It *worked*. And this young kid Liked Fred;
    sensational. Fred went out of his fucking Headdd,
drew his profile for me: crew cut, big jaw, cute lad;
Fred was a good draftsman; the Firm he worked for had
    thought him Talented for layouts. He sketched Very Good;
    he could have been a Great Illustrator, he could.

His letter must have been One Wow of a camperooo
with this marine's Portrait and Full Description tooo
    describing Everything. What's this letter do Then?
    Gets itself turned over to CID—you know: Those Men
who confront Fred with it, without Warning, just like That:
"*You* Wrote This?" His own commanding officer asked: "What
    is the Meaning of *this?*" Fred said: "Well, sir, it don't Meannn
    Nothing. It's just a Joke—in Bad Taste." Get that quean.

Who'd believe Fred? There wasn't One small Shadow of doubt
what his Whole silly sincere letter was About.
    They didn't exactly Arrest him; held him Confined
    in the best hotel. He started to Lose his Mind,
wired Meee. Then, it wasn't easy to catch a plane quick:
Norfolk, wartime, two-motor plane. I was Quite sick:
    I get sick when it's at all bumpy, sometimes when Not.
    I thought: Gloria, If Ize in some Christless spot

Who'd I turn to? Fred, natch. So the Least poor I could do—
try and help Himmm. Hotel room in Norfolk with *Whooo*
    but a marine guard. Get the Picture? I had to get
    permission from his commandant before they'd let
me Innn. They left the door Open so they could listen and
needn't Buggg it. Now I begin to Understand
    it's a Court-Martial offenssse; but—they better Be Sure
    and Prove it. Just get us a good lawyer, but your

Sainted Mother now found that Some people are just Viiile.
They had No idea of letting Fred stand trialll;
    without no Prrooof, just this letter and sketch, like Fred said:
    a joke; in rather poor Taste. Fred was real well bred;

slips me a note: tells me: "Go this certain gay bar Where"
his marine would sure probably Beee—but when?—there-
    sooo, if Anyone asked Questions not to say One Thing,
    quel horreur, though Fred said Jack would Nnneverrr sing.

I'll do anything for Friends, but I didn't know:
What Could I do? CID watched wherever I'd go;
    Was this *smart?* I'm a sensible girl; curious, too,
    how this one would Look, for Fred's a Real Expert and you
Are curious when somebody's Gorgeous. You wanta Seee.
I'm only Human: would this, his, Jack—be for Meee?
    Hon . . . Bar was filled with mad numbers. Remember the Warrr?
    Like a friggin floor show. But no Jack. I drank farrr

Into the night. Next morning I saw Fred, my poor friend,
in a Horrible state. He looked just like the *End*.
    Those lousy CID's. What had they now Gone and Done?
    You wouldn't Believe it. My grey hair *curled*. That S O N
of a bitch the marine guard who brung in poor Fred's food
wasn't allowed to talk to him; this same guy who'd
    been sent in last night, late, with an old hospital tray:
    milk and fruit; then this marine slips Away.

At the time Fred didn't notice. He was too Down to eat—
finds on his plate a thoughtful extra-added Treattt:
    a loaded service revolver. Man, I never knew
    what the old United States Navy could *do* to you.
Soooo . . . your sainted Mother had Quite a time keeping Fred
From putting a bullet through his pretty head.
    I pleaded with him, begged really: the best I could;
    they'd nothing on him At All; so What is the good

In *Suicide?* He wrote a letter. Assuming it's true
(which it was)—it's not the First time. It's nothing New.
    But Fred Collapsed. He broke down. He cried, he cried and cried.
    But no hara-kiri. I saw his captain, Lied
like a real character witness, though I couldn't quite telll
what Cap thought. Told him about Fred's broads. Oh welll. . . .
    I got down on my Kneeess. I prayed for Common Sense.
    This captain, splendid man, loved Fred; was just Immense;

Said Fred was a good man for a good job—in his Way;
told me, very kind: Go back. You tell him: O.K.
  they'd fix something up, but for High Heaven's Sweet Sake
  don't write no more *Letters*. This time he'd get a break.
This puts hope into Freddy-boy. He cheers up a bit,
saw the light; then on in we laughed a lot at it.
  I smuggled beer; gave some to that marine guard and he
  winked. From then on in, it went rather Easily.

But Fred had an Idea proving he's not so Bright;
in some ways he's stupid. Now he thought it all right
  since he's in the Clear and since I had to get Back
  (I was just a working girl, didn't want the sack),
I should cruise that bar again, try to make One last try,
see if I could actually contact this guy;
  couldn't Bear to think he'd never see Junior anywhere.
  How'd I tell which jack Jack was with all them jacks there?

But he needn't ask mother *twice*. I went. Found myself one
Sensational number. No kin to Jack, though *fun*.
  We had beers. You can't help try to make some Try.
  I didn't tell Fred. Him so Depressed. Why should I?
That's about *It*. Today, he'll still say I saved his life;
us camping, I cast myself as his divorced wife,
  we kid about Him paying Me my own alimony. . . .
  End of Story? Not quite. (One more beer?). . . I agree:

Hasn't much *Point*. That's The point of this here story:
they let him resign for the good of Old Glory.
  Soooo . . . then what does this Foooll do? Joins the Marines, he does:
  Ferocious combat training. It was
Murder. Shave you. Beat you. Feed you live ammunition.
Fred did great. He had military ambition.
  So then some Bastard dug up his old Papers and found
  his Navy Records and, natch, they could make it sound

Bad. Marines chuck him out. You think That's it? You ain't seen
Nothing yet. Sooo, now he joins the merchant marine:
  him a mere merchant seaman after all he's been Through.
  Then They got his records Too. They chuck him out Toooo.

My poor Freddy was now a three-time loser for Keeps.
He gave up. I got drafted but you needn't weep
    for your Sainted Mother. Europe? A Ball, for three years.
    Fred? Took it like a Man. Shed no more tears,

Just sat the rest of This war out. Grim fairy tale?
Fred a failure? No, sir, though I watched him fail
    three times, perfectly cast as that Navy juvenile,
    adoring the Service, a good officer, while
when I spoke to his sweet commandant I *did* get Notions
that old salt Liked Fred. Honest, hon, the fucking ocean's
    Full of Strange fish. After the war, Fred makes more than me,
    a first-rate illustrator and No tragedy.

I see him less when I get back from Over Seas. . . .
Now—you Leaving? Please, hon; please. Sir, one more. Sir. Please.

Syko

Doc Young says I got new roses   hell   new roses he says
    You ought to hear the questions he ask me   doc   I said
    You the one thats nuts not me   he said

Sex shun 8   what did I do crazy Id like to know
    I socked Hansen   what was I suppose to do   if you
    was me I bet you sock Hansen too

I try to be nice   lookit   I dont want no fight never
    He pick on me from the first   he didn like my face
    Well   I didn like his ugly face

One night we get frenl and intmat   talking   I mean
    I told him things I nevr told no one before
    It was a load off my mind   whats more

He told me stuff I never heard talked out loud at all
    I guess it was true and so if you think the word friend
    means anything we were friends

One day skuttlebut   all them roomers said we had to move
    Half of us moving so the other half have to stay
    I start to worry   half night all day

Would Hansen stay or would Hansen ship out   would he leave me
    No one knew   Hansen didn know   did he wanta go
    or stay   I hoped he woodn go

Then he start act so mean he woodn even say hi
    Some times I followd him round askn what I done
    Done   he said   done   just leave me all own

Thats it   leave him all own   so I leave him so   I doan care
    if thats the way he wants it   who does he think he is
    Just a big dumb swede   thats who he is

It turns out to be true   they decide to ship Hansen out
    I see his name posted and my name not on the list
    But mite have been   howd I get missed

I hunt for Hansen for I want to know if he new
    He had his bag and gear laid out on his bunk almost packed
    I stood there   I said   no   thing   he cracked

some wise crack how glad he was to get ship out   he said more
    a lot more   too much   I took it but then saw red
    If I hit him harder   hed   be   d

So I didn hit him too hard because he hit me right back
    We trade punch and he could hit real good   I let him hit
    me   it felt good   like the man said   it

feels good after you stop hitting a brick wall with your head
    I fell on his sack   after he gone I will take on his bed
    Partings sweet sorrow   like the man said

One collossal punch and G O D   witness fratercideal site
       He woodn let His boy down   H E show of in bright light
       a commando knife right there   we fight

Batteries flushing evil from my overtack brain
       short circuit so I got to getem recharge again
       My blood circulate back ward in vain

I zoom to top level level   find all tough problems clear
       Trees are more green   birds galore   D O G S o so near an D E E R
       An no snak cree ping in con flick or f e a r

All con flicx are with my s e l f and atually may I so o o n die
       My big trubl alway sbin with I I I   I   I
       I never find no wors averseraye

Whil G O D love me me me Me Me M E M E Me he says Hansens my angl brothr
       and I must pass if eye him from evry othr
       for we was born from the sam Mother M O T H E R M O T   H

G O D   G O D   G O D say so an god G O D has M E rkuperatin in thjs plajc
       But he stars to luck lik ths doc ter hjs fajc
       r semb ls doc Y O U N G while thjs ratracje

they run half lik a hrspitl hav like F R E S N O jail
       A gang o skinjy nurses wid no tit and no tale
       G O D   G O D forget me   I rcjeev no mail

I dree dreeaem Th S A C R E T   H E A R T J E E Z Z in rubbeez o flam fire
       But not in blackan white in tekncolr S H E   I desr
       What you think I am some lousy liar?????

Just kayn rember how they got M E put awa
       N X Q R R T $ % # say I am coprting lts betr ech da
       & whr in hel is H A N S E N any waaaaa # & & &

132

Spec. No.

In our Service there are bodies who as Specialists are known
Eye Be Emmed for special skills in carving stew or baking stone.

All the civil Baker Masons shall fulfill a martial need;
Requests stamped HURRY URGENT snap us through at sonic speed.

Able Baker at Fort Benning, Master Mason in Camp Meade,
Who've sweated months on shit-details from shit-details are freed.

Shit-detail is special duty presupposing skill and haste
With special unique requirements there be no immediate waste

Of energy expounded on each useful pressing task,
So treason is one reason one must slightly never ask

Why must I pry gum from gravel, and me a Ph.D.,
Or process gunk from garbage? It is a mystery.

Hence shot with special vaccine, cutting secret special orders,
Assigned to seize the first flight out that soars atop our borders,

Where we are aimed stays SECRET. One may risk it: OVERSEA
To Theaters of Operations, where'er these spots may be.

The Theater of Europe's got the hots for home-baked cooks;
Pacific hells need deep-fried wells against them screaming gooks.

My captain grips my mit for luck: "Now, fella. Give 'em hell."
Implies he's almost envious, bidding a stern farewell.

My strident sergeant's furious; presumes our wars are lost
If such dumb clucks the likes of us are shipped out at such cost.

A temporary brief snafu. Arriving at the field;
To me, an Officer is told, his pre-set seat, to yield.

This mere preposterous Specialist must needs possess his plane;
Baker and Mason outclass brass. Full colonels fume in vain.

Transport outrides the tempest, deposits High and Dry
Baker brung here to broil a wall, Mason to kill a pie.

Thus, specially delivered to Advanced Invasion Base,
Clerks sweating quintuplicates to save whose fucking face?

Basin's a minor problem, but why's Maker here at all?
There's apple pie for every pal, nor call to fry a wall.

Despite Special Orders, super-dooper trip by plane,
Specialists Faker and Bacon are on shit-detail again.

Obstacle Course

Here we are now, all well or ill met,
Quite sure this isn't It—not yet.
We wait, steady on. Get set
    For the obstacle course.

It is sampling of battle in small,
Lacking crisis or casual,
Practical dress rehearsal
    Of invasion in force.

Master sergeant and brass hang around
Overlooking tank trap and mound,
Swamp, quicksand—treacherous ground
    To try untried recruits

Handicapped in this steeple chase.
Desk, shop, farm was hardly the place
To train for so fleet a pace
    Shod in thick combat boots;

Too spavined or puny for such game,
But age, weight, height, color, or name
Each screens his riddle the same:
    Will I make it or not?

On your mark. Ready. Get set. Now: go!
Pistols crack; police whistles blow.
Careless run fast, cautious slow,
    Ambling off at a trot,

Without haste at the thick milling start;
This takes far more muscle than art;
It's not my mind; it's my heart;
    Ticker may tucker out.

Limp swung rope drops from jungle-gym tree,
Hangman knots to grip gingerly;
They make a monkey of me,
    Boy (emeritus) Scout.

Hold fast. Swing this deep rattlesnake ditch,
Barbed wire, palisado's steep pitch;
Straight run, abrupt reverse switch
    Primes (thump thump) the old pump.

Thorny brake, rocky creek, crumbly cliff:
Ankles twist, breath breaks, backbones stiff.
We'll make that final spurt if
    We take the water jump.

Machine-gun fire ahead. This *is* It.
Brave sound-effects: pop pop, pit pit.
Heads! No one aims to get hit
    Save some lunkhead ahead.

Bellies flat to the motherless dirt
Protect idiot or inexpert,
Yet this son's got himself hurt
    Or, as rumors run, dead.

Push on. He's past all maternal good.
He looks like Sarge said we all would.
Boom. It's a poor neighborhood.
    Pow. His body brews blood—

As we nudge him, brushing close by
Averting a shy craven eye,
Guessing we also may die
    Blotting up ruddy mud.

This, thank Christ, was the end of the race,
Each whole one saved his filthy face,
None tamed by outright disgrace
    Save the one with the wound.

What of his obese carcase? It bled;
Possessor played pompously dead.
Glimpsing his poor puréed head,
    Several stragglers swooned.

Sergeant glowed with legitimate joy;
This corpse was his cute plastic toy:
Hot air infused dummy boy.
    Blood was ketchup for real.

We've been cheated. Our hard triumph sours,
This exercise poor test of powers.
We can't claim courage as ours,
    Robbed of wounds that won't heal.

Fixer

Sol Factor was a fixer; it's very grateful I'm
To him, snatching from self-murder—me—marking penal time,
    Fourteen months stoking one stove from hot to cold.
        Sol Factor fixed me up, the punk,
With a flagrantly unexpected, still fragrantly recollected,
        Irrelevant, six-foot hunk
    Of Mormon gold.

One year, two months? A lifetime. Stir-crazy I've become.
I'm not lazy, Sarge; I lack a knack; nor am I playing dumb.
    Nightly I bank hot coals with my furtive pat;
        Hours before Sergeant's awake,
Scamper over, tamp her, fiddle her clinkers, diddle her damper,
        Give her a shiver and shake.
    She's out cold, flat.

"College fella? Jerk. What they teach you that there college?"
Anent this stubborn stove, naught but needless knowledge.
    "You've stuck here long enough. Can't you pull a wire?
        There must be some slot you can fill—
So be like me; go and see. Why, I'd try, I'd cry, I'd damn near die—
        Sure as hell I'd not lie still
    Friggin a fire."

Boing! A light goes me up—one frantic, prurient flame;
Filed among long unsavored names, one of well-favored fame—
    Sol Factor, Pop's old pal from dank, stagnant Lynn.
        Like Dad, a lad with boundless gall,
Chutzpah (nerve); joins a ward-heeler's staff; coins his graft with cobweb craft;
        In trouble? Just go see Sol:
    This Factor's *in*.

In what? South Boston's Dublin Club. Canny tactics, too:
Wid all dem shanty Oirish they could use one Yiddish Jew.
    Fixed bail double-quick in his bailiwick;
        Pulled the strings but spurned renown.
You want ice cut? Some crumb shut up, sprung, or fastidiously hung?
        Sol's the slickest trick in town
    For kike or mick.

Time marches on. A war needs brains—Factor's not the least;
Washington's a kosher Barmecide's posh political feast.
    Sol's pitched his post in Old State-Navy-and-War.
        Lincoln's lank ghost, Wilson's grey shade—
Masters of lost American wars haunt these massive corridors.
      Sol's the Most. One's got it made
    Once past his door.

"Whadja want?" Shark tooth, snake eye, fish flesh, skinned turtle nose.
Undone, I blushed in caitiff heat. Maiden sweat arose.
    "I heard you're here. . . ." He blenched, betrayed: "So, and well?"
      "Pop just said to look you up, though
Everyone's here now, somehow, anyhow. . . ." I know; I'd better blow.
      Snake eyes broil. Sol slurs: "We'll go
    To my hotel."

At the desk he claimed his key. A servile clerk inclined.
All Pow'r corrupts; abs'lute pow'r . . . I'm spineless, Lord; resigned,
    When wings from Heav'n, as if God's mind was in it,
      A mortal seraph, beauteous:
Burnished brass, blazing boots, snappy cap, tailored suit—he sure shoots
      The Works. Sol burps: "Excuse us,
    For a minute."

It's a warrant officer—strange rank, rare animal—
Interstitial, above us men, below the brass, yet all
    I've met incarnate their lonesome dignity.
      They prize their place. What's Buster's game?
Roughhewn jaw, suave supple lips, stropped blue chin, Choctaw tuft, belted hips
      Mean business. It's a shame
    He's not for me.

He's Factor's man, perquisite of egregious duty.
Sol's alarmed how hot I've got staring at blatant beauty.
    Comment's called for: "A guy I help now and then. . . ."
      I'll bet. Let's us three have a drink.
"No siree"—sternly—"Bill has his problems. I help lick 'em, fix 'em."
      Blinks his coy octipoid wink.
    Jay zus. Aye, men.

Upstairs, at least, real whisky. I'm starved, get fuzzy drunk.
No eats. Cheapskate. He wants me buzzed. O.K. God keep me, stunk.
    Nightmare exercise, the seamier side of war.
        Crut is dirt, so it tastes dirty
But grows absurd. We utter no word. Sol flutters, a girly bird.
        Time drags its ass. 10:30.
    Whoring's a bore.

Twin beds turned back; Fort Belvoir, long leagues away, by bus.
This bridal-suite's avid for the unlikely likes of us.
    Sol slinks to the john; hear his weak leak and hawk.
        I've missed my boat and lost my bet.
If I stay on, all else is lost. Grab the last of his liquor fast;
        Save my sacred honor—yet.
    I click his lock.

And make it! Lobby abandoned. Lone night-clerk, whilst there—
Ensconced in Morpheus' lap or an overstuffed easy chair—
    Lies Buster Bill snoozing, stupefiedly.
        Hah! Had Sol told him to return?
"Mister . . ." (Warrant officers aren't ranked "sir"; call him "mister")
        "Don't sleep here"—since who shan't learn
    To swipe what's free.

Opal panther eyes peep ope in ripe astonishment:
Me, Sol's current trade, made so soon? He don't dig what it meant.
    "Bill"—man-to-man—"how about a hot square meal?"
        "You know a place?" We share the way.
Near by: The Shore Shack; straight rye, swordfish, pecan pie for a late dish.
        His move: "You got a place to stay?"
    "With you." It's real.

Hail Joseph Smith! Praise Brigham Young! Mormons bred my Bill;
An angel his ma, a saint his pa, winged from Cumorah Hill.
    Apostles schooled their corn sprout, ruled him thus:
        Gentiles shun their God-given sun;
Treasure pleasure it's due measure; the unusual's a refresher;
        Individuals: have fun,
    But make no fuss.

There's a Mormon hostel run for sainted servicemen.
The joint's shut; it's 2 a.m. Yet they let us in. So then
    We shower, hit one soft sack—where, nothing loath,
        Street-lamps pour florins o'er his chest.
Quoth Kit Marlowe: "I'll tell ye how smoothe his brest was & his bellie."
        "Bless Sol Factor for this nest,"
    Was what we quoth.

Bless Sol at sunrise (Sunday), a few more sunny days.
War plays its pawns in a funny madcap cat's-cradle maze,
    Whence my sergeant charges in: "Hot news, kid!
        You're shipping out, man. You know *when?*
Pronto. Chop-chop. *Overseas.* Now. Wow! Special Orders. Holy Cow!"
        I didn't see Bill again.
    Perhaps Sol did.

Next of Kin

It's just one of those days,
Like the rest in their streaky, tiresome ways.
    Young Bobby's been naughty so maybe, actually, he's sick;
    He struck his sister, broke his wooden stick.
Grandpa agrees to take them off her neck for the afternoon.
They go. She prays they won't reappear soon.

The empty house, alone;
Interim breather for thoughts all her own
    Untidily stacked like dishes slanting a full sink;
    Tries to concentrate. She can't begin to think.
Glances at her mirror image. No startling beauty lurks there
To reassure an incurious stare.

Doorbell abruptly rings;
Answering, in her absent voice she sings
    A tune she almost remembers; repeats its first phrase.
    Walks unhurried towards the door in a daze.
Doorbell again; then again, again. What's your hurry (unworried).
Hurry, hurry; I will not be hurried.

Damn that stubborn bell.
The boy waits. Has he magazines to sell?
    He seems overeager to hand her the thing in his hand.
    She takes it, signs for it, hesitates, and
Goes back to the hall desk for some dimes or a quarter; finds one.
Slips him his tip. Thanks. The door clicks. That's done.

Telegram in light clasp;
Crumpled paper in her double-take grasp.
    It's sheer nonsense. We regret to inform you, it said—
    An odd practical joke—your husband is dead.
An attractive widow of thirty; two kids, one to be born;
Makes no sense feeling faint, lost, or forlorn.

Shrapnel? Flak? Leagues away
Spun through a shortened night to her whole day,
    Wounding live weather to land hard on a bridebed here,
    An infertile seedling to start a tear
Which only aborts. She begins to watch herself like a hawk:
I'm all right as long as I just don't talk.

Who puts cables in form?
She pictures wounded clerks, after a storm
    Of bloody murder compiling fractured lists, somehow;
    Names misspelled; error. No errors here, now.
His name correctly writ; her address undeniably right.
Permits her cautious mind its measure of fright.

Can she stand it or not?
She delays the decision, won't be caught
    In any reckless knot of hope or unfocused threats
    Recalling lucky or unlucky bets
On former stunning occasions. Surprise stabs, using his name:
Robert, Robert—mumbling shades of half-blame.

It's your fault, yours alone,
Robert—ending in an animal moan
    Which, thank God, none can hear. Still, what will become of me?
    Haste stoppers rank freshets of misery.
She'd best put his house in order. Her family comes home soon;
A dizzy neatness busies her immune.

Of course he had to go;
I know. I know. Stop it. He loved me. So
    Unkillable embers stir, warm on nothing at all
    Save firm throbbing echoes having no call
On valid faith or reliable prophecy, while of course,
It takes time to tame or disarm remorse.

Sensible girl she knows
She is. From now on, she'll have to get through
    As she can, her next day, week, month; years, one at a time;
    She, mild victim of his insolent crime
In getting killed. Clean house. Thank heaven for so tedious a task.
Bob! What was it like? Stop it. Never ask.

Proceed. Yes. And do it the
Quickest you can. Fix your face. She knows she
    Is better. Convalescence by forcing it couldn't
    Let feelings swell as they ought. Grief shouldn't
Spoil existence entire nor, indeed, should sorrow foretell
Her failure. The children ring her doorbell.

Buddies

New Year's Day. 19 hundred 52. No! Fifty-*three!*
Dear Ronnie:
    I bet you agree it just can't be 10 years. Gee,
    Time flies. But some things remain always the same:
Those Xmas cookies Mary's kind enough to send us. *Quel Dame!*
Quel? Quelle? Can she cook! Jean wishes she only knew how
    To bake 'em so light & *tasty.* Here it's New Year's again now.
    For Jean & me, same as last year. No better, No worse.
But New Year's will always remind me the time I met you the first
Time. You'd just ship in from the Pacific & I
    Hadn't got Overseas yet. Ron, at first you made me shy.
    I was no soldier. You'd had all those screaming Japs.
Of all chaps I ever met you were the most glamorous of chaps.
You were russet, rangy, sleek, a prize Irish setter.
    23, you hailed from Waco, Texas; called your pecker a wetter.
    You were wounded on Rabaul, bad. Below the left knee.
I thought a great deal of you, Ron. You kinda liked me.
You were weak & bushed, looked forward to getting married.
    I was headed Overseas not too eager to be buried
    'neath poppies or daisies to the old tune: "Over There."
So you & me hung together & we'd go anywhere
We could. Since you rated as vet you could wangle a pass
    For two of us & thumb rides to town, hunt that piece of ass
    The whole barracks yakked about. Only it wasn't true.
You'd rather get drunk with me, Ron. I rather'd drink with you.
Ronald; remember New Year's '43. Snowing like hell.
    We got to O'Donnell's early; tons of bluepoints on the half shell.
    Fresh ones. Two dozen old fashions; maybe more.
I said some mean thing to you I didn't mean. You got goddam sore.
We had a Christ awful quarrel. I got very upset, & scared.
    You sulked. We drank a lot more. Lots more. I dared
    Unconsciously, it was unconscious, to make a bad scene.
Somewhere in my deep unconscious hysteria got crowned reigning queen.
I'd got spinal meningitis. Back at Belvoir, some had got it.
    My spine more frozen than alcoholized. I knew I'd caught it.
    You look at me hard as if I am one prime prick.
How can you get sick so quick? Was this s.o.b. *really* sick?

You found a cab. I am then dying. Where to go
    With a major infectious disease. We both like to know.
    You ask an MP, how come your friend here is ill.
He says: "Take him to the Naval Hospital over that hill."
In the taxi, I start dying all over again.
    Maybe I'm hysterical. It feels 100% like pain.
    We drive to that Naval Hospital. It is very late.
No one up but one medical corpsman who stares me down with real hate.
"Man, you do not have spinal meningitis at all."
    How can he tell without examination. I'm ready to bawl.
    He's right, of course. In 10 minutes we drive back to town.
In the cab I unlock. Fear subsides. I am coming around.
So are you. You put your big arms around me & said:
    "Louis. I'm glad you're well. I like you better alive than dead."
    Back to Belvoir around 3. No. Later: 4.
Hit the sack quietly. Sleep well. Don't refer to this incident more.
Why bring it up now 10 years after the original fact?
    I realize now it was a silly or shameful act.
    I now admit this deal was about affection or fear.
You'd been in landings, on Rabaul. Japs were near.
They just got shorts on, bitty cocks; no balls at all.
    Hid small grenades in their crotch for final curtain call.
    You sliced their nude yellow skin with fire
& much more happened to you and you were no liar.
What you seen & survived maybe I would, too. Maybe not.
    One thing I didn't want to happen was to get me shot.
    So I took it all out in meningitis or probably love
Which soldiers as well as ordinary civilians end up thinking of.
After ten years, Ronald, I recall that snowy night.
    Whatever happened then happen to turn out for both of us alright.
    10 years later now. A decade. Those cookies taste swell.
I hope you, the kids, the new baby & Mary keep busy & well.
Ron: this year, try & make it North. We sure like to see you.
    New York is actually fabulous.
              Cheers to you both from us both.
              Lou.

P. O. E.

THIS IS IT and so: so long.
    We're soldiers now, all set to sail.
We may not sing one sad old song
    Herded within a dark dock-rail.

Self-pity pools its furtive tear;
    Expect the Worst, discount the Best.
Insurance as a form of fear
    Tickles the terror in each chest.

So: THIS IS IT—yet not the sheer
    Crude crisis we've been trained to take,
For many a female volunteer
    Doles out thin cocoa with thick cake.

They've parked their limousines the while;
    Their natty uniform is spick
And span, their hairdo and their smile
    Pronounces patriotic chic;

And THIS IS IT for these dames too.
    We strive to fake a grateful note
But goddam duffel bag and pack,
    Gas mask, rifle, helmet, coat

Too heavy are, so each sad sack
    Must flop and gripe: This is *some* shit.
Up On Your Feet, our orders crack.
    It's All Aboard for THIS IS IT.

U. K.

Convoy

Luxury liner "Britannia," mail carrier, 30,000 ton,
Once shipped sophomore and cardsharp to Le Havre and Southampton,
Hauling in happier season broker and buyer abroad,
Now transports monthly to battle thrice her tourist load.

"Britannia," rechristened "Alliance," altering former runs,
Was sunk first by Japanese claim, twice since by *untersee* Huns.
At 1100 hours, 10,000 Yankees, black and white,
Cram each open inch of deck room, subway rush, sardine-can tight.

This enables seasick details to police up sleeping space
Stuffed in lounge, bar, kindergarten, cinema, or grand staircase.
At 1200 ten loudspeakers, in accents hard to understand,
BBCeed from shores approaching, cough up news of war on land:

"Ah yew theah?" or "Cahn yew heah meh?" "Kerreh awn. Thet's awl foh naogh."
Theah King's English amplified heah mixes mirth from stern to bow.
Decks below, incipient tension tends to aggravate the scene;
Negro troops rip down the notice barring them a white latrine.

At 0600 hours and at 1600 too
In six shifts 10,000 swallow gooey beans in beany goo.
Above, in less congested quarters, brass chomps three shifts as it should:
Fruit cup, soup, steak, sweet, and coffee, off china, glass, and polished wood.

Then at twenty hundred, blackout. Every soldier should be sleeping
Or if not, then horizontal, place his soul in Captain's keeping.
Is my life preserver handy? Have I clothes in layers three?
Count knife, light, compass, candy, 'gainst the cold black open sea.

And with dawn, arises rumor: submarine just spied, or wreck.
Enemy plane near. Escort routed. Epidemic on D Deck.
Thus we roll through apprehension, weird malaise at every hand,
Till fresh white and black replacements stumble sea-legged onto land.

Troop Train

We'd heard such Areas dubbed Depressed
      And everywhere the squalid sight
Of worker's blasted shop and hut
      Deepen in economic blight.

We'd slight idea that here it was
      The bigger bombs preferred to fall
Though even now the neat control
      Of rubble all but hides it all.

As we roll quick from north to south,
      Working people flag our train,
Tossing V signs at our coach.
      We sling V signs back again.

A daisy in a cracked old pot,
      One gold tooth in a hungry mouth . . .
For half an hour we believed
      We might be welcome in the south.

In our car, fetid poker game
      Or crossword puzzle's trim design
Don't dope us strong enough to drug
      Adams, Babbitt, Davis, Klein.

Our wheels drone on. The blackout shuts
      All nightscape out from bleary eye.
Behind these shutters there must sleep
      Beleaguered cities slipping by.

We are crusaders and our Cross
      Is rigged for dumb draftees to bear.
If there be peril—bring it on.
      This engine won't get anywhere.

Night blacks all greys. Our CO frowns,
      Clamps down our games, commands we doze.
It is the Army we are in,
      Where dawn is friend to all our foes.

Pub

Along rural British bypaths
    Rustic infants blond or sandy
Beg the GI: "Any gum, chum?"
    Answer is: "No candy, Andy."
At Bell & Bush, at Prince of Wales,
    At Bird in Hand or Bull & Bear,
Thirsty Yanks, we beg for Bitter,
    But there's no beer anywhere.
"Not a Drop" at George. From White Hart
    "Dry as Dust" we tikes our text
And the scrawl on Happy Dick's door:
    "Out of Beer till Thursday Next."

So we sprawls in public 'ouses
    Quaffing peppermint-and-gin
With released Eyetalian prisoners
    Who are pleased to be let in.
Some real wops with Yankee dagos
    Cop the taproom of their club,
Though the Home Guard in the backroom
    Feel put out of their own pub.
Comes the closing, nigh eleven;
    Doubled wartime's bright as day;
Farmer's been abed for hours
    While his lassies toss in hay.

As we pedal back to billet
    "Any gum, chum?" 's nighty-night.
"Not a stick, Dick" 's the wrong word now.
    "Gotta sister, mister?" 's right.

Tea

Embattled men of Britain
    Defend their native shore
Four long years, now nearly five—
    Bayeux to Bangalore.

These English needed allies;
    Their cousins came to aid.
With higher pay and better teeth
    Our coup de grâce is made.

English wives are widders
    Or we treats 'em much the sime;
Five years without an 'usband,
    It is a bloody shime.
A Yankee corporal's sitting
    In a dull provincial slum,
Upon his lap the son of a chap
    Who never seems to come.

It is true he may not,
    But then again, he may.
It's been so long it's really like
    Bert's always been away.
Corporal, himself an exile,
    Almost feels her a friend
Who puts her kid to cradle,
    Returns his blouse to mend.

It will not be forever;
    Orders are coming through.
We've just begun to whip the Hun;
    We'll need the corporal too.
Some time at last, presumably,
    Our corporal won't have gone;
He may be staying on to tea
    When Bert comes home.

Bert grasps the situation—
    After five long years,
Young Bertie in a Yankee's arms—
    And bursts into tears.
Bert will not try to kill him
    As the corporal thinks he might:
He's had his fill of fighting;
    He wants no fight.

He falters towards his teapot.
    She offers him a scone.
They know this time tomorrow night
    Each one will be alone.

Evensong

Though barely a believer,
    It happened recently
My errant feet conducted me
    Near sanctuary;
Not really to seek solace
    Nor atone for sinful acts.
The noble meter in a prayer
    Is what me most attracts.

Last night I went to Evensong;
    The sun was at low tide.
Blown roses on a tower glowed
    Like painted glass, inside.
One felt the tone of Jesu
    Was very seldom heard;
Parish and priest both mumbled
    His clearly uttered word.

But this was not significant:
    Far more impressive was
The domestic county feeling
    Of the curate for His cause.
He might have been a family friend
    Dropping by for tea,
Facing a cross, vaguely to ask
    Aid of some deity—

For King, country, and allies
    On land, at sea, in air;
Workers in factories or farms,
    Docks, mines, or anywhere
Their Imperial Ensign floats;
    For those we've hurt, for those we've lost—
Imprisoned, dead; for those we love;
    For those unloved who swell our host—

Thy mercy, Lord. That selfish roll
    Includes some villagers, a few
American enlisted men,
    Five aircraftsmen in tidy blue,
And me. All praise, thank, and rejoice
    Despite our bleak incurious eye,
Our absent automatic voice.
    Theirs and my humbling God is nigh.

Engineer

Quitting his old outfit, a combat engineer
Rides Cheshire noon to Berkshire dusk but his heart's not here.

A sanitary engineer he was in civil life,
Now grasps the tinted snapshot of his sprightly wife.

Around her neck cheap plastic beads lend their shy, stylish airs;
He says such gems attract the tint of any dress she wears.

We stare from out our two-ton truck, straining to understand
A Kodakchromatic sunset from glory's lavish hand.

His ikon he relinquishes. Its gorgeous image fails.
Great nature all but vanquishes. Art palls. Love, even, pales.

Our engineer to science turns: "You know? I'll bet that you
Can't find in a large thesaurus words to describe that view."

What he meant was only that all through his life,
Sunset, jewel, beauty will remind him of his wife.

Riverscape

Relaxing by the river of Spenser's marriage rhyme,
Three GI's at Sunday tea enjoy relaxing time.

The stream's hereditary swan sailed past with queenly grace.
Six cygnets plowing in her path could scarce maintain the pace.

As they seemed sure to falter she swung her wake aside
To scoop her young upon her back, a cargo of white pride.

After tea, GI's digested upon a bud-banked glade;
Overhead swift Spitfires their stern vibration made.

Crossing these smart Mustangs stung cloud and thin ozone
While, shuttling through, trim Bostons flew on business of their own.

Behind us, in a forest, clamor in shadowy trees;
A blind owl beats its branches. Spiteful squirrels tease.

Abruptly, through the rushes, a furious flutter's heard:
Leda's enormous lover by some deep mystery stirred—

Biped, voice, or aircraft—this swan assaults these men;
In a vast fury, sensing some threat to its six young.

Awed by th' inhuman protest, its thrashing neck and wing,
We watch great nature lashing back, at us, the human thing.

Swan, cygnet, owl, and squirrel from Thames and tree exiled,
Forbid the sky by bomber, grow wilder and more wild.

These are their last offensive, against our grand campaign
Where we, compulsive, sweep across to spread the general pain.

Tudoresque

One adores the glory of England. When I was a scamp at school,
  The poet James Agee
And I listed the names of English kings, dates of their ev'ry rule—
  (Exeter's library);
Sketched coats-of-arms with sable bend and even a sinister bar,
  Baron or baronet;
We savored the fame of Tower jewel, Kohinoor and India's Star.
  Late afternoons we met
To devour the epic of England in ancient magazine views
  (Periodical stacks),
From leather-backed rusty volumes of the *Illustrated London News*.
  My first Shakespeare contacts
Were Jim's reading parts from the Histories aloud, fresh as current events.
  Favorite rôles were those
Of Bolingbroke, Hal, and Hotspur in bloody fine incidents
  Where bled the Tudor rose
Within the bosom of lover and friend: Prince Hamlet, Horatio.

  Often Hamlet was Jim;
We got drunk on Shakespeare's iambics and Britain's dynastic rainbow.
  I most remember him
Flipping the pages of portraits vignetted for the *London News*—
  The First War's English dead,
Glorious young men all, each a university graduate.
  Fate haloed every head,
All officers, baron or baronet, not one a mere private;
  History was alive.
Jim had such charm as Hamlet, I was happy Horatio, his friend,

On four days out of five,
Though always I deem myself Denmark and shall play him to the end.
At Harvard before long,
The casting is switched by Agee. He prepares the high comic schools,
Sings us another song:
The chilly end of *Love's Labour's Lost* and *Twelfth Night*'s solemn fools,
And Jim, setting forth strong,
Read me his own sug'red sonnets, which made noises like poetry
Back then as they still do,
And Agee will dwell in English verse whilst, as for merely me,
In footnotes I'll dwell too
For having first printed his verses in the quarterly *Hound & Horn*
(A quote from Ezra Pound
Deeply revered in '26 before most Young Poets were born).
Long since I've turned around;
I've had my fill of Fair Harvard, her Twentieth-Century Men;
Theodore Spencer's dead
Who taught us the Age of Shakespeare, and his polymath Shakespeare then
Was less of heart than head;
Our tutor was friend to Eliot, a nineteenth-century man
From the seventeenth century,
So when we rewrote us our poems, the stanzas were wont to scan.

What meant England to me
Apart from bards on Widener's shelves and Jim Agee's brandied voice?

Britain: its earth, as well.
My people gave me a pilgrim's scrip, bade me make a scholar's choice:
Tintagel's drear hotel—
Its Table Round of Morris fumed oak besprent with thumbed Debrett's;
Cathedral Close at Wells,
Where paddled a white-marble pride of swans with invisible coronets,
Tugged at the moat-house bells.
And I scaled the heights of Bloomsbury; I took rooms in Gordon Square.
I found some English friends.
At dazzling soirees, Lytton, Maynard, Clive, and Virginia were there.
Lydia superintends
Our *pas de deux*. Lopokova and I perform a world *première*
When I'm but sweet sixteen,
For the London seasons *entre les guerres* were Heaven and Vanity Fair,
The like since seldom seen.

At the head of St. James's Street, silence. Crowds hush at brisk rattling brass:
      The Household Cavalry.
An open coach thrones George the Fifth. From Paul's I see him pass:
      "God bless Your Majesty!"
His mask salvaged from mortal ill, very model of some carved king.
      He also is *my* king.

So here am I back in the ole U.K., endeavoring for to bring
      Whatever decent thing
I can to repay my bad Yankee debts to English poesie.
      It isn't hard at all.
England encourages allies with hearts and hearth, and I
      Have billets within call
Of Third Army Headquarters, leased from a kind P.O. employee—
      A Manchester suburb.
It's a tiny Tudoresque villa, but he's cleared a room for me;
      The service is superb.
From Invasion Exercises I drag in bushed. Always, there he waits,
      Tea on his hob, and toast.
We prattle of the state of England and my own United States;
      We make our Allied boast
Of our present Grand Alliance and those futures we're fighting for.
      I tote him PX gum
For the brats of his son, at sea, who's actually winning this war;
      Splicing a brace of rum,
Since his boy's been absent from home five years, we drink deep to his luck—
      An *officer*, no less—
A tall fair youth with starry eyes, like Raleigh or Rupert Brooke
      (His snapshots show me this).
The *Illustrated London News* taught me that specific look
      From World War No. 1,
And declares my P.O. employee: Old England's come very far;
      Now, often things are done
Unthinkable thirty years ago when he'd fought a private's war:
      "Officer? Me? My eye!"
Yet look at his own Bertie now. And Bert's mother, at the door:
      "Daad, coöm ta baid." Hence I
Apologize for keeping him up. It's not that she hates us Yanks;
      She wishes we'd go home,
Though courteous as can be and decently renders her thanks,

Yet I lack the aplomb
To make her love me for me myself or for my Amediken style:
Intruder, and too fat.
She thinks I think this war's a lark and her suffering not worth while.
Still, what she's getting at
Is part of a complex problem of country and class and taste
Useless to ponder on.
'Er 'usband disagrees. We're buddies, though our friendship be a waste,
For soon it will be dawn,
Nearer that day I fare for France where wars are actually faced.

We smother a sheepish yawn,
Ole Limey and young GI, hands-across-the-sea.
I quit my foster home
Shelved full of PX food,
To bivouac nights in a circus ground from the which I may not roam
Unless I plan it good.
Our circus ground is guarded by fairly reliable MP's
With itchy Tommy guns.
Often almost courageous, I've irrational fears of these
Amongst some other ones
Mainly about a prepaid tour in a rational modern war
Beyond this circus ground:
What lurks for Third (censored-dash-censored) Army, on foreign shore.
Joe Sentry on his round
Lets nary a whisper drop on when we ship out or how we sail,
But I'm not wholly lost.
I read in a week-old journal, th'invaluable *Daily Mail*,
Snuck in here at some cost:
John Gielgud opens *Hamlet* in Manchester, right this selfsame week—
Perchance this very night!
I start to charge batteries, low voltage of the terrible meek;
Whether it's wrong or right,
John Gielgud I intend to view, granted Official Permission or not.
Of course it's bad to go;
Deserters from imminent invasions all deserve to be shot,
But I will see this show,
So I trickle out of our circus ground, nab a fast tram into town
As quick as you'd say "knife,"
And it *is* the Opening Night! My ticket costs me arf-a-crown—

The best night in my life
(In a theater). The house is packed; stuffed in a balcony sit
        I, tight against a wall,
But knowing the words and the music and how the plot will fit,
        I miss nothing at all
Of this greatest Hamlet of an epoch that saw Jack Barrymore.
        My father, years ago,
Graded me all his Hamlets; awarded *grand prix* of princes for
        Black Edwin Booth, although
He conceded Sir Henry Irving possessed the more argent voice.
        Johnston Forbes-Robertson
(At least from photographs) had, until tonight, been my personal choice.

        Soon is our drama done:
Ophelia (Peggy Ashcroft) was sideswiped by a flying bomb
        Only two days before.
She goes daft with a bandaged wrist; her performance gains pow'r therefrom:
        That's what Theater's *for*.
Gielgud beggars description; if its begetter could only have seen
        His Hamlet to the life.
Our hearts are cleft in twain. He cradles, he cozens his mother-queen—
        Minx, sister, mistress, wife.
No sweet prince ever drew breath dowered by dynasty or demesne,
        Peer to his taffeta air,
His consonant hysteria, his generous insane
        Cool canny candid stare
When he transfixes his schoolday chums, snapped links with a charmed lost youth—
        Rosencrantz, Guildenstern.
But now this production assumes a superfetation of truth.
        In my mind's eye still burn
That sunset end, that music at the close, that final scene of all,
        That feast of corpses strewn:
(*Enter Fortinbras & British Ambassadors . . .*) We bite on breath:
        Bright midnight on black noon.
(*Drums, colours, attendants . . .*): "This quarry cries on havoc. O proud Death. . . ."
        What did those English find?
An empty throne (*stage center*). Loyal Horatio at post, on guard,
        Nor has he lost his mind—
Snatches the crown from his bleeding prince, ill-starred and starry eyed.
        He sets that hollow crown
Upon its siege imperial. Hail! The king lives nor ever has died.

Then kneels Fortinbras down,
And this piece is no longer Gielgud's nor is it Shakespeare's either,
      Though both make all come true.
It blazons the armour of England in every sort of weather:
      Treason or buzz bomb too.
England shares actor and poet with soldier, civilian, and all
      Allies, of whom I'm one.
England, what thou wert, thou art. Bang hands. Roar throats. Teary curtain call.
      Thus all her wars are won.

Boy Scout

Above a target harbor in the wood of a private park
Cowers our marshalling area 'neath its pre-invasion dark;
    No pinpoint matchstrike warns the sky where our alerted armies wait
    The long expected last command to ship us to our drastic fate.

A youth from Sacramento gags, throbbing in his tongue-tied fright:
"I have so much to live for still," sweating it into Hampshire night,
    South of that "Southern England" where buzz bombs drone and fall.
    "We have so much to live for still" is sincerely echoed by all
His buddies, noncoms, officers—some fazed but most of whom won't budge,
Including medics and nurses who, in a blacked-out tent, boil luscious fudge.

Our Sacramento soldier leans on a nubile tree,
Extracts an ancient Scout knife to carve initials three:
    "I'll brand my name on England deep in this sapling tall;
    Until this sapling wax to wood, in France I shall not fall."

His glance above at its branches discovers the treetop is dying;
His heart contracts at the omen, but instinct, death-defying,
    Hunts him an older stouter trunk, a Robin Hooded bolt of oak
    To hack his three initials deep with an Eagle Scout's unflinching stroke:
"My name shall live forever," though as he finishes
Feels the next bright buzz bomb burst in a field beyond these trees.

Bobby

O I am in Southampton,
        Brave port for ships at war.
I gets my bleeding orders:
        World wars are what they're for.
My orders are for France, sir,
        And this is what they say:
"You drive your jeep to dock, boy,
        Nor lose your lousy way."

I drive my jeep through town, sir;
        All traffic stands at halt.
Buzz bombs impend as smashers
        But are they worth my salt?
They are not worth my salt, sir,
        (As so this Bobby said):
"You've stalled your bloody jeep, son,
        An' you ain't even dead."

"Am I not really dead, mate?"
        Then shitless scared I am.
Another buzz bomb cruising
        Claims I'm not worth a damn.
We are not worth two damns, man.
        This Bobby hops right in.
"I'll spin you to the dock, lad."
        It is a solemn spin.

Buzz bombs fizz but miss us.
        My sergeant chills to ice.
I hunch beside him, sweaty, warm;
        His substance feels quite nice.
Foul weather rather worsens.
        Clouds clatter iron or flame.
A Limey cop, a pissless Yank
        Fuse smallish shards of shame.

This copper is a Briton,
        No soldier of his King;
Just a goddamned good policeman
        Used to this sort of thing.
He keeps more calm than I keep.
        I cherish Bobby bold.
We share one common prayer, Lord;
        In mateyness grow old.

"In climate such as this, boy,
        What we need most is gin."
Hence I suggest to Robert
        I'd just as lief pull in.
Proposal is arrested
        By festive lash of hail.
He parks my jeep beside his pub:
        Here one still quaffs good ale.

We swear we'll meet again, men—
        Slim hope at meager most.
GOTT STRAFE ENGLAND!
        Smart riposte to our toast.
Pledge we twain pints of bitter
        To long-range victory
Which 'spite frantic trumps of doom
        He's surer of than me.

Anti-aircraft pops like snappers
        Whilst we sip ale upright.
Behemoth smites our pantry.
        We issue to the night.
I strive to spot my vehicle
        Which Bob parked vaguely nigh:
"Why, blimey, myte, your bloody jeep—
        It's tyken to the sky!"

Junior

Junior had his hair cut the night before we sailed;
Barber cropped his childish skull as if he'd just been jailed.
When we dragged up the gangplank I was ten feet behind
And saw his shiny nob ahead, so kept him in my mind.

I knew we all were wary, a few quite terrified,
But I'd *my* fears to foster and needed none beside.
Our crew of merchant seamen gaily prepared our boat;
We soldiers marked their easy way and envied them their lot.

Fog floated in and found us. We lost all ships around.
Our danger was collision unless we ran aground.
Also there were submarines waiting for it to clear—
Torpedo boat and strafing plane and floating mine to fear.

I heard a merchant seaman no longer laugh. He cursed:
"Of all my forty crossings, tonight's the very worst."
Thus we knew THIS WAS IT again and wished to Christ that we
Were safe at home or snug abed beyond the mortal sea.

Then Junior, through our nightmare, came stalking quick but dead;
As I absorbed his fright from him, the mist on his shaved head
Stood out like sweat. His two wild paws in helpless animal fright
Trapped me in the clamp of love to nurse him through this night.

He was in peril. So was I. Be with us to the end
Where every selfish soldier is rationed half a friend.

France

Black Joe

This Norman coastal meadow lies in a chill grey haze of light;
A soldier first sees France by day; he'd hit the beach at night.

Stepping over snoring men, he tries to find him fire;
Uncle Tom cooks for Uncle Sam as once he had for hire.

Our soldier thanks the happy black, returns to his own group,
And from those borrowed embers brought, a sharp new flame flares up.

One by one his drowsy gang uncoils from each stern bed,
Stiffens to stretch, scratch, realize not one of them is dead.

Around our fire, like bugs to light, amble a few dazed oxenstray
Negro troops who've slogged all night, orchard from beachhead, miles away.

We whites, with gummy eye, but brave, as our blond blood stirs to its round
Stare hard the dark intruders down to stand our own usurpèd ground.

With psyches sound, but half-awake, we keep possession of our pyre,
Warding the somber soldiers off; this shall remain a white-man's fire.

Thus hard arrayed, fright against fright, upon the first dawn of our fight
In common against a common foe, smoulders their wrong against our right.

Bed Check

Everyone's a wee bit nicer if we sniff some danger nigh,
Kindlier to one another when we think we're going to die.

Sleep is scarcely absolution; by half-past one or two
Their engines hum; our ack-ack barks; an enemy is needling through.

A drumbeat detonation of their cannonading drum
Spits out machine-made murder to startle every chum.

We feel the sinister low drone of Jerry—deeper than our planes'—
And sense him circle low to take a dose of tracer for his pains.

Should we haul on our helmet or roll in our foxhole?
I nudge my moron tentmate. How best to save the soul?

He mumbles for a moment, shoves over with a sigh,
Grumbling it's immaterial whether we live or die.

So I shake him: "Listen, Buddy; Bed-Check Charlie's overhead;
We had better take to cover or risk the falling lead."

Then Bud and me, we shudder, our rancor half forgot,
To hear the Jerry plane buzz off, goosed by a parting shot—

Laid out like lovers, tense but tamed, coupled within sin's droll device,
Worried and married, damp and lame, to let our pauper hearts de-ice.

Vet

A tired new trooper scans the beach
    Where but some twenty dawns before
He, with those thousands of his force,
    Barely achieved this shallow shore.

Through hip-high water over flats
    Gritty cross fire cracked its knife;
Aching blasts sucked all the air
    From quick collapsing sacks of life.

Here where near-misses lapped his craft
    Landings by dozens scar the sand;
There where scratched-off bombers plunged
    Beetle-boats swarm the busy strand.

Across the bay, blunt puffs of smoke;
    A war seems somewhere—miles from here.
He feels its desultory bang:
    Land mines blown by engineers.

Just three weeks after our great act
    He can't recall half his own wild
Sobbing advance. High on a dune,
    This prematurely aging child,

A mite of history he helped make,
    Rubs stubble chin, and spends a sigh.
Tomorrow he'll be down the line
    Waiting one more chance to die.

Ants

Our foes worked here the toil of ants
        within these folds of hill and vale.
A riddled landscape near our camp
        pockets such shallow holes in shale.
Nazis looped lank their lines and wove
        wire webbing, heaping high steel carts
melding a mix of rubble marl,
        liquid and lime in proper parts
to cast vast floors of dense cement,
        hefty enough to bolster tons
of doom-crack blasters equal to
        cosmic collisions of small suns.

Entrenching from concrete platforms
        runways canted angles steep
rails for launching winged typhoons
        skywards up top from tunneled deep.
What was the gimmick? Rocket? Gun?
        Freak wizard warhead still concealed?
We'll not soon know. Two months ago
        our bombers blew them from this field.
Now cone-carved craters dent lumped rock;
        snapped steel uncoils; wires whip atwist.
Trash, track and dumptruck scatter wide;
        no ten square yards our missiles missed.

Aeons ago when Grandad Gene
　　　　seduced a consort in some slime
Grandpa's descendants ran to ants;
　　　　Grandma's commenced the human climb.
Somewhere way up the ladder we
　　　　branched ant-tracks off to grub it where
big bugs wheeled smartly from their soil
　　　　to heap up teeming anthills here.
At what crossroad on our steep trek
　　　　did systems summon ants and then
with capital indifferent thumb
　　　　destine their dynasties as men?

Ants begot aunts, piled higher hills.
　　　　Uncles got gold, wit, glee and tongue,
pigment for pelt; bone, lung and heart
　　　　with some affection for their young
which, for what reason? we suspend
　　　　each generation more or less
marching our juniors off to join
　　　　the mad unmanning we profess.
Conscripted ants close-ordered drill
　　　　to delve and dig with no large scope
locked in insectile strategies
　　　　reiterate a dearth of hope.

We promised who? Who promised what?
　　　　More luck than virtue rashly grants
us spurn free-play as any goal.
　　　　About-face spin the mutant ants.
Where fouled that fine discrepant flaw
　　　　condoning blanket rivalry?
An energetic batblind rule
　　　　endorses pismire butchery.
The Nazi works unfinished rust;
　　　　they'll launch no mayhem just this year
and soon shrewd tourist turnstiles must
　　　　cash in—on whose big failures here?
Trippers from half the world across
　　　　uncles and aunts of those who fought
will gape at gross insectile dross
　　　　and shy from texts some ants have taught.

Tent-Mates

It's no cinch to live together
    In a field three acres square
With your noncoms and your officers
    Sleeping and eating there.
Soldiers aren't chosen wisely
    To be four-season friends;
Neither lovers nor companions,
    We were picked for rougher ends.
Hence our interest seems to lessen
    In snapshots of buddies' wives,
Nor are we all-absorbed by
    Incidents in lurid lives
Which startlingly resemble
    Our own grim or comic tale
But which, on other lips than ours,
    In passion tend to pale.
From living in each other's laps,
    From sniffing at each other's pores,
From glimpsing every function of
    The human mechanism's chores,
From dozing next to unloved flesh,
    From swimming in the common stew,
We're trigger happy to the touch
    At our compulsive rendezvous.
I do not mind my own shit.
    Why then avoid another's?
Answers are articles of war:
    Men are seldom brothers.

Lucky Pierre

Golden bees swarm honeypots; in apple butter foul wire wings
Or tickle lips which cocoa sip or tease our tongue with testy sting.
Hoverers hive on spoon and mug. Chow hounds sure do hate them bees
Miring their buzz in condiments better disposed of by KP's.
Rather than let bugs gorge upon the ordure of our noonday mess,
Mess Sergeant chucks out slop enough to fill a regiment or less.

Pierre's an apt, slight lad of eight. He's learned the Boche nigh on four year.
He did not lunch well when they lunched, nor did his kin residing near.
But now, when liberating Yanks arrive to them their fields restore
This infant hugs our cook tent close, insists he be a bloody bore.
Cook asks, & one can't blame him much, who's taught the kid both *hell* & *damn*
With other funnier phrases, too; "Why can't the little cocker scram?"

Hungry he's not. We've stuffed him tight, though in his picturesque maisong
'Midst lofty antique salongs bare, we'd find his attitude all wrong.
Remoter than his neighbor farms, by friend and foe alike forgot,
Our bombs fell, forty to a field. They pinked Maman and cows with shot.
Pierre's Papa, a Norman dour, dispatches Pierre to forage:
The Free French Radio proclaims it is the generous war we wage.

Except those Boches were generous, too, until they shot his eldest son.
Papa's not quit his farm for months. Now he can risk the youngest one.
The boy must go. If we hold him, it makes its difference, but less,
Whilst Pa waits Peter with a strap, which is why Pierrot haunts our mess.
Papa is gaunt. He's plain half-mad. Odd-nights he howls so young Pete hates
To pass the time too much *chez lui*. This social problem now awaits
Our Rehabilitation Corps. As yet there is none hereabout:
But why cain't this lil ole runt shag his ole lil frog ass Out?

Pierre's enchanted by the bees who, drenched to death in honey taste,
Flutter gilt down shallow drain, casualties of waste or haste.

Foresight

Previsioning death in advance, our doom is delayed.
I guess mine:
I'm driving for some dumb officer on this raid:

I can't doubt his sense of direction, his perfect right.
Still, he's wrong.
I hint we're too far front. Been warned plenty about this before.

Base far off. No lights may be shown. He starts to get sore.
Lost, our road.
He feels he's failed. Abruptly down drops night.

Anticipate panic: his, mine, contagions fear takes.
THIS IS IT.
Not good. I invoke calm plus prayer for both our sakes.

Calm makes sense. Prayer is less useful than gin or a smoke.
Where are we?
If this ass hadn't tried to crack his great big joke,

Pushing beyond where he knew well we were told to go,
We'd be safe.
Checking my estimate, my unvoiced I Told You So,

Granite bang-bangs blossom all over hell and gone.
Let me Out!
My foreseen fright swells, a warm swarm and we're sure done

In by Mistake, including his fright, faking him brave;
Me the same,
Making me clam tight when I oughta had the brains to save

Our skins, sparing official pride by baring my fear:
(Please, sir. *Turn*.)
Sharing his shame with me, who, also, deserve some. Oh dear,

It's too late. The end of two nervous careers,
Of dear me,
And him, dear doubtless to someone, worth her dear tears.

La Grange

This farm is France entire, in peacetime as in war;
Its order and its amplitude, now as ever before:

The house, more grand than farmhouse; its yard more court- than farm-;
Its peeled pink crust of plaster—pale, flaky, fresh-loaf warm;

The pear espaliered on old brick—complete: farm, garden, manse—
The frugal elegance of man, all that is best of France

Has been within the last four years invaded from both east and west.
The Germans killed the bulls and boys, and now we Yanks condemn the rest.

We sad sacks don't think much of France; it's rainy, poor, and cold.
The cider tastes like vinegar and all the girls are old.

This farmer waters cattle; his good wife scrubs her pan;
How dare they, shod in wooden shoon, deem us barbarian?

We dial our radio on New York and, hypnotized, all but forget
The state of war, the facts of life; the dirt, the distance, and the wet.

A cow, two years unserviced, blood burning, makes her choice:
She mounts a sister. We stare rapt. Jazz lends its Technicolor voice.

"I'll be goddamned," a Bronx boy vows, who's heard his pa report this place:
"Them frogs certainly seem to be a queer preverted type of race."

The frustrate cow slides off her mate; the silly pair rejoin their troupe.
The farmer comes to call his kine. His wife rubs garlic in her soup.

The Bronx boy and his hungry chums flow chow-wards with vast appetite:
Dried Klim, canned butter cellophaned, a bite-sized feastlet packaged right.

Red Cross

Come, fellas, all: react with glee. A special treat's in store today.
At half past nine, peculiar time, the Red Cross will a visit pay.
    We are not wounded; no, nor slain; but there's real pain in every breast:
    We're filthy homesick and we crave the cushion of a female chest.

The Red Cross operates a van endowed by Kohn's Department Store,
Equipped with hot plate, radio, and society virgins three or four.
    Our CO sniggered when he said we'd best change shirts and scrape our chins,
    And even officers are glimpsed abluting shyly, trim as pins.

Three girlies aren't much use to our three acres of gaunt GI's,
But what the hell, we'll have a smell: any can win a sweepstake prize.
    So hear the dulcet strains of jazz. Their truck has rolled onto our ground;
    A long queue swiftly sweeps its tail our ladyless encampment 'round.

Standing in line, three hundred joes grin boylike and self-consciously,
Nudging the quicker ones ahead step up for doughnut and coffee.
    Doughnuts are tender cakes with holes which Yankee maids of standards pure
    Substitute symbolically for many acts they mayn't endure.

Doughnuts are token too of home, and coffee also, cool and weak,
And here am I to pour my pint and sight them knockers, lips, and cheek.
    Pat, the svelte cute Redcrosstitute has left Lake Forest far to heel;
    Mechanic, stainless steel intact; sisterly, wholly unreal:

"Now, soldier, where do you hail from? Utah Dakota well that's fine
Step lively please we've lots to serve you're all too sweet the war's divine."
    Yet her efficient insincere hard-boiled charm and stenciled smile
    Are quite undone by her machine; for, honestly, we're touched the while

That radio bass-baritone incanting o'er her doughnut stove
Sings innocently "Water Boy," making us all think thoughts of love—
    Of mother, mistress, kiddy, wife; melting each eye by simple song:
    "Jack O'Diamonds, Water Boy . . ." sobs home is far as war is long.

AWOL

Three shots sting our resounding night; three scattered shots. Then all is still.
Dreamers raise their heads from bed—at what alarm, attack, or kill?
Listen again: no sound at all, save a roused cock in a barnyard
Or convoys pouring down the pike. Roll back to sleep. Men stand our guard.

By morning we learned who shot what: a Texan combat engineer
Pounding our points for seven weeks mixed feral fright with frisky fear.
Finally something has to snap. A bottle full the fellow finds,
An empty jeep, roads to the rear; from this man's army he resigns.

His joy ride dumps him in a ditch. Our drunken craven lands him hard;
Arises, cracks his piece three times; bumps into our alerted guard.
Sentries with ready weapons drawn advance on him as toward a foe,
Back him against a barnyard wall while some are glad to see him so.

An officer comes to command, arranges his correct arrest
Paternally and patiently as if it all is for the best.
Grins our deserter: "Thank you, sir. Was I scared pissless! Now I'm great.
Give me a break, boss. Call my base. It's Lucky Conqueror 468."

Whether he did we never knew, and later no one seemed to care;
A guy told me who'd been on guard and seen this soldier sweating there
Badgered by some bully boys whom battle had not bit till then,
Their trigger fingers itching in conceit they too were veteran.

Courts-martial grade delinquency as frantic terror plus strong drink.
Cowardice? No; hysteria. Heroes recover in the clink.

Sentry

On post a sentry stalks him past
        his cramped encampment's stiffset ground
eavesdropping on limp men-at-arms
        on brief reprieve from feud or wound.
Ripe fancies drone on dawn's default
        spurring dazed tattle-tongues to speak

stunned oracle of throat or gut,
        curbed outcries of the rebel meek.
Faint-heart and fear suborn our man
        seducing one lone mutineer.
He murmurs: *"Don't. Oh, go away.*
        And stay away. Please now. Not here."

Sentry patrols stuffed supine sacks;
        shifts his cold carbine as in pain.
Chafing against laggard relief
        feels his low sluggard pulse complain.
Infected earshot, storm-stacked air,
        stern heavy darkness, sullen space—
sulky bravado taunts tense nerves
        to measure his misgiven pace.
Halted by spectral barricades
        his countersign frowns: *"Stay away.*
My guardmount hosts a mortal troop
        chartered to serve the coming day."

Our sentinel infiltrates murk.
        Gutturals fade, pale threats suggest
scant beleaguered snickering clues
        scuffed from his footfalls' shuffled test.
Soft demons melt love's partisan;
        his valor falters flouting dread.
Yon shade's a foe? Perchance—a friend
        warm from a wish-filled empty bed.
"I know. It's you again. Oh no.
        Not here. Not now. Oh go away. . . ."
He begs a false-fleshed phantom off.
        Dearly relentless, she shall stay.

Chimbly

So it is the Cotentin Peninsula middle July 1944
When took place unusual incidents of our great second world war.
Of them the first time it is I tell now at full length
Result of overemphasis of military strength.

The date is late afternoon on a Friday warm and fair
Major William S. J. Dabeney is the officer in charge there.
This character is known often as Silly Willy to his men
In energy and efficiency a fine civilian specimen.

His unit has its orders U.S. Civil Affairs Unit C34(b)
Trained to take over all town management in all Germany
When Germany is all overtook then seems a long way off
An event at times we laugh our heads off to scoff.

Fact is, Jerry (as we call all them enemy Huns right then)
A last desperate stand he makes Cherbug right acrost to KN
We are midway waiting something good for it to break
Having nothing to do Dabeney didn't want our morale to slake.

Major W. S. J. Dabeney USCAU C34(b) our company did command
The vim and vigor he makes us in every way demonstrate is grand.
Before this he was town manager in some old Mississippi town
A sanitary engineer he come in with fame and renown.

Dabeney he figger busy fingers keep us outta pecks a trouble
Often sounding off you all come here men on the double.
At first at his enthusiasm we poke considerable fun
But in time fine out he is sure one son of a gun.

He pitch his tent we sleep puptents then on orchard ground
Nice set up with invention and appliances his area did abound.
We build him duck-board floor and slat wooden bedstead
Painting railings around his cot blue white and fire-house red.

He insist strict cleanliness good policy all times to pursue
He organize our pipe system two punched cans on us all to spew
Hot and running cold water with deep drain down rock and earth
Enjoying hot and cold water showers was to us often much worth.

We dig up wild flowers and stick them each in painted pots
Ornamenting our medic tent where we go get shot our shots.
All pretty and nice as nice and pretty can be
To set up some new project took lots of ingeneuity.

Dabeney hopes to construct a fireplace in summer warm
At first a fireplace middle July seemed not too much harm?

178

Nevertheless we got no fire brick our immediate area
So some fellows and me we exappropriate a medium weapons carrier.

We tear down past old Isigny too past old Carentan
In front an old church where must of been wunst a front lawn
A fair size brick pile of smooth brown grey beauty
To liberate this here pile of brick become our immediate duty.

Dabeney due to several delays he become ornery and mean
We hope his temper improve wunst this excellent brick he seen.
This way it work out he grins and is very glad
And tells us men erect a tall chimbly no more sore or sad.

Them bricks are nice in the hand well made and smooth
Perfect surface and edge smelly faintly of spice or clove?
A few crumbles most baked hard lays out nice and firm
All are eager to light fire in this chimbly and watch it burn.

We don't wait long sunny July temperature is very fine
Sun sets. Movies after chow where we all stand in line.
Major Dabeney sticks around to try his new falicity
Only one left behind to test it with himself was he.

I forget the name this film. It had been good I'd remember it.
Colossal explosion. Brother. Jerry finally got us all hit?
We gallop up where bright fire flame and screaming sound
Old Silly Willy knocked out cold on the hard ground.

Lucky he isn't hurt worse. Minor cuts and bruises
When he comes to all medical aid he bravely now refuses.
He wants to get back to his fireplace staggers up there
He look at that big hole and stare and stare and stare.

Colonel comes up. "Say Major why are you standing there?"
Dabeney answers "Sir a mystery is here I declare
I light my perfect fireplace it blew sky high
Miracle many personnel and I didn't actually die."

Colonel looked peculiar at Silly Bill shaking his head
He picking up bitty brick bits offen the ground and said
"Major Dabeney I swear you are smart and right bright
How come build chimbly out of abandoned Jerry dynamite?"

Inter-Service

I.

September morn in Norman June: slack sag of middle age in folds;
A comfy tum, a flabby bum refreshed by wet, astringent cold.
Behold our British officer. For forty years he's briskly passed
From town- to country-house to hunt, yet bathes before he breaks his fast.

Even upon this rawbone dawn when brass revelly boasts no sun
Espy him sluice his tingling buff; long e'er we're up, his douche is done.
On rosy, prickling epiderm th' Anglican offertory's spilt.
How he ablutes and scrubs his roots! It is his prime, imperial guilt.

Thus did he douse on Khyber Hill amid a border station's rocks,
Rinsing the taint of hard-set caste, pulled on a pair of clean white socks.
With mineral waters cleansed himself despite the Blue Nile's fetid stain
And sponged away fellahin clay sullied by pharaoh's rotten strain.

Staunch as pounds sterling, all awash, his skin keeps fresh in ambience foul;
Around his world the Union Jack has served as pup tent and as towel.
He's bid our Bud to light his fire. Bud's no mere batman born to be;
He orders me to boil him tea, which in our ranks ain't S.O.P.

He does not dig us Yanks as yet; stout fellas, aye; but rude, but odd.
Whose big idea has hauled him here to boss our unit, poor old sod?
On paper, Ike's plan looked real great: one-half of us, enlisted men
With British officers; at Caen, there, English own Amediken

Officers. We bet they're snafu too. Well—every trick we gotta try,
Though such arcane experiment is doubtless doomed to early die.
Such coils made us wage wars before, o'er Common Sense, Tea Party too,
And 1812. Hence, here we are, wondering, at Caen, who's fooling who.

'Is Lordship's at 'is ruddy ole rub, prize product of the Public School.
We are not serfs claim Bud and I, beneath British colonial rule.

II.

So what? So he's a Scotsman born and bathes each dawn, a marvel rare.
Thrice he's cadged water from our fire; today we caught him ling'ring there—
Enemy, ally, and at once, gentleman, alien, officer.
Puir dog-fices, we keeps our plice, repelling him with curt snapped "Sir."

A pity. He needs room to think; begs pardon for the place he took;
We scarce can credit our sharp eyes when we behold his precious book.
In our vexation we ignore, though Britain share our General Staff,
She's enlisted Chaucer's weather, Hamlet's humors, Falstaff's laugh.

England condemned my boyhood gods; gave Wilde a gaol, Byron exile;
Owen, David Jones, Sassoon, honored their General Staffs in style.
Indignant verses mayn't absolve the snob, the tyrant, or the fool,
But, peace or war, when foolish games the snob ordains by tyrant rule,

British poets have always purged the curse of class or pride of purse.
Pardon the sponge bath. Thank God for the Oxford Book of English Verse.

Château

I.

France, our enchantress, Europa's ripest daughter,
Waits wide-eyed, trembling over bloodied water.
Among French ladies, and the least unripe,
A restless widow stars as prototype
Of classic womanhood, drowsy or waking,
Apprehensive of our huge undertaking.
Kindled by swarming low-flown glider planes,
Chilly in her big bed, she tries to sleep again.
Woman in war, full blown, loveless, alone,
A recluse throbbing in a combat zone,
She keeps one maid, more comrade than a slave,
Lower by birth but every whit as brave—
Cheerful, ingenious, constant Marguerite
Swallows what's bitter, savors all the sweet.

Captain Rick Adams holds in his command—
Bodyguard, chauffeur, and staunch right hand,
Not one to worry, gay at savage game—
Salvator Bardi is this esquire's name.
He takes his young captain in easy stride,
Steers each catastrophe a smoother ride;
Breasting the wars in frolic haziness,

Peasant sagacity condones some laziness.
"Adams—" he figures, "poor bastard's nervous,
Lacking a central aptness for our service.
There's something specious in his public stance;
He's got the willies. Give the guy a chance.
Heroic soldiering's his masquerade;
What that lad needs is just to get him laid."

Both have bit battle: bog-oak's splintered roots
Rear snap-haft trunks to harvest parachutes:
Harness fouled, vast lustrous silks stained red
With all unchampioned jumpers dangling dead.
They spot their target drop from dubious maps;
Landmarks switch, shrink, vanish. Perhaps
They're lost or luckless—what to judge it by?
Waiting on reinforcement from the sky . . .
Six Jerry tanks roll up and wipe them out—
All save Adams and Bardi, his smart scout. . . .
Our beaches build. They find a stranded jeep,
In which this precious pair fresh vict'ries reap.
Prospecting possible command-post sites, they go
Straight up the *allée* of her trim château.

Tires crunch a grass-grown court; Adams hops down.
Framed by her portal, in an old tea-gown,
A Norman lady; by her, Marguerite:
Twin anxious welcomes sneaky Yankees greet
Who would pre-empt this house. Shut, rigid, shy,
Captain averts his sly appraising eye.
Mistress routes them through room on room,
Pausing in salon to enumerate heirloom—
Portrait bust, Gobelin, sunburst chandelier:
A race of gentlefolk held high state here.
Captain confesses to the valor of a louse:
Has he got guts enough to commandeer her house?
Mere social visit should have been a raid;
His sergeant lags behind to date the maid.

Champagne erupts, a sacramental drink.
Adams may touch no drop but marks Sal Bardi wink:
Refusal is unmannerly, might muster trouble.
Protestant lips boggle on popping bubble.

Missing no hint, the countess plies his cup,
Whilst Richard, getting giddy, laps it up.
Things are going great, if too damn quick:
Sergeant Bardi won't want his captain sick.
Better get cracking—Isigny, miles away—
A good beginning—let's call this a day.
Little is mentioned of headquarters' claim;
Contact's been made. Four hearts beat each the same—
In principle. Provocative farewell—
Captain to countess; sergeant, mam'selle.

II.

Americans recross the glimmering *bocage*,
Advancing towards imminent Marivauxdage.
Adams must gain his leasehold on her place
By main compulsion, though he'll strive for grace.
Bardi withdraws, beckoned by Marguerite;
They launch a brave campaign on armagnac, neat.
Captain has plans no woman may defer;
He shall be masterful, but can he count on her?
Her bed reiterates it could comfort two
If she'll teach him the least of what to do.
He takes experiment for scientific investigation,
No worse than a thorough physical examination.
She plays night nurse—or, rather, little sister.
Our rascal might, just for kicks, have kissed her.

Rick, our avenging angel, bison from the sea,
Foam-flecked, flame-licked in nude theophany,
Offers stark solos of flirtatious fun
To spike all hints of rapine unbegun;
Gauging handstands before her small log fire—
Flexed flank, abdomen—tan suede on copper wire—
Sports every flashy caper in the book.
A misfired backflip crystal pendants shook.
She stares amazed, amused at such charade,
His transfixed public. Now must he parade
Somersault, cartwheel. Had there only been,
Replacing oak parquet, a springboard trampoline! . . .
None's needed: moist with flushed aromatic roses,
Upon her cozy hearth the sweaty idiot dozes.

She too's quite conquered by his cabaret—
La fille de Minos et de Pasiphaë—
Outraged Europa by a bullock daunted.
His heifer breathing, measured insult, taunted
A widow wiser than this wastrel's mother,
Nor can she compare him with any other
Lover. Phaedra is prophetess. He's stormed her shore
Risking stupendous parts to win her war,
Yet wants too little. She concedes defeat;
But who's won what? Ungenerous retreat
Of victor vanquished. Can this churlish boy
Be freed to treat the world as his new toy?
She strokes his milky virtue like a pet.
A man-size dreamer nuzzles vain regret.

Air Strike

This was the morning to recall: steep azure, stunning, diamond-bright,
An empty cloudless bell-clear shell, stupendous scale for such a sight.
We groundlings held our bivouac field, the ordinary work in hand,
Protected by a pasture plot, busy and far from battle land.

Abruptly up from out our west, heralded by a droning hive,
Swept over level throbbing air, the stinging squadrons, death alive.
Hand upon hip in proud amaze, soldiers dropped hatchet, nail, and saw:
Four thousand planes roared overhead. We all were speechless in our awe
Of Yaveh, Thunderer, Battle God, who in His just, avenging wrath
Hath lent us much matériel bigger and better than Jerry hath.

This mathematic vision showed four thousand planes complete with crew,
Servant mechanics back at base, whilst over oceans, not a few
Tinkers who'd tooled, sailors who'd shipped, these marvels matchless oversea.
Conceive the method and the mind controlling such dread formulae.

To many, it meant money spent; to others, some vague Bad or Good,
Trying to render in tight terms the vast logistics as we could.
An amateur, I multiplied my balance of equivalents,

How I would handle so much cash, or bad, or good, and how events
Always propel hectic techniques to end up in the hands of those
Who ever manfully insist on any program save repose.

In any case, four thousand planes flew overhead and we were there.
That night, we listened for the news. It was not mentioned on the air,
But at the morrow's trumpet-sun, the big guns sounded strong and slow.
We'd cracked their salient, and we were some kilometers past St. Lô.

Ville Lumière

Free! Open wide! Arteries unloosed
        as if a tourniquet's undone.
Wounds pool new blood. Scars fresh-healed throb.
        Under a covert misty sun
we brave, on cobbles, blank suburbs
        which through terror's atrocious times
had their cancelled ration-cards
        torn for treason's bankrupt crimes.

Posters proud oppressors spread
        on quaint kiosks lack every eye;
scratched-out traitors stare undone
        blind to the neutral unsold sky.
Shade slants mansard streetscape fronts,
        grand promenade routes connect
composed imperious thoroughfares,
        uniform, civil, wide, correct.

Tough brats patrol their boulevards,
        tug hard at each shy soldier's hand,
blessing us for the bread we've brought,
        bidding us into post-card land.
Only from trifling rifle-fire
        chipping pits in smoke-stained stone
or feeble trampled barricade
        are any signs of struggle shown.

Bronze statuary's melted down
　　　　in cannon by a greedy foe.
Pedestals' deep-cut gilt names
　　　　of scornful masters still can show
fame's firm enduring debonair
　　　　whose stubborn grandeur utters where
a temple-city's altars flared:
　　　　Villon, Molière, Voltaire, Baudelaire.

Now their dense absence looms immense.
　　　　We pilgrims gape at headless base
wondering what sort of idol here
　　　　rears lack of vesture, form or face.
Can literature translate rhymed verse
　　　　for ex-boy scouts out our Mid-West?
Yet even these may recognize
　　　　that here high fashion feasts it best.

For luxury's a prize of war:
　　　　sleek skirts on knockouts only seen
as mannequins in Main Street shops
　　　　or featured in some magazine.
Thus bewitched tourists itemize
　　　　from sculpture, silk and kid's caress,
the odor of a garden-town—
　　　　ardor and fancy. Grace. Largesse.

And like some youth who's only just
　　　　unwitting how—yet now has won
a fervent woman—tender, wise:
　　　　mistress and mother, friend in one—
surrenders to such sacrament,
　　　　this freshet bloom, bouquet or wine.
It's us she frees! So now: Hear This!
　　　　"PARIS (by V-Mail), IS DIVINE!"

Hijack

We drive all day from mildly picturesque Coumbes-sur-Seine
Through impressionist landscape it's nice to be seeing again;
My colonel, no companion of choice, uncorks his private pint of pain.

I've driven for this old pre-World-War-I crock before.
He doesn't like me for stink; I deem him a snobby old bore;
But we're inextricably linked by certain tensions ingrained in this war.

His grief derives from a grandson he's crazy about
Whom he's learned was captured two days ago in a censored rout
Of U.S. troops. Now we ride up front fast trying to find something out.

North, ever north; then northeast. Disturbing tableaux abound—
Relics of men and machinery, busted husks tossed around.
As we roll through sinister buzzings, nervous-making mysterious sound

Upsets us and—bang—we stall in a small market square—
But how best to describe it? A pitched battle takes place right there
While the parties engaged wear one uniform: ours. Interpret this scare

As some insane gag, but now a big gasoline truck
Overturns. Jerry-cans bounce on fierce combatants striking or struck
By fist, gun butt, monkey wrench. If we have only average luck

Things won't pop, someone get hurt: us. I watch Colonel stand
In our dead jeep shouting orders, though none obey his command
Sensible as it sounds: "Stop, boys; stop right now," and then his good right hand

Reaches for side arms. I yank him down, jerk our jeep back.
Bodies swivel around the vehicle and dusk dyes to deep black
While it all gets more unreal although staying real enough. Absolute lack

Of discipline or authority. Colonel slumps down
Sulking through this crazy vague riot in a French border town
Where American soldiers sock one another for some obscure renown.

Hence: construe this authentic hilarious scene,
Melodramatic yet stereoscopic. What has just been
Logical chaos stems from hysteria mainly about gasoline.

Our motorized units forged so wildly far ahead
Many imagined they'd seized victory but were then stopped dead.
Whichever eager beaver planned this mad push should have stood in bed.

Hence we hijack gas from whom gas has to hijack;
There's nowhere near enough to make up our present serious lack,
Not alone to sustain an advance but to stop being shoved way back.

Colonel and I, in sort of a bad spot, are safe enough.
I still have, thank Christ, my own tank half full of the sacred stuff,
Which brings us back to base though driving blackout routes by night is rough.

My pre-World-War-I officer sweats in the dirt
Clinging to a great American army losing its lousy shirt—
HIs adored grandson captured by the enemy; lost, maybe hurt. . . .

School

Stol'n from homes of ill-repute near an Estonian garrison,
Paired females, supple courtesans, served a passionate conqueror's fun.
Now their conquerors conquered are, while abandoned harem queens
Languish amongst refugees starting to delve their own latrines.

Leonine harlots in the sun bawdy in blonde languor are,
Scandal of decent folk who try to prop propriety in war.
They nip at neck. They suck at lip. They press with clinging digits hard,
In vicious innocence ignore the homeless innocents on guard.

Also, on guard, is Captain Young. In civil dress he taught some school;
Intelligent, American; suckled upon the Golden Rule.
Watching a shameless spectacle his avid flesh cannot avert,
While whores feast on rousèd flesh, his Mind—ah, more: his heart—is hurt.

Scanning two maids worry their itch. Can he admit Disgust,
Is Sincere in his feeble heat? Embarrassment confuses Lust.
A year ago, he had not viewed a man he'd known spread out for dead,
Nor felt some fears he still can fear, nor said some words he since has said.

So, here's one lesson more to learn, a variation on Love's theme.
Two practiced tarts amuse themselves nor is it in some dirty dream.
Mind rejects such a show as Bad. Heart, made muscular by much
He's seen, felt, thought since he's been In, permits itself a transient touch

Of Wisdom. No. His earlier schools affirm their paltry form.
Captain commands his heart to numb. Asserts the academic norm.

Patton

Skirting a scrub-pine forest there's a scent of snow in air;
Scattered sentries in smart combat dress accord us their sharp stare;
My chaplain for the first time now allows as where we are:
      At the core of this campaign.

Detroit's vast ingenuity subsumes our plans for doom,
Commandeers an auto-trailer to serve as a map-room;
Hermetic and impersonal, one may reasonably assume
      This is Third Army's brain.

I spy a female nurse pass by, baiting a white bull-pup,
Official pet of General's and a humane cover-up
For isolated living or affection's leaky cup
      At secret headquarters.

Nurse accepts my chaplain's solemn amateur salute;
He lets the pup lick and sniff his shiny combat boot,
Shoots her a semiprecious smile which all agree is cute—
      Raps on that map-room door.

Should I from sloppy jeep jump out and to attention snap?
Patton's informal entrance seems some sort of booby trap,
But his easy stoic manner is devoid of any crap,
      So I stick right in my car.

Measuring our morality or elegance in war,
I marked our nurse compose herself. Starch-white, she primly wore
A gold-filled heart-shaped locket on her chest, and this was for
      Second, minute, hour.

Time's analysis is portable and only time can tell
What's in the works for all of us—nurse, chaplain, general.
Syllables in separate hour, minute, second, simply spell
       Military power.

Our brass cut short their conference, and Patton turns to me:
"Well, soldier, how about a cup of hot delicious tea?
Unless I am mistaken, Nurse may even add whisky."
       "Oh, thank you, sir," I said.

"Chaplain says you come from Boston. Then you know it is my home;
Now both of us are many miles from Bulfinch's golden dome.
By springtime it is where I hope the both of us may come
       Provided we ain't dead."

Nurse's watch ticked its temporal tune. Chaplain and I returned
To our base of operations whilst vict'ries blazed and burned.
Reckless Patton's vehicle one year later overturned:
       I see him as a saint.

Angels who flanked his final fling to martial glory's niche
Named Lucifer as honor guard, for that son of a bitch
My immortal captain's mortal, and also he touched pitch;
       His stars tarnished from taint.

In *Stars & Stripes* we read it when he slapped that soldier down
Cringing in a psycho-ward to play the coward clown,
Presuming to a state of shock (he'd smashed a stubborn town),
       But Patton blew his stack.

For me and my companions whom slap and shock stung too
Though minimal responsible find other factors true:
The pathos in enlisted men's not special to the few;
       It is the generals' lack.

Inspecting cots of amputees, unshaken obviously,
Approves the stitch above the wrist, the slice below the knee;
Hides in th' enlisted men's latrine so he can quietly
       Have one good hearty cry.

This soldier has to take a leak, finds someone sobbing there.
To my horror it's an officer; his stars make this quite clear.
I gasp: "Oh, sir; are you all right?" Patton grumbles: "Fair.
     Something's in my eye."

With vict'ry's brittle climax pity's never far away;
Patton feels only wounds should hurt which help him win the day.
But wounds have casual exits and it's often hard to say
     If blood flows in or out.

When endowed as a fine artist you can fling the paint around;
Or, called to seek salvation, you can make a solemn sound.
But crafty priestlike soldiers keep one premise as their ground:
     Loose fright ends up as rout.

Patton's a combat artist; hence his palette runs to red;
Makes superior generals anxious he's prone to lose his head,
Spoil pretty Rhenish landscapes with an April coat of lead:
     Our man may go too far.

The British and Canadians are ordered to push through;
Patton learns he's just their anchor with nothing much to do
But cultivate impatience, curse and sweat or curse and stew—
     Not his concept of war.

He vows: "Now you go fuck yourselves. I'm taking off from here."
He vanishes, nor hide nor hair. At SHAEF there is grave fear.
They bid him halt; he wires 'em straight: "I HAVE JUST TAKEN TRIER,
     SO SHALL I GIVE IT BACK?"

Military governor, Bavaria's shattered state,
He had a naïve notion which was not so all-fired great;
Hired him all former Nazis who'd nicely coöperate.
     For this he gets the sack.

And yet—it's not entirely fair. Since war is done and won,
Patton fears peace as idleness, peacetime as seldom fun;
Idleness is devil's business, and for the devil's son
     Good Nazis don't rank least.

This old pro was an innocent. Thank Christ for simple souls,
Pearl pistol-packin' poppa, prince of polo's thousand goals,
And I'm not fooling you, my friend: he starred three major rôles:
      Warrior, craftsman, priest.

We were rained right out of Nancy. Firm Metz we could not free.
Floods muddied fields; his bogged-down tanks less use than cavalry;
Came his orders: ALL PERSONNEL WILL PRAY THAT THESE UNSEA-
      SONABLE RAINS SHALL CEASE.

George Patton through proper channels forwards his request.
There comes logical reply to logistical behest;
Who am I to testify it's some joker's sorry jest?
      Rains cease. His tanks make peace.

Spy

They don't reveal the whole deal. You proceed without clue.
Sometimes I can guess, but more often not.
The duty is: Drive straight, keep your trap shut,
Pretend you're not present, get 'em there. But
It's hard to act dumb knowing someone's got to be shot.

Eavesdropping helps, so today I deciphered it through
The tense stance of official reporters
Detailed to observe the last throes of those
Whom gallantry tempted, recklessness froze
To a wall at the rear of Third Army Headquarters.

I was assigned a prize committee from our G2:
Colonel, in real life a lawyer of weight;
Major, a fatty at home in his bank;
Chaplain, an athlete whose fair hair and frank
Grin made me happy to drive for him early or late.

To the stockade I drove them, set them down with relief,
Parked in the staff motorpool right behind,
Checked with Motor Sergeant, a man I knew,
Hung on, trying to pry hints from him too.
No soap; waiting, turned off my motor, turned on my mind.

Soon they emerged. Which mask betrayed personal grief?
Slumped in their seats none seemed eager to go—
Where? Nowhere, anywhere; back to home base. . . .
I strove to deduce from every shut face
What all had been shown. Not a one would easily show.

Colonel Law said: "You'll admit he had a fair trial."
Sighed Major Gold: "It's the price to be paid."
Chaplain: "He certainly was a brave lad."
Smiling, stared hard at me, truly sad:
"Right to the end yet never the least bit afraid."

Did he fall crying Heil Hitler or Deutschland Heil?
Fanatic student or patriot brute?
What meager disguise had we trapped him in?
I saw me, his unidentical twin
But unable to muster a similar salute.

A spy judged and shot kept us worried mile after mile.
His busy echo blurred its short breath.
Was there one thing we'd die for as he had—
Land, leader, any notion—good or bad?
What was worth it? Were we all, then, unworthy of death?

Interpreter

In her cold, unlighted piece
    Six flights above the street
She's pinned by us inquisitors
    Who brutally repeat
Questions she's already sworn
    Answers she doesn't know.
But that was to their dull police
    While we are different, though
We have our style of charm quite like
    Her friend, a Francophile;
Both of us are generous
    With cigarette and guile.
My captain speaks no French. He feels
    Futile in his distress;

He formulates a foolish trap
    Which even he must guess
May never net so sly a doe:
    "Ask her," he orders me,
"Was she—intimate—with this joe?"
    And she: "What's intimacy?"
"Well, did she have—goddam it, man—
    Relations with this kid?"
"*Bien. Relations . . . on peut dire.*"
    So try again we did.
"If what you mean is what I think"—
    She frowns; her cigarette
Has smouldered out and she won't ask
    For another one just yet—
"Why, yes. He's sweet. I like him well.
    And what is wrong with that?"
Stretches, yawns, purrs, spreads herself
    To curl, a svelte house-cat.
Commands my captain: "Ask her more,"
    But senses his defeat,
So after further feeble jabs
    We issue to the street.
My captain never will confide
    In this enlisted dough;
Aside from rude conjecture I
    May never really know
What's here involved; what these kids did,
    Who caught more than a kiss
Though on some profounder plane
    There's nothing much to miss.
Six tall flights up, the pretty puss
    Leans at her windowpane,
Idly wondering which of us
    Will scale her stairs again.

Rank

Differences between rich and poor, king and queen,
Cat and dog, hot and cold, day and night, now and then,
Are less clearly distinct than all those between
Officers and us: enlisted men.

Not by brass may you guess nor their private latrine
Since distinctions obtain in any real well-run war;
It's when off duty, drunk, one acts nice or mean
In a sawdust-strewn bistro-type bar.

Ours was on a short street near the small market square;
Farmers dropped by for some beer or oftener to tease
The Gargantuan bartender Jean-Pierre
About his sweet wife, Marie-Louise.

GI's got the habit who liked French movies or books,
Tried to talk French or were happy to be left alone;
It was our kinda club; we played chess in nooks
With the farmers. We made it our own.

To this haven one night came an officer bold;
Crocked and ugly, he'd had it in five bars before.
A lurid luster glazed his eye which foretold
He'd better stay out of our shut door,

But did not. He barged in, slung his cap on the zinc:
"Dewbelle veesky," knowing well there was little but beer.
Jean-Pierre showed the list of what one could drink:
"What sorta jerk joint you running here?"

Jean-Pierre had wine but no whisky to sell.
Wine loves the soul. Hard liquor hots up bloody fun,
And it's our rule noncommissioned personnel
Must keep by them their piece called a gun.

As well we are taught, enlisted soldiers may never
Ever surrender this piece—M1, carbine, or rifle—
With which no mere officer whomsoever
May freely or foolishly trifle.

A porcelain stove glowed in its niche, white and warm.
Jean-Pierre made jokes with us French-speaking boys.
Marie-Louise lay warm in bed far from harm;
Upstairs, snored through the ensuing noise.

This captain swilled beer with minimal grace. He began:
"Shit. What you-all are drinkin's not liquor. It's piss."
Two privates (first class) now consider some plan
To avoid what may result from this.

Captain Stearnes is an Old Army joe. Eighteen years
In the ranks, man and boy; bad luck, small promotion;
Without brains or cash, not the cream of careers.
Frustration makes plenty emotion.

"Now, Mac," Stearnes grins (Buster's name is not Mac; it is Jack),
"Toss me your gun an' I'll show you an old army trick;
At forty feet, with one hand, I'll crack that stove, smack."
"Let's not," drawls Jack back, scared of this prick.

"You young punk," Stearnes now storms, growing moody but mean,
"Do you dream I daren't pull my superior rank?"
His hand snatches Jack's light clean bright carbine.
What riddles the roof is no blank.

The rifle is loaded as combat zones ever require.
His arm kicks back without hurt to a porcelain stove.
Steel drilling plaster and plank, thin paths of fire
Plug Marie-Louise sleeping above.

Formal enquiry subsequent to this shootin'
Had truth and justice separately demanded.
Was Stearnes found guilty? You are darned tootin':
Fined, demoted. More: reprimanded.

The charge was not murder, mayhem, mischief malicious,
Yet something worse, and this they brought out time and again:
Clearly criminal and caddishly vicious
Was his: Drinking With Enlisted Men.

I'm serious. It's what the Judge Advocate said:
Strict maintenance of rank or our system is sunk.
Stearnes saluted. Jean-Pierre wept his dead.
Jack and I got see-double drunk.

Guts

In its seat 'twixt bowel and bladder
Sits the nerve that insists he must dance.
Now he's tense, but what surly disaster
Might mar him a clean pair of pants?
No sense in anticipation;
When it comes, the man says, it sure comes.
This world holds small harvest of heroes
In its gross annual crop of sly crumbs.
Louse he is, but sustains the slim notion
Salvaging him even from fear,
Like curiosity, subtle emotion,
More selfless than first might appear.

When he was a big boy in britches
He got a girl in his daddy's sedan.
It was also the first time for her and
Almost over before it began.
Before he undid she was bloody;
What happened before he was in?
She was only paying her monthly
Wage to original sin.

He should have stopped there but he did not.
Was it courage compelled him to crime?
He was new, hot, hard; and he wanted
To savor the treasure of time.
Bathed in lamb's blood, dried on lamb's wool,
Baptized Buster becomes him a man.
The spunk to buck distaste or habit
Learns you more than a good high-school can.

In a farmer's field five miles from Nancy,
On a dark winter morn, '44.
I drove back alone from Thionville
To Third Army Headquarters Corps.
This here field ploughed with raw furrows
In swipes of wide violent earth:
Two medium tanks held disputation
On the essence of death and rebirth.
On its slung treads one tank was flipped over,
The other a crushed can of beer—
Two beetles squashed on their cat-tracks,
Me the one live thing anywhere near.
I parked my vehicle by the roadside,
Pursued tank tracks o'er the spoiled snow;
Implored my morale to quit stalling
Till I'd probed the fierce fate of a foe.

It was rather richer in bloodshed
Than the lass in my daddy's sedan.
You can feature what can't help but happen
When fire grills a thin-armored can,
Such container containing live persons
Who'd climbed in as enlisted men.
If you think this pageant smelled holy
Then you can say that again.

One question, one answer, acquits us;
Caught cheating, we only confess:
"Who the hell do you think you are, man?"
"No worse than that bloody mess."
They're dead and I'm living: it's nonsense.
They're shattered; I'm whole: it's a lie.
Between us, identification:
I am you, men; and, men, you are I.
Tests of failure, dishonor can hardly
Be matters of all-out degree.
Fresh earth will smother you sweetly;
A warm bath can take care of me.
Gruesome glimpses we stare down, maintain us,
Sin and squalor partly appeased.
Such scale bravery may even sustain us,
Our psyches released or increased.

We've endured the Worst That Can Happen.
Hallelujah! There can't be much more,
But the ghastly surprises of history
Hide their inexhaustible store,
And exams in a peace that we pray for
Make dunces of scholars at war.

Vaudeville

Pete Petersen, before this bit, a professional entertainer;
He and a partner tossed two girls on the Two-a-Day,
Swung them by their heels and snatched them in mid-air,
Billed as "Pete's Meteors: Acrobatic Adagio & Classical Ballet."

His vulnerable grin, efficiency, or bland physique
Lands him in Graves Registration, a slot few strive to seek.
He follows death around picking up pieces,
Recovering men and portions of men so that by dawn
Only the landscape bares its wounds, the dead are gone.

Near Echternach, after the last stand they had the heart to make
With much personal slaughter by small arms at close range,
I drive for an officer sent down to look things over.
There is Pete slouched on a stump, catching his wind.

On your feet: salute. "Yes, sir?"
"Bad here, what?" "Yes, sir."

Good manners or knowing no word can ever condone
What happened, what he had to do, has done,
Spares further grief. Pete sits down.
A shimmering pulsation of exhaustion fixes him
In its throbbing aura like footlights when the curtain rises.

His act is over. Nothing now till the next show.

He takes his break while stagehands move the scenery,
And the performing dogs are led up from below.

Trip Ticket

Implacable fireworks bang wide-eyed in bursting;
    Fat young clouds of shocked smoke and red-orange fire
Hoist fingers from steering and freeze them. The first thing
    To blow is my right rear tire.

Mortars square in; I'm sighted in their magnetic vector.
    Small comfort to know in all fairness I really am not—
Their trajectory sprays any object moving in this sector
    For a random rhetorical shot.

Boy: you'd better jump. Jeeps are cheaper than you are.
    Slow motion drags its loose lurch, taut tympani pounding;
This man's torso subtracting thrusts forward, bounds too far
    To cushion the jounce in grounding.

My four-wheeled bargain takes off from its dizzy roadbed,
    Skips a pert miniature loop-the-loop in mid-air,
Flops gently to settle in orchard, its load dead
    On all fours, somersaulting where

Percussion subsides, though silence is patent deception.
    Tense, but intact, risk a cursory look all around:
No bad breaks—safety windshield the solo exception,
    Smashed when its frame hit the ground.

Next problem: how to get back without actually paying
    A worse price than shifting my one stubborn spare?
Two bursts tersely boast they haven't quit playing.
    Clamber under my car; lie there

Confused by so outlandish a manifestation:
    Who'll ever believe I turned turtle landing all but upright?
A shattered windshield offers no plausible documentation.
    When I drag in, way past midnight

Motorpool sergeant is snoring till morning inspection.
    I must fill out a trip ticket with some wild story or other,
Less lurid than truth, which prompts the sobering reflection:
    The inexplicable is a bother.

DP's

In boxcars displaced persons howl hymns of home like wolves at bay.
Accordions support their choir: *Praschai.* We're cast on song, away.
For them it seems all holiday. For those in charge, quite something less—
Insuring thirteen hundred souls plus their accumulating mess
Leave a point north of nearly here, a treasure hunt which ends in hell,
For an undetermined turn on a blind gear-stripped carousel,
To hit a siding where ten trucks with bread and blankets lie in wait.
Estimate movement: twenty-eight hours. We are forty-eight hours late.

Paragraph I, Subsection I: the hypodermic numbing cold,
Far worse for them in open cars, infant or pregnant, sick or old.
Subsection 2: electric fright. Each scheduled stop an ambush seems
To petrify their timid guard and verify my livid dreams.
Boy with a granulating wound has dropped his pants for Doc to see—
My flashlight white upon his red; my hand that holds it shaking me.
The halts. The starts. The startling stops. Their wailing tunes and tundra wails;
Then, to surpass apocalypse, at 2:13 the train derails.

Its shuddered brakes. Disaster sure. It cannot be as bad as this,
While all it means to our dazed mob is one more chance to grab a piss.
The shy sun, blinded, oversleeps. Dawn, like our train, 's derailed by night.
A wrecking crew arrives by five to bang in a blaze of target light.
I do not care who else is slain; from strafing spare the undersigned:
"Where did you put my goddamned gun?" "I'm sorry, sir. I've lost my mind."
For cheap insurance let us bet where lucky Jerry's falcon-burst
Can easiest ignite our gas to repay worry with the worst.

The worst is spared us. Nigh on noon, the switch is patched, engines put-put.
We're really rolling. Feel them wheels. Sit still, my heart. Unknot, my gut.
Thus, o'er eroded Europe's map, her bridges blown, her signals crossed,
Filter ten thousand scrambled trains, unclocked and aimless; shunted, lost.
All you who catch the 8:18 to make your office sharp by nine
Consider your timetable may seldom correspond to mine,
Where Mars the testy anarch twists unscheduled stateless cars
To give thumbscrews the one turn more he keeps for first-class global wars.

Joseph Jones, Jr.

A bit bigger than most, this athletic specimen was quite complete
In pectoral, bicep, and deltoid, stoutly spanning six spruce feet;
Firm as a sound birch, it would take unseasonal storms to shake him;
Brisk as a diet of wheat-germ and ball-game could make him.

A big boy, big all over; big hands, big chest, very big heart;
Impossible to think of him alone, always the most agile part
Of job or joke; the nimblest, most limber, while his special magic
Lay in being what everyone else wanted to be. As for the tragic

Element, which in so muscular a mortal is usually lurking,
It was only his mind one might find slack or even shirking.
A self-starter, always set for the kickoff, such stalwart physique
Is fated to magnetize metal. Dependent on an instinctive mystique

Of muscle, you have to expect strain or snap sooner than late.
At the rate he raced through this war, he wouldn't have long to wait.
Adorers dogged him. There were problems, of course, but few if any
Seemed uncomfortable, perplexing, nor were there ever too many.

Oh, sure: some mornings he'd like less that nice face in his glass,
But self-knowledge isn't stylish; left to themselves, doubts pass.
When he decided he'd had enough of our routine life and inane duty,
I wasn't alone in being robbed of his baked-fresh-daily beauty.

So, when the word came down he, among lesser men, was very dead,
We felt his aura effectively pushing up daisies, as he'd often said,
Scouting perils, sulking days away. The most common wildflowers
Bless any path, cross-stitched by perennial suns and domestic showers,

Not at all unusual save in fulfilling the trim limits of some homespun form:
Personal tragedy. In second-growth birch groves a hungry storm
Devours boughs, strips frail tree trunks raw with the heavier ones.
Thunder. Chain lightning rips birch bark; gash and sap. Gnawing guns

Digest twenty-two summers to artless echoes of modest grief
For this Joe and his genial hulk. His quick exit tried belief:
He'd been so alive and kicking. When I'd first seen him, we were sitting up late,
Six months back, drinking—charlatans, wanly trying to simulate

202

Intimacy, acting friendlier than we felt, that tired old makeshift
For friendship. Then his gymnastic entrance gave us its real lift
Into the luxury of loving—spry warmth, more cordial than gin;
Physical attraction lit up our gang electrically, welcoming him in.

We felt: new and unknown to us, Joe: you hit the right spot.
Dead and gone your merit heats us still, like liquor, a straight shot.

Tony

A midget-type Mexican stud, tough as a range pony,
      Was our Tony:
Eyebrows lustrous as silk; the eyes—ebony, agate, or steel;
      No phony.
Queer as a three-dollar bill, hard as hell,
He could tap-dance, sing, do ballet, tell jokes pretty well.
      Universally popular, never hid a thing—
      Take me or leave me—yet did he bring,
To some tense situation, sterling joy.
Tony was quite a boy.

Plans for his program seemed fine, though one might guess what could grow
      To a drag show—
Uncomic gags, too damn many male prima donnas and stars
      Only go
To spoil great entertainment. From the start
There's our Special Services officer, that old fart
      Who bleats: "We cahn't be dirty; we don't think *that's* funny."
      What's humor about? Sex or money.
Jokes about money in a modern war
Aren't what the men ask for.

Our troupe includes a baritone-tenor M.C.; a clown
      Like Joe E. Brown;
"Carmen Verandah" (no Carmen Miranda): Tony Marón.
      Her gold gown

Once was a bedspread from some inn near Metz
Where she gets the idea for this show: "Fellas, let's
    Dream up some kind ole-fashion burleycue smoker stag
    Party." So she tied a crimson rag
Round her curls, managed to look almost cute.
Playing the quean don't suit

Everyone. Tony Marón played it exactly O.K.,
      The only way
To ridicule the bull shit we heard, habitually talked.
      When he'd say:
"Gooohood Niight; Guhoood Mawnin' "—put us in stitches;
Invent choruses like: "All you poor sonza bitchez—
    We got you Surrounded!" or "Each time we camp this way
    Boys wanna play but Girlz gotta stay
OFF LIMITS." It's not witty now, but then
Amused most of the men.

Particularly those up forward. So, that's where we go.
      Our minstrel show
Plays Pont-à-Mousson, a charming old town now hotly aglow.
      We don't know—
Can we work here at all? Unload, try to kid
A collection of half-dead, shot-at GI's amid
    Intermittent murder. Fanfare. Several crack wise.
    Half a laugh. Snare drum. Footlights arise
Simulated by shells traced bright and clear—
Thrilling, but too damn near.

Program formally opens as Fatso (tenor M.C.)
      Brays "Rose Marie,"
Shoots two lousy flat jokes. A fruity trombone introduces
      La Tony,
Who grabs at her cue. Dialogue goes
Sorta like this: "Hey you gotta fulla bag there, Rose
    Marie sweetheart; what's" (rolling her eyes) "you got *in* it?"
    "Just like you, sista: it's fulla shit."
(Groans.) Now: the chorus. In tutus, six boys:
Indescribable noise.

Arm in arm they prance in; ruffles flounce, pink pony-ballet
        Trying to stay
In step. They almost give up. Christ, whatsa *use?* But, justa same—
        It's a play—
Professional as far as place allows,
Though now time and place worsen. Through the roof of the house
    More spectacular spectacles Begin Their Beguine:
    Krauts, closer than one hoped for, I mean.
We better get the Christ outta here, man.
Whilst the Christ we still can.

In shellings, we're not allowed to crawl under our truck,
        But, what the fuck,
Where else is there to crawl? Our full cast makes its rapid exit
        With some luck;
Rip back to base, where we learn we're all crossed
Off the chow list. Past midnight, cooks abed. So we lost
    Our supper to hit the sack hungry, thirsty, and mad—
    Grease paint still on. However, we had
Brought laughs to an audience of grown men
Who mayn't laugh much again.

After such terrific performances, brilliant success,
        Artists, I guess
Might find the Real Thing can pall. Tony Marón, a true trouper,
        Nonetheless
The Dance still adores. Right after the war,
Runs to pick up His Career where he'd parked it before;
    Trots to his Union; explains he's been four years away;
    They say there's FOUR YEARS back-dues to pay—
And he risked his Life for his Land! SHE RESIGNS.
"Sign here, girl." Tony signs.

Snatch

Stained-glass panels shed their red as in a chapel to endow
With rose reflection brass and bench, and bathe the bar in ruddy glow.
Exhausted though still unrelieved, some GI's lounge against the glass
To sip warm beer and drag dead butts and wait their rationed piece of ass.

Near two full hours before high noon but in this whore-home's smoky air
A stupefied narcotic pulse vibrates the muzzy atmosphere.
Too bright and early to make love; nervous fatigue harasses haste.
We've just been dumped upon this town. We've fucking little time to waste,

And vice versa. Here she comes, with nothing on but rhinestone drawers,
To toss her tit and wink her twat and cense her scent of musky pores.
Our soldier feels his courage stir, although he'd almost just as soon
Hang around, bull-shit, drink and piss, and make it back to chow by noon.

Yet sullen dreams of luxury unspent for starveling months to come
Inspire a blackmail base for lust to activate our beat-up chum.
Though he's no expert, still he can manage five-minutes' stiff routine
As skillfully as grease a jeep or service other mild machine.

Slips off his brakes; gives her the gas; dog tag and rosary entwine;
Moistures distilled from tenderness lubricate the kinky spine.
Well: up and at 'em. Now downstairs, the other joes have had theirs, too;
They're waiting on him. Buzzy and smug, beer makes 'em feel a shade less blue.

He slicks his cowlick in the glass; unchanged his mug her mirror shows.
His pecker limp, he pats her ass and blindly back to business goes.

Big Deal

I.

Speaking of genuine characters, Major McGeek was a case.
One's detailed to every division. At our Taxeville base,
Tall, dark, handsome, we believed he shat by the book—
A model of army-manual deportment and a common crook.

Marvin McGeek: to you I raise half a nostalgic glass;
I was mad to see Paris. You got me my pass.

You were motorpool major; a hound's tooth stained but clean;
I had to explain to an FFI liaison officer what you'd been
In civil life. Translating word for word, could one tell
Which was autobiography, which the bargain you had to sell?
Frenchy was begging that spare part he knew you kept in stock;
Your concept of lend-lease came as a nasty shock.

McGeek specialized in motor equipment. In automotive war
One thing most officers can't do without is a command car.
One thing command cars can't do without is a complex dingus
Of which he held local monopoly, which must bring us
To incidents attending Xmas holidays, 1944–45.
I didn't get to make Paris but stayed alive.

McGeek had been a big P.R. man for Better Business Machines;
His family is long used to service in the U.S. Marines.
Due to errors in Personnel it's still disloyal to reveal
He's sent to a mere service company. (Here one can feel
The charm, assurance, and enterprise of a talented thief;
Officers breed respect, salesmen valid belief.)

FFI's Gaston withdrew, unserviced, with a Gallic sneer,
Leaving McGeek empty-handed, me gaping awkwardly near.
He snorts: "What's aching that slob? You do what you do;
These bastards rather lose their lousy war in spite of you.
Son, you're a smart lad. How about taking a flyer for fun?
I can spot guys with guts. I'm betting you are one."

Was he kidding? Marvin McGeek, wavy brunette, near six-foot-three,
Had not, as claimed, graduated from a good military academy
But indeed studied in schools of hard knocks and high kicks
Plus taking a few prizes in small percentages and the big fix.
I plead no moral or ethical advantage. It was clear
We'd caught the same nonfilterable virus: fear.

Headquarters' beehive routine secretes extralegal events.
I had guard duty. When the Lord God of Battles relents,
The awkward, craven, incompetent, or hysteric to pardon,

May he spot me in moth-eaten moonlight, drastically harden
A psychotic sentry's backbone, limp in fungal fright;
It was the classic locus for air raids by night.

McGeek stumbled past my post; I presented him arms O.K.,
He, a stickler for ceremony, each detail done the right way;
It was too dim to see me fumble in thick anticipatory gloom
While numerous indications promised imminent doom,
In zinc clouds, steely air, breathless X-ray stealth
Of buzz-saw noises inimical to human health.

"Hey, man," he gasps, "it's you." I smell his musk of relief,
He more jittery than me. It takes thieves to catch a thief.
"I'm that pissed," he moans, "I'm blind." A silly lie.
"You know where I live?" "No, but show me, sir," volunteer I.
"See me home, son." It's an order? Do I abandon my post?
Is this a test or a trap? All indeed may be lost

Yielding to magnetic attraction in this genus of male.
His intensity betrays indiscreet need. I feel him quail
So my valor rises. With less than a sketchy salute
I, carbine cocked, lead paths he shows. Then begin to shoot
Star shells, anti-aircraft fireworks, while grumbling thunder
Augments respect for ballistics in wide wonder.

I see him safe back to his billet. He offers gin to drink.
Noise has been briefly stunning. Its brevity makes me think
I shouldn't press luck too hard on this peculiar night.
Thank him kindly, tear back to my post, guess just right:
My relief man turns up on the dot; he'd been hunting me;
Palming it off, I joke about slipshod artillery.

Time passed fast. Christmas approached. Rain for days.
McGeek hunts me in chow-line, pulls me aside. He says:
"Soldier, you've drawn an important mission. Prepare
For detached duty for an indefinite period. Take care
Of instructions. Orders are being cut. You won't go alone.
But, kid: It's Your Ass; you're Operating on Your Own."

II.

So, ho! for Paris, fair city of high style, cuisine, and fine art;
I love thee so much I can taste thee; my little ole hungry heart
Is set on Paree. In peacetime, thou art all things to all men;
In war, bright gold at the rainbow's end, wine, soft beds, orgies, and when
You're horny and starved any passport is cheap. McGeek said just be sure
To contact that motor mechanic in a garage near Point du Jour.

Paris! How many leagues to thy perfumed breast? Whereby lies my route?
We're in Lorraine, on her borders. Signal corpsmen only map out
Main highways. Metz isn't ours; the bridge at Pont-à-Mousson a worry;
But Major McGeek and me his man are in one hell of a hurry.
My Marvin trusts me implicitly, yet to tape it all supersafe
He ships along three overstuffed brass wild to get back to SHAEF.

Nancy is queen of our dark duchy, her artists sublime: Jean Lamour
Forged floral gilt iron for Stanislas; Georges du Mesnil de la Tour
By candlelight limned Sebastien's corpse mourned by St. Irene;
Callot first etched the disasters of war, his needle tiny but keen—
Court painters to Alsace's twin sister whose sorrows never cease.
Eternal as art and suffering are, none warned me of terre-glisse.

Terre-glisse is slippery clay, mud laced in stiff oil greased by glue;
You float on its soup, you sink in its muck; you cannot navigate through
Black miles of sheer glassy roads with hard tires intended for tar
Surfaces. We managed at first and, leaving early, got even as far
As Bar-le-Duc, named for a delicious dessert, as well the former home
Of dukes of Bar and Lorraine. There, terre-glisse foundered in foam.

Our command car slid its fated skid; skimmed off the slick of the road
Doing drastic damages to our supernumerary SHAEF-bound load.
Driver was stunned; on the back seat, three officers took it hard—
Broken bones, crushed pelvis, internal injuries. My sole reward
Was, counting the hazards, a simple scratch, for, grazing the door, my head
Tore on its frame in my flop to the mud. By taillights, ropy red

Leaked through my thumbs. I tried to see how clotted gore would freeze.
Hyperaware, yet feeling no pain, I reclined in rich terre-glisse;
Finally sat up, ministered as I might to those more broken than I.
Aeons later, ten degrees colder, trundled a weapons-carrier by.

Emboldened by soft exhortations from Negroes manning this truck,
In no time at all we're safe and sound, Base Hospital, Bar-le-Duc.

When we'd quit Nancy for Paris, blithesome, insouciant, and bright,
Ninety miles north our troops and tanks bled in an extreme plight,
Malignly attacked by Nazis masquerading in GI combat dress;
The Battle of the Bulge's initial phase was a rabid loused-up mess.
For anxious hours, touch and go. Tall youth on both sides was killed.
Wounded, as many as might be sent south, Bar-le-Duc's hospital filled,

So when we checked in at 4:30 a.m., the place seemed black and shut;
Though bloody and weak, all I claimed for my pains was a superficial cut.
The pooped staff, at surgery since dawn, had just tottered to bed.
An orderly, looking up from his desk, cast a hasty glance at my head:
Did I require a surgeon, or might he lend his capable hand?
As for me—sure, anything, though I never will understand

How capillaries cram a scalp; you can't credit the beakers of blood
Filtering through skin with no pain at all. My skull felt carved from wood.
He scrubbed it hard; the green soap stung. He looped a masculine stitch.
I felt hilarious yet grateful I'd not been left dead in a ditch.
He led me to the head-wound ward. There, all seemed drugged or dead;
Showed me the john; gave me a shot. I died in my boots on a bed.

In the morning it made like Christmas; tinsel, crêpe-paper festoons.
On the ward walls thumbtacked cutouts from Disney's cute cartoons.
Some of the men propped up were shaved, giddy at tea and toast;
Screens 'round cots in the corners showed who were paying the most.
Hero lying next to me, swathed thick in his Pharaoh's trim cap,
Assumed I'd been at Bastogne too. This ironic, affable chap

Kidded about dem Poiple Hartz all of us were undoubtedly due—
"All of us" counting those present, which included imposters who
Had not bled with McAuliffe, who'd been bought by Marvin McGeek,
While the enterprise I got skinned in held its signal lack of chic
Which was later underscored at Chief Surgeon's morning round;
He created a scene by my bedside with stereophonic sound.

Surgeon, a Texan crew-cut with a temper to match his red hair,
Scanned me with a wrangler's eye; I cringed at his clinical stare.
"What in Hell is Wrong with You? Who sewed up your Lousy Head?"

He ripped off my loose slack bandages. I could only pretend I was dead.
Spasms of guilt adorned my gut. He glared at his staff; he said:
"How often you-all been tole not to use circumcision-thread

On head wounds? Who's the Mad Genius who thinks he's so damn smart?"
Both our temperatures soared to meet peak standards of surgical art.
"We'll fix you Up, and Fast," quoth he, my occiput throbbing to burn;
"You don't need a welt like a rope." That clear, now it's the next bed's turn.
Surgeon wasn't so hard on him; pats his Egyptian mummy's quaint hat.
I'm left to blush at the business I'm caught thus short-haired at.

Without a whimper of protest, fourteen stitches they deftly removed.
After-shock, when it shortly struck, this racketeer's conscience reproved.
Scar healed like an excellent reweave job; my scalp no blemish shows.
My records read it's an honest wound, good as got against true foes.
Scar tissue absorbs disappointment. For my shabby personal part
I never appeared in Paris nor got pinned to a Purple Heart.

Why

Why why should it never be I?
        It was this that he always had thought.
My eyes, they are keen. I am nearly nineteen.
        If they teach me then I can be taught.

Also there were six friends of his
        Who thought the identical thing:
Wait for us, Joe, you old so-and-so.
        They joined the same fighter group wing.

They trained and they trained. They sure trained.
        They flew. Did they fly! And they flew.
Before they knew it they all could do it
        As some of us could have done, too.

But our Joe had to stay on the ground
        And watch six friends skimming the sky.
While they were all hot, he was not so hot.
        He never learned how to fly.

A pilot he wanted to be:
　　　　If they all can do it, can't I?
My eyes they are good though my hands may be wood.
　　　　If they wash me out now, then I'll die.

They kidded him kindly. They said:
　　　　Why, son. You don't even rate.
This Joe should not fly. If he does so he'll die.
　　　　You couldn't handle a crate.

He didn't entirely wash out.
　　　　A gunner he finally became.
Unlike Sam, Rusty, Jim, Bill, Bud, and Dusty
　　　　He isn't stone dead. He's lame.

Sam sank in a flash and a puff.
　　　　Rusty hit rocks in a cloud.
Jim got lost in the hail, snow, or frost
　　　　Or the rain or for crying out loud.

Bill, Bud, and Dusty bailed out
　　　　On a steep sideswipe late coming home.
Flash rhymes with dash. So does crash smash & hash.
　　　　Home with never to roam.

Now he's asking: Why why was it I
　　　　The hand of just providence stayed?
I drank more than they; cursed and laid more than they.
　　　　I prayed a lot less than they prayed.

I'm asking why why why and why.
　　　　Best friends are best friends. So what.
They burned up bright blue. I didn't burn too.
　　　　But I might have but but but and but.

Hence he lies there, survivor unique
　　　　And his head, like a prop is atwirl.
Can't figure it out. What is it about?
　　　　Waits for a redheaded girl.

She comes as she does, every day:
      Red hair, white skin, green eye.
He's not going to die. He'll stop asking why,
      Take her on faith in the sweet by-and-bye.

Zone

Where does a battle begin?
      How far from a beat-up town,
Which had its dose; recovers?
      Now people walk up and down
Fighting's over for them;
      All that's left to be done
Is rethatch a roof, cobble a street.
      This, they've already begun.

Jeep whips out of town quick.
      Ruts bristle with cooled-off scrap.
Fields slashed with tossed-off treads;
      Burned trees bleed stubborn sap.
Dirty old snow unburies
      Farm horses, cattle, and men.
Under grass, fresh and greening
      Earth tries all over again.

Soon the going gets tense,
      Taut as a stinging wire.
Ears hook on to the solid rip
      Of valley-masked mortar fire.
At Marnach, cresting a hill,
      My jeep stopped, and my breath.
Scattered all over the sprouting vale
      Spat separate nests of death.

Air unraveled and tore,
      Too mean to sustain a man.
Combat parties crept into brush.
      Here a battle began.

Breakdown

Upon a hillcrest in a swarm of snow
    This driver holds his citadel alone.
High in the cab, he's left to staff a truck
    And feel each toe and finger numb to stone.
His pump's leaked pressure; the battery's gone;
    This bus rolled up the slope but can't fly down.
He squints beyond his windshield's flake-sagged frame
    Where prism lights wink out upon some town—

Nivelange, Dudelange, Longwy, or Eich,
    Wiltz, Berg, Esch, Mersch? Where did he miss that fork?
Route 6? Route 9? Here's no alternate
    To the old drag from Pittsburgh through New York.
The shawls and veils of snow in whipping sleet
    Frost on the glass, reflect his cigarette.
Our next twelve weeks of winter wind and wet
    Lock his big wheels in their glazed slipknot net.

His buddy's gone to get him help. How long
    Depends on phoning for another truck;
Delays from blown-up trestles, scrambled wires,
    And the short circuits of unhurried luck.
He is a fortunate joe who in this dark
    Merely endures, nor strives to sift from night
Salvage in chill nor wastefulness from time,
    Nor worry comfort from his trivial plight.

Shivers and puffs. His smoke's hot dot
    Glows like a pilot light to feed its flame.
Time stops. A season sets. Night's blind stare shows
    Shut-eyed or open-eyed a snowy same.
Our chauffeur's dream embracing summer sun,
    Stateside hammock, and suburban green
Fades with his Chesterfield. Grey-hooded cold
    Mantles hilltop and swamped machine.

K P

A Tec 3 pulls KP three times in ten days: is he sore!
He'd plans for this night. They are shot.
No one loves him, less than dirt, and what the fuck for
Is this war? Death were better: a lot.

Then some creepy jerk, he knows the type well, blows in where
He strips grease from the pots of his silly platoon:
"Report to the captain in charge. Wipe your ass, comb your hair,
Get a shave, son. Snap to it and soon."

"So what's this? Goddam Captain, the Army, and God;
What have I done? They've nothing on me now nor can
I've goofed and not known it; still it's odd
My luck stinks since this saga began."

He comes off KP, gets shine, shampoo, and some sort of a shave,
Hunts his captain in a weak storm of fury and gloom;
Kept fretting five minutes, he worries himself almost brave.
Then he's called to a small inner room.

"My boy," his captain commences, "I have Bad News for you,
Be a Man; it happens to all of us some time or other"—
Hands over the sheet writ in square type and true:
DAD IS DYING COME HOME LOVE MOTHER.

With interest his captain surveys him. How will he react—
Quick breakup or stiff upper lip? So they stare yet avert
Orbs which mirror the soul. When a fact is a fact
It's not blink nor a sob; it's a blurt.

So: it's dying he is. I request, sir, compassionate leave.
Granted. Catch a plane from the airstrip at nine.
Twin snappy salutes. He shan't grieve
Till he's given a sign.

Grief lurks in its lair to unleash in appropriate season.
Adjustment takes time. As for Father—who he?
(This character, dead or still dying.) With reason
He asks himself: What's he to me?

He returns to his mess-hall. Lamps low, they're all nearly through.
His secret stays shut, though indeed some notice a change.
Yet no one dares risk: What the hell's eating you?
Clenched tight, he buffs a gas range.

Daddy, where have you been all my life? Now from where
Hidest thou thy hard face from thy prodigal son?
Before you take off for the wan thankless air,
Bid me know what I've done.

Guilt boils from his loins up the vascular spine of his youth,
Simmering liver and lights to their slim broth of shame.
Sincerely—I do not give one damn. It's the truth.
Am I wholly to blame?

I'm a heel, I'm abnormal, I'm happy the bastard is dead;
Now Mom, Bud, and I have a chance to live in some peace.
He surrenders to moderate sobs while his head
Drains with mucous, tears, and release.

This gets me nowhere. Blow my nose. Wipe my eyes.
I'm no kid. I'm a man. What is more: I am free.
Choirs, swelling the end of film epics, arise:
Dad, we thank thee.

G2

Intelligence is Common-Sense or Knowledge-of-the-Enemy,
      Hence due-in-part to birth-and-brain,
      A busted-back and growing-pain,
      Lorraine's long night and winter rain,
      Our rear-headquarter's nervous-strain—
Intelligence is where I pray they soon may transfer me.

My company-commander quips: "Fah-Pete's-sake-whazit-eatin-you?
      Ya stem from all them Ivy-Leagues;
      Ya doan-look-good in ole-fatigues;
      Ya'd make-a-hit in deep-intrigues;
      I shall-appeal-to-my-colleagues:
Fill out these forms sextuplicate. We'll see-what-we-can-do."

Miracles happen. Here I pine on secret-project off-the-track;
      It's how I help to Cross-the-Rhine,
      And I can sniff from every sign
      By what intelligence is mine
      Uncommon-sense is just-my-line,
Absorbing poop from two ex-cops whom we'll call Jack and Mack.

Mack is a bum from Alabam', the dumbest of all classic dicks.
      So-what? Police-work-is-his-trade;
      His papers proved it, got-him-grade,
      A looey, too; he has-it-made;
      His biggest battle, whorehouse-raid,
Till he pursued such tactics here, risking stickier tricks.

A-ramblin'-wreck-from-Geogah-Tec, Jack's a rough-diamon' private-eye;
      He's bright-as-brass for sports at dawn;
      Surprised with brisk accusing brawn
      Faithless husband, the well-paid pawn
      Of faithful wife. Now has he gone
To more strategic enterprise with wider scope to spy.

Security-Is-Classified. Top-Secrecy we-gotta-keep.
      Mum-Is-the-Word they inculcate:
      Ya-doan-ask-questions. You await
      Ultimate-briefing soon-or-late.
      Meanwhile my work's to correlate
The price-of-liquor hereabouts—and, chum, it-ain't-so-cheap.

For dry-champagne (i.e., quite-dry) the cost in Chesterfields is—well,
    More cartons than you'd quite expect.
    Quetsch (plum brandy) many reject,
    That local liquor I elect:
    Six dozen packs. If you select
A blander blend, Bourbon-or-Scotch, it's any loot ya wanna sell.

Whadja want? We recommend our commissary repertoire:
    K-rations, tires, candy in stacks;
    Canned-ham, tinned-chicken, scrumptious snacks;
    Shirts, secondhand from-off-our-backs,
    And lethal tool and fierce knicknacks
Partial-security protects a tenderfoot conspirator.

I have-the-duty, more-or-less. I'm on-the-job. I fill-the-bill.
    I get promoted; duty pays
    In-a-variety-of-ways.
    On one of my dizzier days
    Jack toddles up. He tautly says:
"Ya just made corporal, buddy-boy." Twin stripes; a dubious thrill.

Part leer, part mystic paradox reveal enigmas of police:
    "There's a black market somewhere near. . . ."
    I am amazed, show it too clear.
    "We've spotted the black marketeer;
    He mayn't escape. This racketeer
Is kinda-coony, in-a-way, but: all-such-shit-must-cease."

Vow Jack and Mack, twain burlesque goons, a sister-act from vaudeville:
    "It's time for you to now know who
    Our villain is. Man, this-means-you
    (We gotta keep ourselves from view).
    The lad's a damn smart jig-a-boo;
Some frog-gang pays-the-fellow-off. Find how-he-makes-his-kill.

"So you can sock him easy-like, here's extry applesauce for bait.
    Peddle him bourbon twice-the-price;
    He'll hike it high and heist the ice.
    Doan-look-so-shocked. No-war-is-nice.
    This bugger wants a bigger slice
Both of gross-markup-plus-percent. Is-that-legitimate?"

The Economics I knew-cold; the Ethics were-a-different-case.
       Valor's a soldier's first virtue;
       Loyalty next, though to the few
       Obedience boils its bitter brew.
       When put-in-false-positions you
Reread-the-Articles-of-War and pull-a-double-face.

Our cobby jeep we heaped replete with barter-stuff of jungle-cheer;
       Jack slips me road maps and a gun;
       Mack swears I'll have-a-lotta-fun.
       They learn me rules, and No. 1
       Is to ensure this simpleton
Woan-nevah-squeal-whar-he-come-from. He swears it, nevah-feah.

The road to Thionville I took. About halfway it turns hard right.
       Terre-glisse is hub-high; weather, fair.
       I take-my-time in getting there.
       Just-after-noon I pull up where,
       Framed in slim birch: my brigand's lair,
A Louis-Treize pink-brick château, some Grade-B-mystery's site.

I park-the-jeep and ring-the-bell. I case-the-joint. The-place-is-dead.
       I check-my-map; my-route-is-clear,
       No human-error coming here,
       Yet something's sorta-kinda-queer.
       I munch-my-lunch and drink-my-beer.
Anticlimax muddled in malt confuzzed a foozy head.

When-I-come-to, it's-almost-dark. Lights may not lamp a homeward road.
       I've gone-and-done-it-that's-for-sure;
       My-first-big-chance: performance-poor.
       Night falls, with it, the temperature,
       When an enormous Black-a-moor,
Electric-torch and Tommy-gun, straight from those birch trees strode.

"White boy, whadja wantin heah?" His manner, eke his voice, are low.
       I rub-my-eyes. So, here's-my-man.
       I hasten to propose-my-plan.
       His mask presents a pained dead-pan;
       Big hard-boiled eyeballs now began
Dilation grand. My parley done: "Perhaps-I-better—go—"

"Ya-stay-right-heah"—this Nigra grins—"gimme ya gun: y'all need it not.
        Just-step-inside. We'll-have-a-talk;
        Unload ya jeep whal Ah'll unlock
        Mah shatow. Whadja gotta hock?"
        His eloquence commenced to mock
Worry in powder trains which wriggle up to getting shot.

He helps me haul my boxes in. He is an-elemental-type;
        We heap square cartons pile-on-pile,
        In annotating each the while
        His eggplant watermelon smile
        Bares tiger-teeth: "Naow, honey chile,
I gotta-Big-Surprise-foh-you." Mah spine is chill though ripe.

"So you hail from Intilligins, an Institooshin excilin;
        It's tough apprenticeship is Hell
        But stick-it-out. Y'all do-right-well
        Since y'all got-goot-goots-ta-sell.
        But, son, ya gotta rottin smell,
An foh a man ta stink like that, it ain't intilligin.

"Betya-who-sentya: Jack and Mack. Them two dumb-clucks ain't smaht-as-you.
        They doan know info that Ah know
        So lissun-to-what's-foh, although
        It's super-flew-us to say so;
        Podnah, to you mah-hand-Ah'll-show:
Unknown to them, unknown to all, Ah'm in ya G2 too.

"Under Suvreyans foh six weeks, Ah reconnoitreh you-all-three
        An evreh move-that-you-three-make
        Ah'd oversee an overtake.
        If you half-hep ya-getta-break;
        Ya eat-ya-cake, ya keep-ya-cake:
This-is-a-Proposishin, bud. Naow, ya-come-wuk-fa-me."

Ah sweat foh Sahjin Bookeh Jones, a whiteh soul Ah'll nevah see.
        No extry motion makes him blench.
        He treats-me-fine. Ah am his hench-
        Man. Foh him Ah win wine-and-wench.
        Ah speak some though he speak no French.
Intelliginsch is Common-Sench-and-Knowlensch-of-the-Enemensch. . . .

F F I

We found his canvas stacked in dust—weak study, landscape, nude, and flower;
One portrait whose well-studied mouth even gives promise of some power.
No date on any sketch is signed much later than five years ago
When the invader came to mar plans for his first big one-man show.

Then he retreated to a site whose cave and cliff he knew by heart
And organized a team of toughs to practice them in abstract art.
He hammered splitting of steel rails, modeled the clipping of high wire;
Designed for roads, impediments; illuminated sudden fire.

In his spare time in hideaways, 'twixt tricks on guard or days alone,
Furtively he first detailed where beauty's sunrise vista shone,
But this was hopeless; always near, the hidden threat, the certain call,
So he renounced his art until he could devote his meager all.

Let us admit, who with disdain, not undeserved, regard this art:
Slavery to a hard career beyond aesthetics tore apart
Promise, pleasure, and that gift about which he was undeceived;
He knew art markets call for more than the notations he achieved.

But compositions in the frame of ambuscade and dynamite
Assumed the scale of masterworks hung on the middle of the night.
As soon betrayed as briefly shot, his pals persevered as he'd planned
Till alien allies, better armed, usurped the posts he first had manned.

Now, all that's left of him is here: sketchbook scribble, flick of taste,
Needless unwanted immortelles dry in a cemetery's waste.
St. Ingres, St. Corot, St. Cézanne, whose shrines our galleries adorn,
On stronger students shed the glow which in his eyes was barely born.

Comité des Forges

This belfry trembles to its tune
        tall in a perforated tower
where mastermasons drilled droll holes
        for chimes gracing each quarter-hour.
War now perfects the carvers' craft;
        by its rasp-edged hacksaw blade
shorn off is surplus ornament
        and cruder decoration's made.
Its big bell bongs: one one and one—
        unsteady measure, swollen tone.
Next noise banged out upon the breeze
        confirms this here's a combat-zone.

The clock clangs Three. By army-time
        it's 15:00. Count it. Hark!
Hard on its dot their first shot slings
        wheedle-hurtling to its odd mark.
Its mark is not an ironworks
        safe past the outskirts of this town
where plump pipe-organ furnaces
        lift stiff-stacked tubes of rusty brown.
Nor is it yet a steep coalmine
        whose elevators groan aloud
with windlass, chain and truckle-tread
        ungarrisoned from ground or cloud.

Mid-afternoon's bombardment slams
        not just at random nor as yet
at any target one would guess
        an enemy might want to get.
Brown ironworks, deep black coalmine
        stay them unscathed since both provide
weapons for someone—mayhap: us?
        wages for workers who reside
way past all open areas
        from which a secret cannon's mouth
lobs brisk combustion on our turf
        beyond the Moselle, east and south.

That no rancor can wreck the works
          won't seem too quaint to our command.
No hurt in this or prior war
          have grazed them once from either hand.
So what's the target? Why waste shot?
          Does mere malpractice warp their fire?
Ask not too often, Mac, nor much;
          a traitor need not be a liar.
Shareholders in such mine and mill
          need not themselves risk battle-ground.
Across the sea snooze some of them;
          across the Rhine dream others sound.

Hard by a river-front café,
          from farther shores a paltry sight
one woman starts to dart to Mass
          fixed in her tearful frozen fright.
She's spotted; struck. She falters; falls.
          Small-arm's fire whetted blasts and barks.
Spite hankers after exercise;
          minimal murder snuffs its sparks.
Where citizens were wont to hunt
          haven within their ancient spire
it's whittled sheer by Act of God
          or oblique artillery fire.

Each day's chime-triggered brusque barrage
          spares the endowed shared treasure in
disputed earth, and handily
          shows two-faced foes how both can win.

Load

Our dirty dreams in ragged sleep:
    Kick off that blanket, creak that cot,
And all our billet, ankle-deep
    In dry-lipped dozing, waits the shot.
Upon some secret siding trained
    Forty miles over the Moselle
Nestles a long-range railroad gun
    Which slings a two-ton super shell.
It splits some slumber, rips a roof,
    Priming our chest-pumps overtime;
Set to sweat out this noisy night
    We mark the hours' quartered chime.

I am a tube, dry at both vents,
    My molars ground, my sphincters tight,
But damp in oxter, palm, and crotch,
    A hose for cowardice or fright.
I am a stack of plastic tubes,
    Liquids and solids to transform;
Bundled in armies, my moist friends
    Frame our vast sieve to strain the storm.
One supple pipe from lip to prick,
    One coiled long loop from mouth to ass,
A modest million drippings drain
    Letting each pissy droplet pass.
These thin-spray every fluent fear,
    Greasing its shudder, gag, and shock.
Wow! Here it comes! Just feel this floor
    Rise to the blast, bend, crack, and rock.

Well aimed from forty miles away
    Are steel-turned tubes the Jerries use,
But the most harm their banging does
    Is stiffen us to self-abuse.
Waiting the next note from their gun,
    A hot hand strokes an aching hard.
Nervousness exceeding fun
    Jacks a poor peter to its yard.

All eyes and ears on fire, in dark;
    Livid the iced, unspoken noise,
Threatening to madden, stunt the growth
    Of me and my lot of naughty boys.
Kraut cannon crouches, skins it back.
    Self-murder's tool is terror's goad.
It crashes about three blocks off.
    Its big load splashes my small load.

Réveillon

It cannot change a thing at home
    to harp on horror happening here.
We certainly won't want to mar
    our homefolk's New Year fireside cheer.
Yet fear and trembling take their toll
    in awe of all ill-will can do.
Solemn musing crams the mind
    on what folks here have just been through.

Such solemnity is sparked
    by hardihood of partisans;
a widowed mother who contrives
    to remedy time's mangled plans
as if these were embroidery ripped,
    design undone, bright pattern torn—
fabric too fine to throw away
    yet weaving now a web outworn.

We skip the war. We sip at tea
    dropped from an Allied parachute
retrieved by manlike unarmed kids
    in pre-dawn heists of risky loot.
Her mourning silks of mauve moiré
    grace ritual evidence. She'll show
the portrait of an hostage heir;
    some snapshots of their burned château.

Thanks to our thrust this year will be
          the first in three she'll have a chance
to take her tears to midnight Mass:
          deliverance. Continuance.
How can faith mean so much to her
          whose every prayer was paid by loss?
Her every taper lit defeat
          and pinned a family to its Cross.

So now, abjuring toast and tea,
          my hostess (no apologies)
conjures time lost as time possessed,
          the missal of her memories.
Outside, new snow mists panes within;
          she bids harsh history warm her pride—
one family's feudal services
          crowned by a splendid suicide.

Good-manners lapse to gaucherie
          as loss unlooses awkward grief.
She proffers paper which proclaims
          how death embraced defeats belief:
her splintered son lashed to the bone—
          rash valor, crisis at its peak.
Obdurate. Ready. Mute, serene
          who leapt five floors but would not speak.

It's getting late. It's time to go.
          I'll hoist carbine and haversack.
Under her waxen mistletoe
          we'll swap the usual New Year luck—
hostess, her hostage—almost friends
          I've never known. Will always know.

Trinity

He is our first to penetrate
      with prudence down this street
hugging sharktooth ruins close,
      firm as dead shocks repeat
where a few guardsmen on their rear
      set final futile charge.
He halts, as smoke-shroud canopies
      on stack and spire enlarge.

Like a young surgeon with his probe
      more curious than afraid—
palpates a town's erupted skin
      which gunnery has made;
pushes a sag-hinged door ajar
      to catch a mortal sound;
steps down a shaken hangnail stair
      where, throbbing underground
lurk twain survivors huddled close
      against a rotten wall.
A woman shields her child within
      the shadow of her shawl.

Scooping small rations from his tin
      he hosts a barebone meal,
one messkit's sacral minimum
      while all three scarcely feel
slinging hotshot overhead
      scuttle past bonepicked roof
and, since mother, corporal, child
      hold fast they stand aloof
in our nightmare's familial trance
      where three make one, a world—
each body self-sufficient breathes
      through everything that's hurled
by noisy neighbors, way upstairs.
      Their sovereign trinity
how often haloed, night and day—
      by our bleak mystery?

A sanguine sentry Joseph is
            typecast as GI Joe:
She's our Lady with her Babe
            out of the Book we know,
while harsh resplendent overhead
            glares angry orient Star;
its iron auroras flick gouged earth
            where Inn and Stable were.
Numb buzz-saw acetylene
            rusts on a bombard coast,
incandescent malevolence
            of what unholy ghost?

These hostel find for holiday:
            three bipeds in a vault
share fare enough to feast them full
            in amnesty of fault
though woman, godson, scapegoat learn
            whom resurrection wait,
instinct pays dear its innocence
            thin armor against hate.
A child that crowed on winter wind
            in Spring is crucified.
Shards of Christ's snowbound Mass explode
            on thorny Eastertide.

So, wiseman soldier, by your wit
            extend our shackled scope,
this mother for a mistress take,
            her babe as last-chance hope
suckling heart and hoarding pulse
            against the dogged guns
till ransack ruin break on dawn's
            determined risen suns.

Lights Out

In this cubed space, a schoolroom, our company settles for bed;
    Blankets draped over French windows where glass was before;
    Kids' desks stacked in the corners; we tuck in on the floor.
    A smudged blackboard still chalk-talks what makes four times four.
One low lamp throws footlight shadows of huge stooper and leaner
Shedding pants and shirt, unpeels the martial biped.
        Someone shouts: "Put out that light!"

It's been a hard day. Unlike most nights in this uncertain site,
    Everybody acts gloomy; no horsing around or noise;
    Reproachful fumbling and stumbling; some two dozen boys
    Subside towards sleep. No strength in loneliness annoys
The single soul striving to snooze alone, a state meaner
Than marriage. Self-love more than true love burrows right
        Into us fidgety men,

Landing us all back here in an old kindergarten again
    If not in wisdom. Won't we learn anything? I guess not,
    Except new and novel ways of getting ourselves shot,
    As if we'd no thought save to forget or get caught
In every trap we've been warned against, which we recognize
As sly boys schooled by enemy adults, trounced when
        We ignored their plainest threats,

As they did, before we were born, with no call to pay bad debts
    For which we were spanked and drafted. Deep torpid earfuls tell
    Who naps. Hard snore, grunt, snort, weak groan, breathy protests, spell
    Out degrees of probing the thick- or thin-skinned shell
Of dreamer or dreamless—chilled, untrusting; primed to be wise
But prone to stay stupid, casting pitiable nets
        Into the deep quicksand dark,

Trying to make medicine of suspicion or envy to mark
    A nightmare truce. So we survive, more quick than dead, but by
    Dozing, not knowing. Rat squeak, cat call, lullaby
    Of ventriloquist blab or somnambulist cry
Learns how sleep leaks its mumbled lecture to transmit a key
To codes where gut or cough read friend or foe. A lark
        Promises, bright-billed but mum,

What we're told love sings like yet can't hum. Conveniently come,
    Lark. Sound off and save. But love is no wonder-drug which makes
    Dog-tired foolish ones sleepy, whatever it takes
    To cure the pain in the neck, the trots, or the shakes.
Damp and unbriefed, all of us wearily twist, wishing we
Common soldiers, eager for kicks, dazed if not dumb,
        Had the sense we ought to want.

Let's pretend we always will sleep wide-awake, all licensed to haunt
    Each paradise we can dream up. Everyone smiles. Soft bowers
    And built-in sofas soothe our all-out powers,
    Beefy, untried. Armies? Worlds—drenched in showers
Of warm intimate glee . . . yet—who do we think we are
Tickling such fancies, not meaning one word, then taunt
        Our failure to make it true?

I give up. It's not in the cards to think this through. As for you,
    Lark—trill that dawn, but let's sleep first. At least, let me sleep;
    Make these planks softer. I'll start in counting docile sheep,
    Pray my Lord this bleary-eyed ill-kempt soul to keep,
In return for which, past billet or bullet, too damned far—
Stand to, supernal sentries. Unsought, unthanked, do
        What can be done for sleepers.

Germany

Charlie Boy

His family was exsanguinated, atomized, and aereated
In a predawn fire-raid on Berlin.
That he alone of nine survived partly explained his power:
He felt himself a destined morsel of flotsam and jetsam,
A choice brand snatched from the burning. So when he met some
Americans near Mainz, we forthwith proved him right and hauled him in
As jester, pet, and pest. In fair return, he'd indicate our
Grim imminent future. Long before he trapped us, exasperated

By status envies, a syndrome seldom dormant in his septic nation's
Permanent incipient madness,
I observed his odd anguish in a big kitchen overtaken
From an old Wehrmacht installation, handily provided
With castered copper cauldrons; two of these collided,
Spilling a lake of soup. He nearly swooned, absurdly shaken.
Mess Sergeant bade him sop the smoking stew, yet his starved sadness
Was such as one might spend for private woes, not on mere wasted rations.

Precocious and prepotent, floridly fleshed, downily upper-lipped,
Fifteen years, a fresh and foul-mouthed lunk,
Learned six four-letter words and like a broken record these rehearsed.
Mess Sergeant slyly pressed seignorial claims and taught him
Some useful lesson daily. Presently he brought him
Apt and eager as a silent partner to his comfy double bunk.
Sergeant in peacetime was a famous headwaiter; he disbursed
Ringside tables to crooners who grazed lordly ulcers and overtipped.

Karl was our baby's name: Karl Schmidt. Sergeant suckled him as his very own.
Karl didn't care; now was fine and clean
In T-shirt, parachute boots, stashed ten times daily. Man—could he stash!
If nights were naughty, cheap enough quittance, for they made him feel
He paid his way and gave him the full wherewithal to squeal.
It rid him of thanks. Bred for blackmail, not exactly mean,
He'd hold his peace for now. Later he'd take it out in cash.
We schooled his queer contralto to a singing commercial's mealy moan:

Parrot and puppet, ground out the hit tunes, his sponsor's top-ten winner;
We called him Charlie Boy. Vas you dere,
Charlie? Sing us a song, Charlie. Charlie, give us the ole one-two.
Charlie, a poor orphan, sweet and sincere as the songs he sang,

Lacking a family or friend, sorta liked to hang
Around our dayroom sampling affection; swipe his triple share
Of Cokes or candy, estimating by shrewd impromptu cue
Which idler's empty lap would let him squirm there, fidgeting until dinner.

It pleased our sergeant to promote his punk; tacked three stripes to his uniform.
The midget martinet infected
By poisoned patronage or *Führer Prinzip*, pulled spurious rank,
Commenced to give us orders. We demurred. Back he'd tattletale,
Report our vain rebellion on some shit-detail,
Stirred mutiny to murder. Sergeant, sensing his game suspected,
Sold the monster he had spawned yet held him dear who could not thank
His tutor loud enough for training him to sponge, toady, and inform.

He was corrupted. Between us all, we cooked his golden goose. Charlie was too
Much. *Auf Wiedersehen*, lover boy.
His sergeant had to break the news. We bet they wept. We knew it broke
Poor Charlie's heart, and all were glad to donate each his dollar
To ship him off to Christ knows where in a clean collar,
Another Displaced Person. When our improved atomic toy
Ticks twenty years from now, watch Charlie rally the German Folk
Slurping his next Führer's soup. Who gave him the first handout of that stew?

Das Schloss

Schloss Voss, built between 1600 and 1650:
Am I our first to arrive? Papery silence schemes
To repeat a stubborn after-image, pale and shifty.
Passing the gatehouse, didn't I see a furtive face
Where everything else spelled newly emptied space,
Blank, yet heavily pregnant? And, speaking of dreams,

Isn't this one I've had often before:
My host waits at his gate bidding me in to what
Funeral or fancy-dress held at the height of war?
This must be me, just on time; so is he, waitful
For whom? Me—with a welcome gracious or hateful?
Yet whether I've actually been here before or not

It's his mother, the Gräfin, who really expects me—
Ogress or angel, she's secreted upstairs, inside;
He conducts me through room after room while he protects me
(From what?) to a dainty meal fit for princelings at least:
Tarts, butter, cream, sugar, berries—a miniature feast.
In its alcove, the countess's vast bed. Does she hide

Under thick winter quilts from our warm end of May?
Embroideries, gilt furnishings from fortune and taste—
This great house an individual dynastic display
Of German legend; from story too, that witch in her bed,
Smothered in covers up to the chin, shamming dead,
Her boots sticking out black below, tightly laced.

For a moment I long to rip off her blankets but then
Doubt my mastery of chance in this fluid situation;
Dull thuds suggest she has several uniformed men
Upstairs or down who can make beds, murder, or cake.
I think it best to swallow her fairly perfunctory fake,
A feigned weakness corresponding to the capitulation

Of her sick nation, never, alas, enough sick to die,
Freeing us for our fun. I accept a strawberry tart
Ignoring its venom if any; pass the plate. Her eye
Marks me nibble nervousness. Then pride, strength, shameless arises,
Fully dressed. Thus betrayed, her son freezes in crisis.
He's dismissed: strangers alone shall learn thoughts near the heart.

"You're a man of the world," she begins, and it's true.
"I can see you're no child—college-trained, gently bred. . . ."
Shall I snarl: "Yes, ma'am. Grandson of a poor German Jew"?
But, being no boor, I urge her to get down to her deal,
Which is old as her castle, always and also for real:
It wouldn't be much that she wanted as so she soon said.

I'd agree. What she begged for was by no means excessive:
My house is historic. Spare my house. We would spare it.
My son is not well. He's wounded—this, overexpressive—
He is ill. Here she halts: a Nazi? By no means; *that*—never!
I'd been silent. I'd said no word. Were we stupid or clever?
She had little to fear. Go ahead: let her dare it.

Ask anything, everything. I felt hope rise like a rocket;
Can't she guess my patience is impotence masking as kindness?
I say: If she has treasure, let her list it and lock it;
Our arms undertake to succor the poor with the wealthy.
We provide what we can for the sick with the healthy.
My feeble fibs supported self-hypnotized blindness.

I wished I meant what I said, though irked at her wheedling;
She ran on, released by my bland passive behavior.
I hate to be needled, yet my manner encouraged her needling.
She asked the moon and, since she was as old as my mother,
And her son, that sad youth, was no worse than another,
I let them presume my vague rôle as effective savior.

Well, what the hell; no skin off my ass what becomes
Of this countess, her castle, this crumbling country.
But when American troops act more like bums than chums
They don't respect Art. I make my ambiguous adieu.
Thanks; just—thanks; if we ever can do anything for you. . . .
She donates her last butter and berries as bounty.

I find my way out via echoing salon and hall.
Mirrors mock an insincere exit. Polished parquet
Scorns my shoes. In the ballroom, soundless footfall;
A harpsichord open, on which Bach's Goldberg Variations.
Something breaks in, pricks my spine with icy vibrations:
Only that heir of the countess, who begs me to play.

I can't, so he sits and makes music for twenty minutes.
Bach begs nothing but absolute all-mastering order;
Nor does great dancing, concerts of finches or linnets,
Fronds of fern, veins in marble, stars in their courses,
The core of design in excellent or malevolent forces
Which lords of chaos or coherence coax into a border.

I thank this young man. In some happier dispensation
He'd have been a close friend; nay, even a lover.
Impulse shoves me to the brink of intense declaration.
Music undoes me. I'll help him, forgive him, restore him,
Unite what is left of our lives, slave for and adore him—
But conscience or caution warns of possible bother.

Driving back to base, I rough out a report in my mind.
Suggestions aren't mine to make, although I may imply them.
Schloss Voss can serve as command post, rest area; we'll find
Ample use for bedroom and ballroom. I needn't mention
Personal problems nor bring to a superior's attention
The Gräfin's greed, her son's need, mine, nor how to supply them.

Festspielhaus

And haven't I also been here before—
In 1923? No, it was 1924,
The first Wagner Festival after the first World War.
My mother, of German descent, liberally educated me;
Loved Beethoven, Brahms, though not Bach, as a virtual necessity;
As for music-drama, Wagner came first, naturally.

When she traveled to any foreign town
She'd hire a carriage and we'd wander easily around
Important streets. Thus I memorized this same ground
Driving from the station, as yet unbombed, sitting back-to, facing her.
We'd reserved rooms in advance at that famous inn, the Schwarze Adler.
When we checked in they would not take us. We felt some rancor.

Bayreuth: Wagner's imperishable shrine,
Noah's Ark of song. Between each act, one full hour to dine:
Würst, Kartoffelsalat, beer; the trumpet's ducal sign
Bids us return to the vast auditorium, half hangar, half shack;
Outside, brick warehouse; inside, a wide fan-shaped barn. Rigid seats sweep back
Cramped steeply. Swamped by such music, comfort's no grievous lack

Where not only Deutschland but all lands swarm
To bask in the Rhine's shimmering gold, the Flying Dutchman's storm.
Meistersinger starts like a Sunday school, sounds calm and warm,
Less the gross Wagner, more Bach-like, and while Ma disliked Bach, thought him a bore,
Even she couldn't resist such strong antiphons, such solid decor—
St. Katherine's choir-screen pierced, through which organ-voices pour.

Finally—the sacramental end:
Full processions, solemn din craftily composed to send
An audience roaring to its feet, the crammed aisles rend
Cheering. Here emotional or political factors scream and shout.
Next to me, a middle-aged black-sacked Jesuit with a pug's blunt snout
Howls *Deutschland über Alles*. Strained cords in his neck stick out.

Deutschland's metaphorical music-play
Performed once more, after defeat, on this red-letter day—
Germany resurgent, while spurning our naïve way
In fraternizing with late enemies, rekindles a chilling burst
Of song, prophesying, celebrating redemption by revenge: thirst
For blood: ours. German soul vows to German soil all the worst

Of what's happened since, bringing me again
To this identical opera house, now upon pain
Of death. One more war, a second, worse, world war. Thin rain
Drips through its fretted roof. Our taut tarpaulins don't do a lot of good;
My Special Services officer, née Metro-Goldwyn, thinks this shed should
Be a recreation area. It even could

Double as stage for our own USO:
And why not? Who won this war? Someone around here might know.
In 1924, quitting this hall was a slow
Process. As aftermath of that daemonic Teutonic battle hymn
All exits jam. An exhilarated public relishes its grim
Retard in leaving. My analytical senses swim

Trying to make art and evil relate—
Aesthetics ambushed by murder. Enthusiastic hate
Spills out its heady surplus, and so it grows quite late.
Ma is exhausted; hence we, having no hotel rooms, are sent off to
A small private home; towels fresh, the bathroom and toilet nice and new,
Reserved for Jewish tourists and kept by an old Hebrew.

And why not? We'll feel much more at home here.
So now I'm back in Wagner's house for a one-night stand where
They'll soon revive his Minnesinging, lending my share
Of salvage to the site's philosophy, invoking more the malice
Than the music: Beckmesser's stolen prize-song, rude envy, and all his
Apoplectic anger: *Deutschland über Alles, Alles.* . . .

Souvenir

Joe's a darn good driver.
       He's got the courier run.
Sometimes he hauls me along.
       We have a peck of fun.
We find Heinie weapons;
       Near Trier a case of wine;
By Vacha twelve binoculars;
       I took four pairs for mine.
Pushing back from Herzbrüch,
       Two miles from Himmerod
We smacked into a blown-out bridge,
       Explored an old back road.

He skidded as we hit a ditch.
       Our jeep tossed off its course.
Brakes screeched and stuck, for we had struck
       The severed head of a horse.
A taxidermied hunk to hit—
       Glazed, somehow stuffed, it lay.
The rest of an animal lacked its skull
       Thirty-five yards away.

Domestic brutes like Joe and me,
       Gun shy, both shun unflinching fact;
Can't stand the sounds of what we see;
       Unglamorous, our stories lack.
Perhaps we might explain in time
       To stay-at-homes what happens here.
We're half afraid we may forget,
       Hence swipe some useless souvenir.

Joe found an early gramophone
       To grind some sad jazz by his bed;
Its horn is lost. He rigs it up
       By lashing on our horsey's head,
To croon the half-truth's past Lights Out,
       A ragtime tune to turn all night:
Half-lost, this half-won war. It hums
       It's all been half more fun than fright.

Bath

Bent benches, no lockers, nor nowhere near nozzles enough—
Still: stacked towel, fresh soap, fresh foamy warm intimate cream.
Disdain crutty layers of uniform wardrobe; husk off
Shoe, sock, shorts, shirt. High luxury's lathery dream

Gargles hair-tonic tenor, brass baritone trill;
Life Buoy's lunatic tunes recollected from hymnbook, high school.
Slosh water by buckets. O brother. Slop, splash, and spill
All over crummy bifurcate buttock, soaked slick supple tool.

Athletes all, man or boy; at the least, what a sculptor might tease
Into classic athletic condition: life class, locker room:
Nudes in wet armor, a small-scale orgy of grandeur at ease
Or daft plastic mockup for votive historical doom.

Snap towel. Sting quirt. Rambunctiously prance, goose, gripe, grope.
Tank runs dry. Drain away all drear ordure, sud, sweat, and dirt.
Immaculate loons in raw hide, slicked hair, red ears rimmed in soap,
Strait-jacket us quick into stinky shorts, dead shoes, sodden shirt.

Off Limits

Under an altar's tabletop
        cowers a quivering bitch in heat,
abandoned puppy. She's disdained
        starved suitors sniffing from the street.
Here she's consigned a nervous wreck
        from our offensive, their retreat;
now, our attack. Amid such din
        her ganglia took quite a beat.

Her chapel, too, endures lopped shock;
        carved wilting saints arrest their droops.
To salvage any relic left
        we post: OFF LIMITS TO ALL TROOPS.

A fane defiled a kennel serves
        and safeguards shards from slipshod war;
expunged are scripts on plaque and tomb
        illegible as local lore.

We cannot read. We cannot count
        on god or martyr, sin or saint.
Martyrs are we if such still be;
        our compline mostly means complaint.
Infants were tricked how He was spelled
        by rebus rendering GEE OH DEE
counterclockwise DEE OH GEE.
        Pets mirror-mocked a deity.

Cudgelled and cuffed our warrior wolf,
        a displaced cur to stroke or tease,
this bitch in glory snuffs at hell
        and with real relish gnaws her fleas.

4th Armored

Was I bushed, workin all day: thirteen enlisted men, one officer,
We tole to take this ole town,
Move in, set her on fire; place machine guns at the crossroad.

One ole guy come out; he says: "Sure am glad to see you-all."
I say: "Fuck you are. Git back in line."
Lotsa Heinies—soldiers, civilians—all line up.

I was so damn tired. This guy come up agin. He says
How happy he is to see us, talkin pretty good English.
He says it again.

I smash his jaw with my rifle butt. That kep him in line.

This same ole town; we know damn well womin was shootin;
Them kep soldiers in houses too.
Took this one bitch, her undressed, in unnerwear,
Some Kraut with her. We kill him. Doan know who done it—
Charlie?

Anyway—Charlie he slit the straps on her brazeer;
Two ripe knockers fall out. Was that somethin!
We want to tear her pants off, march her down the street,
But lieutenant come up. He woulden let us.
She'd of fucked too. That damn lieutenant!

Way into town we head up agin a plowed field,
A womin there, plowin. She didn stop never,
But a lot of Heinies start up across her furrows.

I'm a farmer. She was real good with that heavy team—
Two big ones drug her plow, Percherons, Belgium hosses.

We pot them Heinies like pigeons.
Two of em fall into her fresh clean furrow.
She never stops onct, jus plows two of em unner;
Guess she was too scare to stop that fuckin plow
Still I can't see why she couldn turn her furrow one side.
Oh, I guess she done the right thing.

Then one of them SS bastids. We didn take no prisoners after Bastone.
They come in on us there dress-up like real GI's. You hear?
This SS son of a bitch have his piss hot.
Officer, he say. He wantsa surrender to an officer.

Charlie took his bayonit (this Jerry didn have none),
An Charlie have him a Heinie bayonit.
Easy-like, jus let it slide
Past this mother-fucker's ear. It make no difference;
Still kep outa line; still wantsa officer.

Nex time, Charlie says: "Lissen, bub."
I say: "Lissen, man, you doan know Charlie."

Damn fool wantsa die or somethin; open up agin, starts it hot.
Charlie slips that knife in his windpipe like buttah.

Worse thing was cold. Cold, cold; all the time, cold.
I mind the cold most. Weeks we never git warm.
Bastone. We have two K-rations a day. That's all. No warmth.
Cold. Jeez-us. Particularly your fuckin feet.

That Colonel Abrams. He sure saved a lotta lives.
Abrams love his ole radio. He git him inta town;
What a lotta bullshit that man throw;
"Now hear this. Now hear this. We have you surrouned."
Surrouned? My ass, but that's Abrams.

"Hear this, you-all.
We have you poor sonsa bitches completely surrouned.
If you-all doan come out an surrener esatly ten minutes,
Our artillery, which have your town already pinpoint,
Will commence."

In esatly ten minute everyone come out. An surrener.
Like usually they do; sometime, not.
One time we lose four tanks in fifteen minute to some of them
Goddam Hitler youth with panzer fists.
They burn our tanks. Flame-throwers. Cooked. We didn have
A chance. Them Hitler-youth kids. Was they fierce!

We see one stand up with his girl, her about twelve, maybe thirteen,
Both of them with their type bazooka.
Charlie have his Heinie P.38. Wasn use to it then neither.
One hunerd yards, a long shot fera pistol. Hell, long fera carbeen.
Hot damn. That kid drop like a hammer hit him.
Later, went over fera look. Charlie plug him jus unner the left eye.

He was going to pot sister too. I guess it was his sister.
I say: "Charlie, doan do that."

Then this door. I open up, easy-like. Tavern sorta bar;
They sell beer an santwitches?
Inside?
I'm a son of a bitch if weren twenty-eight Heinie officers,
Two machine-gun tripods, mounted low, on tables—
Swing roun angle one huner eighty degree;
Twenty-eight men, all officers. I count three womin too.
I tell you, mac, I had a lotta things go through my head.

I riz my hand jus like to say:
"Not one peep outa you bastids. You-all jus come on out."
I do this cause I know damn well we have evrythin set up, outside.
Atually, this town was very well covered.

Them Krauts come out. They lef their weapons heap on a table.
This here P.38, the one Charlie got; he got it here.
Another time, a bluff like this mightn work.
Atually, these Krauts almos didn believe me or somethin.
Some silly son of a bitch start to open up.

We had 75's, 88's, 101's, evry fuckin gun you kin think of
In hills back of this town, listenin fer one shot.
They hear this one shot.
Christ: we start to fire, just at roof level:
One, two, three.
Then we hit a leetle lower, a leetle lower—an lower.
Special, we pick out any tall tower, like a church steeple.
One, two, three.
Man, was this cute! Like a typewriter:
One, two,
Three.

P. O. W.

Behind tall coils of slack barbed wire
      Fresh prisoners slump and wait
As far from home as sentries are
      From theirs, who guard this gate.
In scarecrow coat, in bandage soiled,
      Crusty with bearded grime,
To well-washed warders claim to be
      Confederates in crime,
Whom crime abandoned on the spot
      Once having used their knives,
Then freed them to captivity
      Whereby they saved their lives.

Such dreams as they've tucked in their kits
　　　　To us seem creased and thin,
Some consolation prize for games
　　　　They took good chances in.
Inspect our thoughtful foe. What thought
　　　　Depends on his decline?
A mirror writing of ideas,
　　　　Echoing yours and mine.
This war is over now—for them;
　　　　A stagnant calendar
Shall intervene before they go
　　　　Back where their kinfolk are.
An equal net of nights and days
　　　　Claps us in our wide jail
To land us locked in judgment where
　　　　We'll never raise the bail.
Tight handcuffed to their loose defeat,
　　　　Stain, cold, indignity,
We're prisoners of their slow revenge
　　　　Which we name victory.
So frisk yon haggard mask for steel,
　　　　Hate, or arrogant glint.
Behind barbed wire, how'd we take on?
　　　　Red, dull eyes lend no hint.
Fear, rancor lights no vivid trace,
　　　　Disdain, nor stiffened pride.
If hatred once was heated here,
　　　　How long ago it died?
P.W.'s framed between the barbs,
　　　　Pinned by strong stake and wire,
Watch us take kindling, split it up,
　　　　To cheat the chill by fire.
Thin as our will, flames flicker up,
　　　　Warm neither them nor me,
But somehow calibrate great wars'
　　　　Level adversity.

Siegfriedslage

Beyond the Isar—*Reichsdrückmeisterei;*
Drück? Dreck. Vast warehouse bulked with Nazi fill
Of drug, gun, uniform—feckless supply.
In leagues of corridor, abandoned room,
We've set High Headquarters, 'midst sloven chill—
Our *ersatz* vict'ry and rankling gloom.

My bureau, a dust-sifted shoe-box cell
Usurps the top floor of which stair is shot.
I serve my Sergeant, Filthy Flaherty. He'll
Tell the World his canned Cagney Irishry;
Bathes once a month, need it or not;
Buzzed up at coffee-break and spat at me:

"Man. Get a load of this. Waiting below,
A wild man's parked, and he allows as he
Wants *you*. He must be nuts, but pronto:
Git. See for yourself. Gawd, it's just a farce—
Some stimulated Major, V.I.P.
Who does not know his silly English arse
From one damned hole in our accursèd sod;
Hies here to Headquarters a lousy mess—
In *carpet*-slippers, yet! Before Gawd,
He lacks his HELMET LINER, and is clad
In uniform which Patton must suppress."

Dunstan, driving from Kempten, else I'm mad—
It's *you*, heaped high in Quixote jeep with loose
Bedding, valay-packs; manned by nordic cook,
Wehrmacht driver, yesterday's P.W.s—

Enemy personnel, but how the hell,
Released to you? It beats for keeps, The Book.
Yet here you are, crummy and very well
To haul me off to supper, talk the night.
Sergeant is useless, never'd let me go;
I skip right o'er his head, which is not right,

Straight to my Captain, piteous pleading thus:
"Sir, an old friend awaits me here below;
May I go with him? Filthy'll make his fuss,
But I'll be back by dawn; inspection stand."

My Captain snickers: "Soldier, is this Ass?"
I play deep hurt: "Don't, sir, misunderstand.
It's (simulated) Major Morden, sir;
His invitation prompts a formal pass—
Of prose and verse th'ingenious author.
Here, his momentous present mission's for
Interrogating Pastor Wiemöller—
Sage U-Boot Kapitän of the Erst Worldwar;
Whom Hitler jailed, or did he? It's obscure.
But Dunstan Morden will prompt, uncover."
"Permission granted. Back by dawn—but sure."

His jeep was comfy, like a busted sack:
Pot, kettle, mattress, a fat case of books,
Floor-lamps, victrola, Wagner's profile plaque,
Discs; a crate of wine, God knows all what—
Salvage or pillage. The teenage cook's
Worried about his steaks, a cute kid, but
The fierce chauffeur will kill us if he can,
Cuts every corner, never honks his horn
And barrels wrongside down the autobahn;

Finally achieves a silk Bavarian lake
For a four-color travel-poster born,
Schloss miniature, pasteboard cut-out fake
Domesticating Rheingold's local name,
Hight S I E G F R I E D S L A G E, mean memorial
To hero Siegfried of operatic fame,
Sieglinde's tenor, Mime's fosterson.

Upstairs, a dormitory; windows all;
Unrolled neat bedding for ten men, each one
An international-type specialist:
Dutch, English, Dane, plus two Americans—

Morden, with chum Tim Burns, complete the list
Tho' Tim is Afro-Irish in addition—
Intellectuals cosmopolitan
Sworn to high secrecy on topflight mission.
What they're now up to here, one may not say:
(Investigating the repentant kraut?
Did he mind bombing more by night or day?
From R.A.F. or from a U.S. plane?)
Has this some use? File and forget? No doubt
Archives are avid; still, it's to *my* gain,
For by this site I learned th'essential score,
Nervous prognosis of hist'ry ahead.

A poet sketched the full orchestral score,
Sight-read symphonic fate precipitate;
Defined some main determinings in man's
Hate which "no man can ever estimate."
Prussians have a sense of status only;
They must be over us all—or under.

Equals are no compeers for these lonely
Infants who've one word: G R O S S—for great, big, grand,
Extraordinary, huge. Their blunder
Is semantic. "To rule" they understand
As enforced order by gross control.
They rest undefeated; this gimcrack peace
Is but a breather for us both, each soul
The same. Unwar, never a victory,
Bequeathed to all our epoch—slight surcease:
"Organized hatred. *That* is unity."

Twenty years on—absolved, rich, competent
To kill again, but next time on "our" side;
Russia an ally who shan't relent
Her quasi-oriental tricks of tension
So all the luck we wait on here—denied
Or distilled to the dreariest dimension
Of mindless spirals in biomorphic daft
Jounce of organs' or organisms' junctures,

As free as pistons in a confined shaft;
Captious hide-and-seek of whimsical guns,
Cops and robbers whose gamesome punctures
Waste random blackmail on risky runs.

I get depressed. One often gets depressed
When pliant minds for whom the human aim
Spell complex logic logically expressed,
Are rendered sanguine by the basest acts,
Discounting tragic or ironic claim,
End up near truth with just the lyric facts,
Yet past complaint or wisecrack cynical
Reducing analysis to partial
Documents of the jejune clinical.
A poet made uncommon common-sense.

I change the subject. Aren't there some martial
Arts safe from ordinary murder? Hence
Asked the silly question—as one must,
Concerning our "war-writers": "What think you
Of Soanso?" whose combat verse was just
Out, Pulitzer-prized, compassionate, fine,
Deeply experienced, sincere; so true
It made me weep. I wished it had been mine.

"Thin stuff," he snapped. I know it then: thin stuff.
"Poetry," he said, " 's not in the pity.
It's in the words. What words are wide enough?"
Yet if one's greedy in our craft or art,
Shrewd, apt, ambitious—here's a recipe
To fix some blood-types for a wounded heart,
Resecting style, or better, grafting tones
Eavesdropped in anguish o'er field-telephones,
Wise walky-talking through our murky mess,
Rococo bingo, gangbang or deathdance,
A microscopic keyhole on distress—
Merciless, willful, exquisite, grim, frank,
As in some masterpiece ironwrought
By that tough butterfly, Ronald Firbank,

From whose *Flower Beneath the Foot* recall
The texts they taught: "What Every Soldier Ought
To Know"; the Hon. Mrs. Victor Smythe's "All
Men Are Animals"; field-manuals' skit.

No epics more. Grand style our wars are not.
Teasing is all. Let's skip the heartfelt bit.

He's restless now. Gossip is done tonight.
Kümmel. Then hit the sack, for *punkt* on 8
Morden rates Wiemöller in his light bite.

  Near dawn I drag his driver deep from sleep
Too soon, but scared I'll make Inspection late;
In chill midsummer mist grope toward his jeep.
Coffeeless, furious, he whirls me fast
Towards Headquarters, through growing light, on time.
Dazed, do I meditate through forests passed:
History's long hurtle, my precious part
In decades left me and the health in rhyme;
How one believes, nay, *must* believe in ART.

  Heavy the burden; indeed so onerous,
I needs must to my Sergeant spill it all.
Better: my Captain. He'll alert our Brass:
"Listen! d'you know what This is all About,
Really—*about?*" Cassandra's howls appall:
OUR PRESENT VICTORY'S BUT OUR FUTURE ROUT.

  No dice. Who'd listen? No use, and, who cares?
With us, stout England, th'enfeebled French
Shall shrink our risks to what dubious shares
Of salvage as th'Imminent Will intends.
Stubborn enseamed inertia shall entrench
Its sturdy virus—blind, complacent, send
Its livid chain through our complacency. . . .

Gripe

Who is a friend? Who is a foe?
      No answer's absolutely clear
But every sign intends to show
      Friends are Up Front; foes To the Rear.
Our own troops, forward—limp or stiff
      At every shell that they sense shot—
Sorta react like we would if
      We were Up with them. We are not.
Safe back, I'll curse my colonel's name
      Whose whimsy aggravates my life;
Griping's an intellectual game
      Absolving me from guilt or strife.
I'll not desert my desk secure
      Nor cede it to some combat man
Whose ruggeder nature shall endure
      A larger love, a shorter span.

Yet should one wander six miles west
      Where mortar barrage splinters night,
I could relieve two for a rest
      Pondering friendship, pluck, or fright.

In a charred stable, on damp grain
      Shock slaughtered cows shan't want to eat,
Shiver twin jokers who remain
      Exposed, in spite of this retreat.
A one, his liver's slit straight through;
      Sob and saliva down it drain.
The most that modern war can do
      Dulls his complexion in his pain;
While Bud, hysterical because
      His frantic nerve is fit to bust,
Cries: "Joe. Don't die," though die he does.
      His slackened lips absorb the dust.

Outside, their other boy friends bleed
      Like murder, while the wilder, they
Work off hot rage or terror, shed
      Layers of self, like skins, away.

Here's a commencement to a show
        Of selfless love we all might spread
From common friend to common foe,
        Sparing our livers from their lead.

Till then, though, I shall bear my brunt,
        Cursing the colonel from my Rear;
Lavishly let lads Up Front
        Spend all their love, share all my fear.

Kristallnacht

Major poet Heinrich Heine
        Sings bitter German songs;
Hamburg hears and hates them,
        Charged with sovereign wrongs.

He sings of Jewish maiden,
        Of baron bold and cruel.
He is a Jewish *Dichter*.
        His rhymes are learned at school.

Still ist die Nacht. . . .
Ruhen die Gassen—hear.
Mädchen mit dem röten Mündchen;
        Nach Frankreich . . . zwei Grenadier. . . .

Would Heinrich Heine
        Were alive today.
I'd feed him German fable
        He'd say in Heine's way.

There is a Jewish maiden;
        In Posen she did dwell.
Before attaining nine years old
        Savored scraps of hell.

Had her family herded
       Into a warehouse bare.
Dawn by dawn she heard them
       Ta'en into open air.

Men who came to take them
       Always appeared by four.
Four, that is, a.m.
       They'd wait no hour more.

One dawn she was wakeful
       Because she could not sleep.
Men came. They took her father.
       He didn't make a peep.

He did not wish to wake her;
       She needed all her rest.
Next day they took her mother;
       At other times the rest.

But God redeemed His daughter
       Of Zion's cursèd brood.
Somehow she crossed the water,
       Because of Quakers good.

Now, she is a grown lady
       Of thirty-two or -three,
Incarnating dignity
       Queens might envy.

Sometimes she remembers
       When she was eight or nine
Nights of crystal clearness
       To thank her God and mine.

On one such night of crystal
       Storm troopers with bold blade
Smashed pretty porcelain and glass
       Which her small home arrayed.

Auschwitz, Belsen, Dachau
　　　Are famous German names
Like Wagner, Goethe, Heine,
　　　But vary in their fames.

When Heine lay dying
　　　Far from High Germany,
He sighed: "Since it's his *métier*,
　　　May God pardon me."

Armistice

Rain runnels helmet, skips the neck,
　　　Drops, spits, and hisses in our fire;
We shudder in each leaky coat,
　　　Boots squelched to ankle-deep in mire;
Really relieved despite the damp,
　　　A dozen buddies here have come
To pool our mutual luck and thanks
　　　And sweat it out till we're shipped home.

Burn fire, rain rain; love, buddies, love
　　　Each other, sure. It keeps us warm;
Battles of braver joes than us
　　　Have kept us clean of scar or harm.
By good sports shared, the wet warmth steams:
　　　A summer's done; a war is won;
Our drizzle downpour's not so bad,
　　　And slight discomfort's not unfun.

Real rain is soothing, for it hums:
　　　Though weather's wet, still pluck is dry,
And not a fellow's near as mean
　　　As I deemed you or you deemed I.
Do not misprize our meager blaze
　　　Snapping the short slant summer night;
Tinder love may still catch fire
　　　To kindle on the next sunlight:

Keep if we can some tender trace
      To carry back to bed again
Salvage of twenty piss-poor months,
      Copper embers in the rain.

Kinderlied

GI's aren't free to "fraternize"
            save with mature kids of 14
(or under)—who, all paws and eyes
            cadge gum or sweetmeat pink or green
and choklat-bar and cola-coke.
            Their straw bangs bob on bucktooth smile;
though spawned by foes these slyly joke
            at intercourse Teutonophile.

We risk: "*Nichts gut. Alles kaput?*
            Wie viel ist deine Schwester hat?"
These be small fry lusting for loot
            within our barracks' orphaned plot.
V-Mail, stray pups, beer, pin-up dames
            lavish domestic substitute
for after-hours carnal claims
            craving too churlish to compute.

My foster-daughter's weird but cute.
            Her vertebrae emerged askew.
She's a mature proud-chested beaut
            except for limbs which never grew.
A runt, she preens beyond the pale
            of our lax "fraternizing" ban,
a hunchbacked sport, a sound female,
            sweet solace for a normal man.

She mooches with her scapegrace crew
            whining Brahms' schmaltzy "Cradle Song."
Our *Kinder* are accustomed to
            haul her for extra luck along.

When sundown clamps our handout streets
        as shriller rise their clatter cries
each merry midget bums its treat
        and my grim goblin snags her prize.

Our M.P.'s have their orders too—
        as Mac who stands late-guard tells me,
lifting the barrier: "What the screw;
        we're all one happy family."

Scraps

1. THE LANDGRAV OF BUSS AND NEUSTADT LORD OF VACHA
      MARRIED THE VERY HIGH-BORN LADY
   MARIA ANNA ELIZABETA COUNTESS OF LAUBACH
        DOWER HEIRESS OF THON
    AND SET THIS SUN CLOCK HERE IN MAY 1528

(Inscription on a garden sundial in a Thuringian castle, wartime refuge of elderly Swedes, Danes, White Russians, and Britons.)

2. THE GIFT OF
RABBI EZRA BEN ORDAO DA SOLA POEL
TO THE PORTUGUESE CONGREGATION OF
AMSTERDAM IN THE LOW COUNTRIES:
HEAR O ISRAEL!

(Inscription on a silver-gilt chalice found in a bushel basket, Sparkasse vault, Hungen.)

3. PAX IN TERRA HOMINIBUS
GOSS MICH CONRAD RATH
MAINTZ: 164—

(Inscription on fragment of bronze bell, Stephankloster, Mainz, after severe bombardment.) "Peace on earth to men: Conrad Rath of Mainz cast me, 164—"

4. SEPTEMB 7 44 AMERICANS TOMMIES IN CASE YOU SHOULD OC-
CUPY THIS COUNTRY DONT FORGET NOT ALL UNS ARE HUNS AS
YOU BELEEF THE MOST UNS ARE YOUR BLUT UND KHARACTER
DONT BE HERTLOSS TO OUR POOR GERMAN PEOPLE LAST ADRES
116 MADISON AVENUE

(On a supply-room wall, Frankfurt.)

5. WIR WERDEN NACH DEM KRIEGE IN JEDER LATRINE EINE NAZI
HÄNGEN

(In SS Kaserne washroom, Nuremberg.) "After the war we will hang a Nazi in every
latrine."

6. REIN DIE EHR: BLANK DIE WEHR

(Over barracks' mirror, Erlangen.) "Thine honor clean: Thine weapon shine."

7. INAUGURATION OF EXPOSITION OF NORTH BAVARIAN
    CULTURE AND EDUCATION
PROGRAM: 7 July, 1939: 11 A.M. BAMBERG
1. Entrance of the Gauleiter into Exposition Precincts (Fanfare)
2. Report of SA Standortsführers to the Gauleiter
3. Review of the Honor Guard and Honor Formations. The Bamberg Symphony
   Orchestra will play during this Schröder's March: Deutschlands Ruhm
4. Overture to "Prometheus": Ludwig van Beethoven
5. Greetings of Kreisleiter. Oberburgermeister and Partymember Zahneisen
6. Reichshauptstellenleiter, Partymember Bartsch, of Munich, speaks

7. OFFICIAL OPENING OF EXPOSITION BY GAULEITER
    PARTYMEMBER WÄCHTLER

8. Sieg Heil and National Anthem
   (Proof of program copy found in Gauleiter Wächtler's house, Bayreuth. He had been
   shot by SS the day before our entry.)

8. LES MAUVAIS JOURS SONT PASSÉS VOTRE PAPA VA TRAVAILLER
EN ALLEMAGNE

(Unmailed postcard, Displaced Persons Center, Ingolstadt.) "Bad times are finished.
Daddy is going to work in Germany."

9. TO HERR WILLY KRAUS
    CASHIER FOREIGN EXCHANGE SECTION
    DEPARTMENT VI: FRANKFURTS REICHSBANK

    6 FEBRUARY 1936

    DEAR SIR:
            YOU WILL KINDLY PRESENT YOURSELF FOR STERILIZA-
    TION 13 FEBRUARY 1936, 0730 HOURS AT THE NEUFRANKFURTER
    KLINIK. PLEASE BRING YOUR OWN BANDAGES AND RECEPTACLE.
    YOU WILL BE PERMITTED TO RECOVER MEMBER. HEIL HITLER!
            (SIGNED) PROFESSOR DOKTOR HANS SCHEIDEMANN
                      COMMISSION FOR RACE PURIFICATION AND
                      HYGIENE
                      FRANKFURT, AM

    (Typewritten practical joke circulated among the foreign-exchange section of the largest Frankfurt bank; first believed authentic, it was later explained as example of middle-class German humor.)

10. IN DEM WOHNZIMMER LAG DER BURGERMEISTER MIT SEINER
    EHEFRAU DURCH KOPFSCHUSS GETÖTET UNMITTELBAR NEBEN
    EINANDER JE IN GROSSER BLUTLACHE.

    (Eyewitness description of charwoman who had entered the Rathaus of a small town, north of Nuremberg, day of the American entry.)

11. DIE ÜBERGABE KOMMT NICHT IN FRAGE. DAS LAGER IST SOFORT
    EVAKUIEREN. KEIN HÄFTLING DARF LEBENDIG IN DIE HÄNDE
    DES FEINDES KOMMEN.

    (Heinrich Himmler's order, April 14, 1945, Dachau, given as a souvenir to Walter Hnaupek, a Polish prisoner, from the copy given SS Camp Officer Dietrich Schwarz.)

12. ARBEIT MACHT FREI

    (Camp motto, over main gate, Dachau.)

13. LATE SUNDAY:

MY VERY DEAR WILLY:

NOW IT IS SO FAR.
PAUL COULD NOT DEFEND MUNICH BECAUSE HE HAD NO TROOPS
HE WENT BACK WITH THE WEHRMACHT
NOW WE ARE TOGETHER

WE DROVE TO HINTERSEE TO THE POST INN WHERE WE WERE RECEIVED WITH THEIR USUAL GREAT KINDNESS AND CONSIDERATION AS ALWAYS SO WE HAVE IT PLEASANT AND NICE FOR OUR LAST HOURS.

IN ORDER TO MAKE NO TROUBLES FOR PEOPLE IN THIS NICE HOUSE WE SHALL TAKE A LITTLE STROLL LATER THIS EVENING ALONG THE SHORES OF THE GREEN LAKE WITH OUR LITTLE MOTHER SWALLOW OUR POWDERS AND THEN MY DEAR LITTLE BOY WILL THROW 2 HANDGRENADES UNDER OUR BENCH IN ORDER TO AVOID HAVING HIS CORPSE ABUSED.

WE SHALL DIE PEACEFULLY, CONSCIOUS OF HAVING KEPT OUR HANDS CLEAN IN THE STREAM OF LIFE. OUR TROUBLED THOUGHTS FLY TO YOU WHOM WE MUST NEEDS LEAVE BEHIND.

WE QUIT THIS EARTH IN FIRM BELIEF THAT OUR FÜHRER WILL ONCE FIND IN HISTORY THE PLACE HE SO RICHLY MERITS ALTHOUGH AT THE PRESENT HOUR EVERYTHING SEEMS TO BE AT END.

ALL LOVE TO YOU AND A FITTING [gnädiges] FATE IN LIFE AND DEATH,
YOUR LITTLE SISTER.

(Letter from the wife of Paul Giesler, Gauleiter of Munich, to her brother, Willy Patt of Bochum.)

Peace

Peace

This was the end of a war:
    Here we were, rounding the bend,
Racing towards peace against time,
    Wild to be in at the end.
The front swept ahead like a flood
    Rolling away from our road;
We chased after the fading guns
    With hope our heaviest load.

For years we'd been one and one—
    Millions of ones, all apart;
The end of this war which everyone won
    Was time to unbuckle the heart.

Only a small border town;
    Bright banners hung to the ground;
Weather sighed thanks, everyone laughed,
    Brooks made a bubbly sound.
They said: "Take any bed here.
    Bathe in the brook by the gate.
Sleep through the steep or fading star.
    Don't wake up till it's late."

I walked into a white room
    And found me a big double bed.
On its fresh crisp counterpane
    Glowed a curly gilt double head.

Its four lips made one mouth:
    His firm tawny arm lay free
Across the pulse of her childish breast.
    They were not startled by me.
I sat on the edge of their bed,
    Held his open hand in my hold;
Our fingers joined beneath the weight
    Of her fair hair's curly gold.

Linen sheets fold back from flesh;
    Tan skin is kissed by white.
Here's where we've all come to play
    Tonight and every night.

Arts & Monuments

We woke up early one morning. My! what a gorgeous day!
We'd crossed Germany's borders to capture a German May;
    Strawberries-in-wine was the weather. All outdoors smelled of fresh heather,
        And my puffy captain had a lousy toothache.

"Get me a dentist; it's an order. This pain's just got to stop."
As dentists, we know the Germans rank at the absolute top,
    But this town was banged all to hell. I didn't speak German too well,
        And where does a good dentist hide out anyway?

Believe it or not, Captain's toothache led to our pulling first prize:
In the street strayed a blond kid with bangs willing to fraternize.
    I puff out my cheeks and I make dumb show like I got a toothache;
        Flirting, I proffer him three sticks of Pep-O-Mint.

With glee he snatched *Kaugummi*, the enemy infants' treat;
He grabbed my hand in both his paws. In step, we chewed down the street.
    O'er a door of Gothic design hung a tooth as gilt ensign.
        The dentist inside spoke quite good Rhenish Englisch.

Captain's wisdom tooth was impacted. Dentist was tops at his trade;
He gabbled more than a barber but his tedious small talk paid—
    Much of it rumor or hot air, but somehow he'd been everywhere
        In the vicinity and really knew plenty.

He was swift to uncover our personal specialized part
In these dubious battles. We protected objects of art
    And here the coincidence was extraordinary because
        His own soldier son was in the same business.

No longer a soldier, he'd resigned from the Wehrmacht as such.
His uniform hung in his garderobe; his Luger he would not touch.
    From his intellectual looks and high shelves of standard art books,
        Big ones, with pictures, he seemed a bona-fide expert.

It took tea and twenty minutes to learn what he had been.
He sent his French wife and child from the room. She brought cognac in.
    So: our war had not taken place. I tried to decipher his face:
        Kind? Dangerous? Servile? Clever? Or quite hopeless?

He'd done his whole duty in Paris, charged with Enemy Art—
Location, salvage, seizure, and sale, all from the very start.
    He'd records of everything done since the project had been begun
        To loot Europe in honor of Hitler's mother.

His price was safe-conduct for himself, his child, and winsome wife—
How should I know this requirement determined a family's life?—
    In return for which he would tell which Jews had been forced to sell
        What, for how much, and where it all was presently.

We couldn't insure his protection. Why had he need of the same?
Urgency clouded his liquor as if some shadow of blame
    Disturbed this anxious charming chap. He explained it as mere mishap:
        Five years he'd been an officer in the SS.

Him! An attractive Prusso-Balt, yet major of dread SS!
Sentiments evinced by confession we'd just better suppress.
    His Courvoisier made us warm. There seemed to be minuscule harm
        Sharing first-rate brandy with such an opponent.

He did not conceal his status, conceding he might be shot;
Not by us: by the Germans. Beloved the SS were not.
    He felt we would understand, whereupon extended his hand;
        Captain lit a cigarette; I nursed my snifter.

We disdained all bargaining. Safe-conducts weren't mentioned again.
He turned over his records with the data copied out plain:
    Title, size, and the exchange rate; metal and marble, their gross weight;
        Catalogues of paintings, manuscripts, ceramics.

I was impressed by this scholar who seemed familiar to me—
Bonn-trained, took graduate work at Harvard University
    Under wise old Kingsley Porter; loved Queensley, his wife. He thought her
        The cleverest mad woman he had ever met.

His thesis had been research on the Abbey of St. Denis;
Professor Porter taught him to parse the stones of Vieux Paris,
    Which all came handily in when he led Göring's museum-men
        In heisting everything they could clamp their claws on.

At first you might think it theft, but later it merely became
Conservation as acquisition, if there's some choice in the name.
    Victory turned much bad into good. In all conscience we almost could
        Forgive his foresight as selfish convenience.

Interrogation ended on a brisk businesslike tone;
I felt free to venture a couple of questions on my own
    Since I wanted to understand how the SS program was manned,
        This type of temperament operated.

"When did you first start to wonder would Germany never win?
When you did what you had to do, did it never seem like sin?"
    In all hypocritical jerks, the query certainly lurks:
        Under just what pressures would I have behaved likewise?

At our first Norman landings he knew they were doomed to lose.
His answers sounded candid; 'twas horrid about the Jews.
    Of these, some had been his best friends; some few met depressing ends;
        At his club he found himself served off Rothschild plate.

We thanked him as we thought apropos, then bade our brief good-bye.
He recalled his wife and child, both beautiful, frightened, and shy.
    He even remembered some more photos he'd forgotten before;
        I loaded our jeep while he checked maps with Captain.

Was that the last of our major? Until about the first of June.
We'd been ordered forward May ninth and had to leave much too soon
    To get the safe-conducts required. Besides, we were much too tired
        To think of anything but important problems.

We'd all but forgot this Nazi who'd helped as much as he could.
His romance ended more or less as one might have guessed it would.
    Despair at our lax ingrate haste propelled a predictable waste:
        He shot his wife, child, and himself in a panic.

However, and all thanks to him, we tracked straight to a mine,
Masses of art inside tons of salt, near the Austrian line—
    An upper-class health resort for Tyrolean winter sport;
        It was now held by a committee of miners.

Lines direct to Hitler's chancery were laid to Altaussee
Warning to blow it to Kingdom Come should he be brought to bay.
    These miners were Austrian born, held Germans in consummate scorn,
        And weren't blasting their own livelihoods foolishly.

Mad orders phoned from bunkers of flaming Volsung gods,
But workers in Salzkammergut were betting on different odds.
    They snipped all the dynamite wires and lit tall victory fires
        Hailing the next army here to liberate them.

We prised open crates at random: contents not to be believed—
Supreme constructs of hand and eye that Western man has achieved.
    Objects like these are sacrosanct, for which the SS may be thanked;
        Everything promised is here for the asking.

In cases swaddled in cotton, Van Eyck's Ghent altar piece:
The Lamb of God sung by All Saints, its glint our Golden Fleece.
    Count Czernin's veristic Vermeer scintillates expensively here—
        He painting Dame Fame's portrait; we, in his studio.

From Bruges in Belgium one huge box cradled a Mother and Child,
Michelangelo's august notion of the massively mild
    Carved in petrified clotted cream, a gently frosted marble dream.
        The edge of the Virgin's robe was chipped in two places.

The worst of it was when we brought out the Van Eyck for close view,
Over his hair shirt St. John's green gown was crisply split in two.
    We studied it under our glass. Now, how could this have come to pass,
        And not for the first time? Weak old glue feeds strong young worms.

How often through the centuries has Ghent's altar piece been cracked?
Obverse of its tempera panels showed which had been rebacked.
    Survival is luck or care. Excellence is canonized where
        It takes a miracle to insure miracles.

Time nicks St. Mary's mantle hem. It rips John Baptist's dress.
Science restores these losses. Art History mops up the mess
    While treasures get shipped home again to hang on the same hooks as when
        They were stolen by Hitler or Napoleon.

Presupposing virtuoso vision—scratched, fragmented, or hacked,
Art's intention is barely marred. The residual artifact
    Glimmers steady through years or blood, enduring rough treatment or good
        Or the suicidal carryings-on of humans.

How marble moulds itself into flesh, paint kindles gold in shafts
Makes me witness salvation first in comely handicrafts.
    It's been often observed before: objects we choose to adore
        Don't prevent war but survive it and us.

Threesome

There was: Corporal Harold Q.-for-Quincy Henderson and
Private (First Class) Leroy J.-for-James Costain. Each may properly stand
For any ordinary average American soldier, but
There are many average ordinary American soldiers one cut
Above or below given norms. Averages need surveys to sell,
And your survey tells every sort of lie about our moderate hell.

Theirs was not hell at all, at the first. It was sheer pure heaven,
Though anyone with a trace of brain who can throw 7-come-11
Might have learned from shooting craps that snow-jobs can't last forever,
While payment is fiercely exacted in kind when, then, and wherever:

A railroad-crossing six kilometers from Hartsholz GHQ
Had a little white-washed peasant-type wooden guardhouse and two
Gables framed with shutters for one bedroom and a window box
Full of blossoms plus one well-stacked babe built-in to cook and wash their socks.

Convenient? My ass. What a setup! She made rabbit stew
Their first night, and wow: was she marvelous! It only goes to show you
After so much shit you've had it up to here—well, man, it's then
God and/or luck, fate, circumstance, coincidence, chance—what all you men
Implore in awful hours as solace or savior—busts right in!

Costain and Henderson never tasted such sweets. Assuredly, sin
Sniffed its bit about. Henderson was Presbyterian born,
And Costain, Roman Catholic, but still stayed the dark relentless morn
Ten hours off. This girl, Mar-ee-ya, not Mar-ee, made beds
Or, rather, one enormous one with fresh sheets for three hot sleepy heads.
It had been better had she a sister, but even this way
Was quite the maddest night any of them played such mature play;
She was good and Harold no slouch, while Leroy, generous man,
Watching those two at games admired Harold's pocket-Herculean can:
That's what basketball does for you; then took his turn, and slow, too.

Maria wasn't the virgin American crusaders deserve, that's true.
But she had all her marbles. While watching Henderson make out,
Costain mused: The prettiest sights on earth often you can't talk about.
He should have meant what he said; instead, told some intimate friends
What went on in that railway hut. Ah, vanity certainly tends
To delete from grace each of us. They were screwed chewed stewed tattooed
And never had it so good. Close friends whom they told never understood
That when rumor uncoils, in the long run, then close friends must pay.

While Costain and Henderson did full duty at their crossing by day,
Pleasuring by night, circumstances past control at GHQ
Were forming a mean premonitory thundercloud which at first view
Was smaller than a man's hand which is what Costain often put
Under Maria's bust or fraternally on his buddy's tight butt.

Sharing is relief, man to man. But come—enough of all that;
There are certain limits beyond which one must not trespass, which is what
Lieutenant George T.-for-Tomlinson Kinicutt swore when told
Something damn queer went on in that railroad hut. Our adult kids were sold
By vain boasting. No one pardons any one or thing in war,
And George Tomlinson was Lieutenant Kinicutt to give what-for
To each and all who hadn't learnt his lore of how you better spell hell. . . .

The rest of this fable is guessable, depressing; messy as well—
A sordid comedy. At once he had them up on charges
Including: Sleeping-on-Guard, Raping-the-Enemy which enlarges
On horror, for, consulting our Judge Advocate's clever boy
He tacked on Malfeasance-of-Funds, Suspicion-of-Sodomy. Destroy
Evil where manifest. He threw The Book at those hapless two
Who were now low as once happy high. Hard doom plus deep disgrace ensue.

Before court-martial he had words with Maria, that same whore
Who might also be blamed, in twin interviews. First: absolutely swore
Nothing went on but mend their socks, make their bed, but soon enough
She allowed as how she loved them; they sincerely loved her. This made it rough.
She shot the works, for which Lieutenant was grateful. Her soft touch
Made him selflessly eager to set her up for himself, although much
Of what made him hound these three trivial tramps for their puerile game
Were thoughts of Costain and Henderson cooling off, and in the same
Bed, which was what Henderson and Costain recalled when all shame and blame
Were wiped out—after stockade, dishonorable discharge, their
Forfeiting all rights, privileges, GI Bill—hard burdens to bear.

They bore them, then. Now, sometimes, their kids worry some why their dad
Often gets vague talking about wars which seem less exciting than sad.

Dear John

"Dear John" such letters begin; thus ever they're styled to begin.
Hers starts "Dear Russell" since she knew her helpmate as Russ.
"I don't know how to say it; still it has to be said.
After you read this I guess you'll wish I was dead.
Russ, this is the end of us."

Russ takes it hard: on the chin;
Continues decoding her skimped script straight through;
Figures how long this took her to write, which draft it was:
"It hurts me as much or more than it must hurt you because,
Russell, believe it or not, I sincerely hate to hurt you.

Please understand." He does; if he bites his lips harder, they'll bleed.
She writes further: "Larry's on the late swing shift with me.
He has his car. I have no car now. I need a car.
I don't blame you, but the factory's so darn far.
Larry acted real kindly."

Larry. . . . Russ quite feels her need;
Still and all, Geez-us, he'd not dreamt it of her.
In his gorge two syllables start to flutter: You Bitch!
Up to now his lips won't mutter aloud this last curse which,
If uttered in air, proclaims all is, actually, Over.

What's Regulation for rage? See Chaplain, get laid, drink some drinks—
In that order. With Russ our S.O.P. is reversed.
Cut grain-alcohol with canned prune-juice. It's not so bad,
Or anyhoo, here and now, that's all to be had
To drench so drastic a thirst:

Stones himself stinko, then thinks
Of nearby supplies of available ass
Which are handy indeed. He takes off, rents him a piece
Perfumed like them raw prune-juice slugs. Therapeutic release
Does not pleasure a partner when she feels how plastered he is.

Chaplain remains. Cur-iced! Feature our shorn lamb back in the fold;
He'll shit or go blind. Chaplain's an ole YMCA man;
Human as Hell, boasting a brain though minus a ball,
"Wid a veree small peckah an' no ballzatall,"
Yet shall do the best he can.

Firm handclasp, supersmile: "Old
Man, sit down. Light a Lucky. Take Your Time.
Nothing's Bad As It Seems. Let's try and work this one: Out."
Russell sips silence; hopes if he pops, he won't scream or shout.
Unfolding her creased page, he surrenders the map of a crime.

Chaplain's read such piteous epistles before. This here's no shock,
Which he shall not admit to his client now waiting.
Muted thoughts buzz like bees but distil little honey.
"Son, I can't blame you for not finding this funny;
Still, it's no cause for hating

Your wife." Broth-urr. "Now, you talk
A bit about: yourself. How you feel right now. . . .
How you *do* feel, not how you're supposed to be feeling."
Risky business: Chaplain, a gambler, is appealing
To Intelligence more than mere Manhood or Pride. Anyhow,

Something clicks. Indignation halts in its tracks. Motors begin
Modest motion. Chaplain's aware of this ignition:
"I'll bet you already got pissed and laid, otherwise
How come see *me?*" Wide extrude Russell's grey-green eyes
With sly roguish admission.

"I know a speck about Sin.
It's my job—even, some days, a trace boring.
We try to help, but what can we do? Just take your case:
What do I try to say? Solve the problem or save the face?
'Fess up. When she was faithful to you, you never went whoring?"

Russell's rocked back on his heels, whose heels are fairly well-rounded.
How does he know all this? For once, the padre's inspected:
Smart lad; bet he played halfback for his seminary;
He don't smell like no usual sky-pilot fairy;
There's always—the Unexpected.

Thus Russ feels an unbounded
Admiration, almost sheer, like attraction;
Smiles: "Sir, you're So Right. So what do you think I should *do?*
Take her *back?*" Chaplain mildly sighs: "Son, she is through with you,"
Waits; puffing at peace; observes Russell's unraveling reaction.

Russ tries thought in depth. Self-pity precludes guilt for transgression.
"You're so right. I'm out." Misery fills its fat bucket.
"A Good Guy, like me—Bitch. Now I said it, I mean it."
Starts picturing Larry. "I'll kill her." How keen it
Cuts. Stop thinking. Oh—fuck it!

What's the Final Impression
Left on the Chaplain? Russ rises, as if to
Make like leaving, sure he'll be asked to sit down again;
Cap in hand, lingers, lost. He feels the world's hate; his own pain.
Somehow he's landed up in the wrong, which he hates. This is new

And novel—analysis—rarely his self-chosen weapon.
Will his wan grin kindle a kindlier confessor?
"Sir, thanks for your time," yet this thin curtain-line doesn't ring right.
Chaplain proffers a paw. In any prize fight,
Even amateur, lesser

In stature can still step on
Brawnier brutes. Concedes he's defeated;
Tries Exit-with-Dignity a trace too greasily.
We won't let Russ get away with all this so easily.
We can't let lover-boy lam out feeling one bit cheated.

"Son, you listen to me. Try using your head. Take a long walk
Through this pretty countryside. Stay by your lonely sad
Self. Ask this Self leading questions, of which some may hurt.
You're no angel; she's no whore." The man can be curt.
"Cut the crap; you're not so bad."

The End, that is, of such talk.
Russ commences his pastoral promenade
Following counsel, through Bavaria's landscape.
Groans with blessed relief. Was this one a narrow escape!
Reflects: In our whole interview he never once mentioned God.

Nor had he need to. Near Russell-Columbus new worlds appear—
Alpine scenery—low Alps beyond bud-bestrewn field;
Ripsaw profiles of pure peaks in ever-living snow.
How, here, do such big blue beautiful bluebells grow?
Begins to feel, nearly, healed.

And God said: "Son, have no fear;
Enough for today. Gaze around thee; relax.
Thou'rt well out of it. Behold my wondrous universe;
'Midst my multiple marvels may not the better be worse—
As well, the reverse? Praise me, nor recoil from anticlimax

When it comes, which it will. Joy thyself. Have fun. Take a new wife,
One more wife. Yea, two, even three. Possibility
Entails children, love, hate, divorce, death—all; even these."
Sun swamps him. Dear Russell almost falls to his knees;
Adores Chaplain's Deity.

Our hero finds a new life
In this German field in the prime of tall youth.
Yonder shine mountains towards which he need now no longer
Wander. Long trek back to base, but he feels him far stronger.
A two-ton truck passing picks him up for his tempering of truth.

Hymn

Front and center: call roll of certain scholars who,
Not thanked too much, somehow saw us through
Mainly intact: splendor traditional—
Salvaging articles of bronze, silver, gold, crystal;
Men famous, others evading fame.
All merit mention in fine arts' name.
        Praise them.

First: our Supreme Commander, Ike Eisenhower,
Painter of sorts in pleasant times, our
Daddy-O in the unpleasing times,
Whose decent manner, common sense, justice, stump weak rhymes;
Who endured stupendous waiting,
Winning worst wars with the least hating.
        Praise him.

Patton's side-kick, attractive Colonel Charles Codman,
Champagne-loving proper Bostonian:
When we must champion some monument
This gentle man his gasoline and influence lent;
Good then to know where one could turn
Lest fragile painting fade, flake, or burn.
        Praise him.

Colonel Geoffrey Webb, learnèd British architect,
Ordered U.S. sectors to protect,
Drove to our Third Army territory.
A hard duty was then assigned inferior me:
Patton wants no damn Limeys here.
Webb forgives me when I make this clear.
        Praise him.

Hutch Huchthausen, Ninth Army's brave Arts Officer,
Slain in his jeep by a Kraut sniper
While driven by Pfc. Sheldon Keck.
Helpless to revenge his boss, managing to save his neck
Deep in German lines, Keck survived;
Renowned damaged paintings since revived.
        Praise them.

Lieutenant John Skilton, no noisy brawny lad:
Sensitive; among loud soldiers, sad.
By ingenuity, guts, energy
Saved the best Breton primitive stone Calvary;
Without help, cool as a church mouse,
Salvaged, from damp, Würzburg's Treppenhaus.
        Praise him.

Kyoto's gravel shrines, Yamoto's cypress halls,
Clean glory still, unscorched by fireballs:
Langdon Warner strong logic extended;
Joint Chiefs of Staff further Kansai fire raids suspended.
Shogun, priest, peasant, tourist—we
Bless his bones walled in Horyu-ji.
        Praise him.

George Stout, Lieutenant, U S N R, first World War,
Had been through this type rat race before;
Instructed me, Harvard, 1930,
How permanent blue is crushed from lapis lazuli;
Back in navy-blue uniform,
Well-cut armor for informal storm.
        Praise him.

Based at Toul, Lorraine, in a French border caserne,
Our colliding gave me quite a turn:
Navy? Here? Yes—with sailors not a few—
Busy bees in loose fatigues of deep navy blue.
Landlocked flotillas seem unreal,
Their hulls and Stout's skull cast from blue steel.
        Praise them.

Near Echternach, Luxembourg, we worked together
In harsh destructive winter weather.
Bridgeheads blown; hid mortars bing-bong-bang!
Bronze bells in their rocked belfry ring merrily rong-rang.
We note shot sculpture we admired;
God's unconcerned with what He inspired.
        Praise Him.

Man was concerned, however. At least George Stout was;
Coolly judged damage: bimb-boom-bomb-buzzzz;
Gravely proceeded to bridgehead's brink,
Watched patron St. Christopher's head crack, tumble, and sink.
George Stout noted precisely where;
After war, hauled up, now it's right back there.
          Praise it.

One more river to cross, which was their bridge-blown Rhine,
Captured quicker than the Siegfried Line;
Navy no more needed, Stout shipped away
To Pacific theaters more useful rôles to play.
There, something happened to him:
Monument Officers' paradigm.
          Praise it.

When Bangkok surrenders, the Japanese assign
Buddha's toenail to His Tokyo shrine.
After Tokyo's fall, Stout sees it return;
Saffron-robed Siamese monks reclaim their sacred urn
Whose outer cover is dull lead.
Inside five more lay this toenail's bed.
          Praise it.

Lead, iron, bronze, silver, gold, and perfect crystal,
One snug inside the other and all
Skillfully interlocked, cut fine to fit;
A masterpiece of packaging. The neat sight of it
Awed Allied commissioners here
Detailed as steward or overseer.
          Praise them.

With soft chaunting, fondling smooth rosaries of jade,
Buddha's bland prayers His mild monks prayed.
The white Western observers hung around
Tolerant of picturesque sight, peculiar sound:
Lead, iron, bronze, silver, gold, and
Flawless crystal passed slow, hand to hand.
          Praise them.

Lieutenant Stout observing this fastidious rite
Was granted a brief profound insight;
Doubting his level well-trained X-ray eyes—
Oriental magic stirs skeptic Western surprise—
Hence quizzed his five companions, who
Shared the vision he'd been vouchsafed too.
       Praise it.

"You saw what I saw?" Christians asked one another
Since smile or faint grin each had to smother:
In lead, iron, bronze, silver, gold, crystal
Reposed in rich sacrosanct vacuum, nothing at all.
Samurai blades had served as thief
Of no booty save Buddhist belief.
       Praise it.

Good *gaijin* manners sustain Gautama's prayer,
Homage to no relic very there
Just as six well-wrought boxes played their part
Maintaining dull mortal credence by immortal art.
No thing grand some thing was: nay, is.
Lord Buddha's toenail indeed is His.
       Praise it.

Scholar-gentlemen laud master-sculptor,-painter,
As guns sound off further or fainter;
Gold or silver brighter and brighter glow
Saved by gentle scholars from our fighters and their foe.
Melt, hot bronze. Iron cannon, rust;
Let no lead shot smash crystal to dust.
       Praise them. Praise them.

Viewers exult, idling peacetime through galleries;
Curators vanquished artilleries.
Praise those who prized objects above themselves.
Some won't arrange them tastefully soon on our rich shelves—
Nor killed, yet kept skill's live spirit
Intact in what grace we inherit.
       Praise them. Praise them.
       Praise them.

Göring

"*Let's get Göring!*" Get him we almost did.
We knew he'd be in hiding. We bet we knew where he hid.
    Albrecht Dürer taught me. *Tod, Teufel, Ritter* brought me
        To Schloss Veldenstein.
All of us image previsions. Dürer's engraving's mine.
        A stubby staunch castle on its crag
        At dawn. The scut of an antlered stag
Vanishing into hemlocks, while, at the base of the hill
    A hunter paunched as DER REICHSMARSCHALL
        Winds his clarion still.

We were strafed in our cots the night before;
An enemy all-but-conquered all but cost us the war.
    Good luck's too good to last. We'd better get cracking fast
        Past Pegnitz River.
Breasting a crest of history kinda makes you shiver.
        How snag *Dritte Reich's* Number Two?
        We'd sue for a protocol interview;
He'd be needing his codeine. Picture his manic dismay.
    We plot a pattern to pull our haul.
        He grabs his getaway.

Here's his last-stand hide-out, with him all gone.
It's only five in the morning. Göring skipped by dawn.
    Lost by an hour or less, we risked our stupendous guess:
        Nuremberg, by Fürst;
Racing blind with carbines cocked for an ambushed hedgerow burst.
        Well—we made it, to lose at the end.
        All of us felt it, rounding the bend
To park in his cobbled courtyard. Polish DP's surround
    Bonfires of von Eppenstein papers
        Documenting this ground.

Tower, portcullis; bone-picked, bone-dry moats:
Fragments—authentic. An *ersatz* mosaic misquotes
    Bits from Gothic builder as current events bewilder
        Me, art historian.

Displaced wan Polish persons, now jobless deft masons, can
      Detail which carving is new or old;
      What battered stonework the sold French sold
From Abbeville's de-roofed abbey to gape as backdrop here
    For our paladin's *kitsch* capers,
      His secondhand veneer.

Parchments stoking a starved Polish bonfire
Pertained to a gentile Jew who stood as foster sire
    To the secondmost modern German, plump airman Hermann.
      Graf *von* Eppenstein,
A circumcised rich Austrian had lent Burg Veldenstein
    To Göring's daddy, his yid *Hausfreund*.
    Games played here by a stepson portend
Dreams of a *Tausendjahr Reich*, when tin Uhlans were his toy,
    Sketching preposterous rôles he'd play,
      Auguring STRENGTH THROUGH JOY.

Sunday galas on Potsdam's broad parade:
Prussian brass bands crash on spiked helmet, glittery blade.
    England thrashes the Boer. Göring adores any old war:
      EIGHTEEN SEVENTY!
Hoch der Kaiser! Deutschland, hoch!
      He, like many likable boys,
      Leaden soldier battalions deploys;
Aligns a plate-glass mirror; doubles his regiments' might,
    Augmenting twice his model array:
      Dubious *Sachlichkeit*.

It's all done with mirrors. But, mirrors crack.
Once his *Ehrenhall* hung with glass. Crystal shatters black.
    Mirrors are tactical portraits, spur practical habits.
      Göring's mirrors lie.
GOTT STRAFE ENGLAND! Queen, she reigns, sov'reign of sea & sky.
      He, lacking bombers to purge her air,
      Tripled his aircraft on paper where
They did small material damage yet plugged immediate needs;
    Swears he has plenty of planes to spare.
      His FÜHRER much misleads.

Double tin soldiers. Triple paper planes.
Hitler fries, cursing him, slight pay for all his pains
  Forging an air force from scratch few in the world could match:
      Göring's Luftwaffe.
  In a stale downstairs bedroom, soiled sheets creased recently,
      Imprint of his gross carcase remains.
      In an unrinsed bathroom, his thumbprint stains
On toilet, razor, vial, scummed as though still he were here.
  Outfaced, we suffer his mirror's stare,
      A cheater souvenir.

The Chosen

Under scant shingles, this unwalled shanty, a brickwork's ratty shed;
  Wide open to airs and damps and drys—
  A vast mass of loose written material lies
      In heedless layers, adherent or scattered wide.
      It is our current tedious task to try to decide
  Of what it consists, making practical choice of what may be saved,
What boxed or burned; initially, what can clearly be read

Of all these old certificates, old records, letters, unfurled scrolls
  From synagogues of ten Dutch cities
  Weighing five hundred years and a thousand pities.
      Its presence, despite much ruination, persists.
      Its chance for conservation accusingly insists
  If only as common courtesy to the slain or enslaved,
Foundering echo of that planned obloquy which still tolls

Through Germany, where in more horrible sheds spoiled a richer treasure.
  Where do we start? Reluctant fingers
  Peck at the parchments. Mildewed, a limp scrap lingers
      Stuck to its rotten binding. Square Hebraic script
      Perfectly readable could I but read it, and tipped
  Between pages, columns of notes writ in late-Spencerian Dutch
As if some genealogist of lore and leisure

Collated these documents to resurrect places and persons
    Until war's envy stopped his good work.
    Sympathizing with his interest, I won't shirk
        Labor, however futile—assortment, salvage—
        Yet a fever infects me caught from such wide ravage,
    Impelling fury. I am perfectly willing to end all such
Untidiness. My touching these corrupted words worsens

Chance for survival. I'd hurry their slovenly, worrisome end
    Blotting out many meaningless facts—
    Bury them at once—scriptures, ledgers, texts, and tracts
        For tribal banishments or dietetic rules
        Of rigid scholars in strict proscribed puritan schools
    Which bred a stubborn descent electing to trim its thinnest skin
Marking them, and me, self-chosen. Obstinate backs won't bend

Easily except to the unique judgment of One Awful Eye
    Winking at the success of mad foes
    Who choose not to know or read. My petulance grows,
        Flipping torn page on page, date after dead blurred date,
        Name on lost name, trying to relate what can't relate
    To anything useful, shriveled poor tendrils of abundant kin
Shrunk on the branch, rooted in fine granite dust from Sinai.

I con these screeds as if by fitful tapers whose curled fetid smoke
    Dimmed ignorance's unfestive light.
    They flare from wicks whose sick wax first makes flame bright
        But then ill vapors rise, swelling a sluggish pall,
        Snuffing out any legible handwriting at all;
    There's left a smothering canopy, an impenetrable haze
Through which no candles glow. Is it faith I cannot invoke,

The faith of my fathers—all those prophets, scholars, lawyers, ancients,
    Whose busheled ash sifts Israel's decline?
    Made firm our road? Why may we never take for sign
        The criminal thorn we chose to set as His crown?
        Let's prise it from His enemy head and lift Him down
    To lie at last among forgiving kindred. We pay; He still pays;
Maybe the solvency in brotherhood all but consents

Not to be chosen, while many Gentile gypsies and infant Jews
    Have no choice. Their ends are made less hard
    By their parents' playing games with their cruel guard,
        Pretending to laugh, who both shove them in hot gas
        And, waving, watch them choke and smoulder through the thick glass.
    They all knew it was never a real game. The guards were also young;
As for choosing, even the young gas-oven guards could choose

To push or not. Some let themselves be pushed and had no cause to kill.
    Old books bleach, faint scrivening left.
    Apart from calligraphy are we much bereft
        Of learning? Could I have read, would I? A choice text
        Compels little but quotation, awaiting the next
    Example of His choosing or chastisement, and psalms simply sung
Remember themselves without prompting scribe or saving skill

On our part, in cleansing fierce covenants of worm hole, mold, or wear.
    Ourselves chose; or were we chosen truly
    Improvising laws for our self-serving school? He,
        Unwilling to cozen His favored children, less
        From rage than to scourge us strong, reveals His wilderness
    Without a word. We praise, wailing; our temple, the collapsed abyss.
We swear, having borne much, it's more than we ever can bear;

Gratefully swear it; then bear it. Jealous vanity bids us hear
    Sacred pride in secret pride: Thy Word
    Echoed from desert utterings, Thy Promise heard
        Abrupt as thunder. Did we ourselves first say it?
        I am that I am. Fear thy God, thine: alone. Pray it
    Illumines the legible pages of wisdom left in all this
Waste. Call it mercy, these blank vellum margins scorched with fear.

Truce

We mark our new month take its turn.
        A dozen idled conquerors stare
at searchlights swung to tickle stars—
        thin probes on pivots, their slim glare
kindles wan conscience as a spur.
        Midsummer swarms its musty heat:
calmed in a simple arc of dark
        we'll try to test twin-edged defeat
part by sure starshine, part by men—
        the grand plan now but partly plain,
weighing the war we're slow to know
        is pittance spent on one campaign.

Faint honey-lindens' whisper breath
        rustling Bavaria's night across
soughs *finis* on twelve seasons' wrath
        to urge us tally up our loss.
It's only been a matter of months
        counted to cost the foretold rate—
so many murdered, maimed or missed
        shortguessed in every estimate.

Have we heft left enough to plead
        in passionate or composed voice
windy answers from some star
        granting our chance was never choice
when we were drafted to be briefed
        how casualty can interfere
with routine's drilled expectancy
        to waste our time in worry here?

Lo! We've scotched dragons. Their blunt plunge
        is blazoned in brute overthrow.
Our stolid, scruffy dogtired ranks
        mumble small thanks while bonfires glow.
But, steady—lest our knuckles nick
        clipped on a brittle champion sword.
Pale bloodstreams clot in sloven phlegm
        envenomed by the monsters gored.

Fuddled on fond self-starters' luck
        ripe sorry riddles lurk unasked.
Distracting questions fumble clues;
        gagged demons in us groan unmasked.
The ache of Sibyl's self-sought curse
        yawns wide tonight in Joe GI:
a deathless beldam told a boy:
        "I, made immortal, long to die."

So we stay sturdy, you and I;
        fat waste bleeds its rich minimum.
Fright, fury, fret pay back dirt-cheap
        the homing veterans old humdrum.
Our duty done, a true debt's due;
        what could be learned we cannot learn
hence licensed drift or dalliance
        steadies our headstrong unconcern.

And thus our trusty braggart myths
        play havoc with a next crop's youth
and if one dares to doubt his dad
        he can be conned by cunning truth.
Tossed on soft lindens' whispering
        searchlights cat's-cradle unborn stars.
We trace a truce by auguries,
        chill windage of what next big wars.

Postscript

Purple Heart

Sure, he's lucky to be alive; those parts of him that feel at all
Throb in their frame. His eyes test ceiling and the blank wall.

His weak wrists on crisp sheets ache, though he knows he'll be all right;
Nurse gives him a sharp look, raises the window, dims the light,

Quits him. Darkness fuses; burns. Spots in his shut eyes spark;
Alone, he worries some more whether burns leave a bad mark.

He tells himself: The worst is over, doing what had to be done.
He did well, but he's not sure if the worst has even begun.

He tries not to dream nor yet doze on what all happened back there—
A bad accident roaring around found and froze him in its glare.

He'd been dreading it months—this menace, test, this end, this worst.
While he waited for it to hit, skies fainted and he burst.

Folks, at least for a while, will be in awe of him. They'll stand
Aside from him or steal luck, patting his back; wringing his hand.

He's sick, naturally; he can't ask what he needs and well knows
He hasn't the stuff to love back; fades into a thin doze.

Not enough love to go around, a blood bank to pull him through
Easily. He'll come out of it, the hard way. Myself, or you,

Seeing him thus are moved to tears. Real tears. We always need
Tours through the wards to make sure real wounds really bleed.

Here Lies

"I who am now but a thought
    Once was a fanciful man;
Blood in my nerve, skin on my bone;
    My cheek took a coppery tan.
While I was breathing I feared
    The nothing I soon might be;
Fun, like my fright, was fantasy,
    Sturdiest part of me.
Mirror grinned: 'Don't worry, Joe.
    Others may possibly die,
But boys with flax hair and green eyes,
    Fast workers like you and I,
Are so firm in fanciful pride
    The elegance crammed in our youth
Is helmet enough to keep us whole,'
    Which we knew was hardly the truth."

I'm thinking of three friends of mine,
    None of them selfless nor strong,
Who loved themselves far more than me,
    And fashion, excitement, and song,
Who now are deader than I,
    Who never fancifully lied:
"We lived for somebody else;
    For somebody else we died."
Fair Harry, red Caleb, dark Fred
    Were lavish in other ways,
And when it came time to be killed
    The flush of their holiday days
Spilled its fancy exuberant light
    On a shadow-long late afternoon;
Flared into dusk like song, and sang
    Ends to a fanciful tune.

GI Bill

So: here's our Joe back home again,
      And tart October nips his ears;
Nothing about his street or room
      Reminds him he's been gone three years.
Schedule the same: habit persists—
      Bed, bath, and breakfast; pipe and book.
Time shrinks it tight, a seamless stitch
      All scarless from the trip he took.

Ex-pilot wires his bombardier
      To hop out West and meet the folks—
A fortnight off for fish and games,
      Air Corps talk and GI jokes;
Whips back to college to cram up,
      Add or subtract what so far fails
To keep his classmates at their sums
      When fires freeze or scrap-iron hails.

Professor waits his heroes home
      Alert and tender to be told,
Astounded at what innocence
      Survives the stories they were sold.
For how can he, poor Ph.D.,
      An idiot AWOL from their war,
Venture to lecture veterans
      On what they've just been fighting for?

Each starved survivor aches to learn;
      Professor has no cause for fear;
Straining towards logic, every son
      Lends a rapt unaccusing ear.
Down the long wards, the walking wounds
      Compare their chances, legs, and eyes
Left to each user, all in luck
      Contrasting fiercer sacrifice.

Lo: the World Wars I, II, and III
      Now test our homework's memory;
Ten months ago what towns were tall
      Whose wrecks date Modern History?

Memorial

By here, where once we came
Along this selfsame road
Back to our base and field,
Perennial pollens yield
Their ragged rusty fame.

Burdock, hard burr, and rose,
Sweet wildrose, dusty burr,
Thistle and aster wild—
Past here a waiting child
Ambushed some noisy boys

To ask: Where are you bound?
Where bound indeed? Where? Where?
They did not know, and we
Who know more than they knew
Have lost more than they found.

This chapel scarce a church
They could ignore. They did;
To them—odd heap of stones,
Old shelter for some bones
Or pigeons on a perch.

Thin and unshadowed shone
Pale panes of window glass.
But color? No; nor glint
Of richness, gleam, or tint;
No texture and no tone.

Why should they stop to pray?
They had their way to win.
They flew far, headlong fast,
Reckless and randy past
Broad daylight and brief day.

All gone. Some gone for good.
Some bad, some still alive,
While those alive, with grace
Have not forgot this place:
We've done the least we could.

We've stuck a window here:
Pure color for clear flesh,
A penetrating fire
To glorify the choir
Or sanctify our fear.

What are these colors fine
That strain the sun; shine clean
In citron, rosy ice,
Mulberry paradise,
Sharp wintergreen, or wine?

This fire is all our air
Which was our airman all.
Our window claims he's here
In warm translucent cheer
And gilt transparent hair.

Blond as the licking sun,
Rosy for tawny cheek,
Frank mirror-eye and green
His candid earth and keen
His fury in his fun.

Glass is sand, sun, and lead
Fixed in a shattered sheet.
All day our star is sight;
At sunset shuttered night
All dust, dust-shot and dead.

In four fierce sheaves of fire
An elemental shock
Has compassed every air
Boxed cardinal to square
Sky, ocean, flame, and mire.

Fuse us our triune saint
Who was boy, bomb, and blast.
Brittle his doubled arm.
Tense still our hard alarm
And strenuous complaint.

For glass, send us some sun.
Blend blood and bone a hymn
To salve our coupled nerve
Preserving us to serve
The wonder in a one.

Notes

A Note on the Notes

The American soldier in his multitude was the most attaching and affecting and withal the most amusing figure of romance conceivable. . . . It was the charmingest, touchingest, dreadfullest thing in the world that my impression of him should have to be somehow of his abandonment to a rueful humor, to a stoic reserve which could yet melt, a relation with him at once established, into a rich communicative confidence; and, in particular, all over the place, of his own scanted and more or less baffled, though constantly and, as I couldn't not have it, pathetically, "knowing" devices.

The great point remained for me at all events that I could afterwards appear to myself to have done nothing but establish with him a relation, that I established it, to my imagination, in several cases—and all in the three or four hours—even to the pitch of the last tenderness of friendship. I recover that, strolling about with honest and so superior fellow-citizens, or sitting with them by the improvised couches of their languid rest, I drew from each his troubled tale, listened to his plaint on his special hard case-taking form, this, in what seemed to me the very poetry of the esoteric vernacular.

Henry James
Portsmouth Grove, Rhode Island, 1862
From *Notes of a Son and Brother*, New York, 1914, Chapter IX, pages 313–14

Notes which follow may rank as overkill, and can be skipped with ease. However, there are some initialed abbreviations referring to commissions or categories which now are meaningless to many. While slang shifts slowly, and is sustained in vernacular habit, historical allusions are more difficult to locate. Interest in World War II wasn't smothered by Viet Nam; indeed it attracts continual curiosity. Its nostalgic recovery is comparable to that attached to The War Between the States.

When, in 1964, this muster first appeared, Alan Pryce-Jones, reviewing it for the *New York Times*, was nice enough to write that it recalled Wordsworth's *Prelude, or Growth of a Poet's Mind.* In its Book X one finds:

I thought of those September massacres,
Divided from me by one little month,
Saw them and touched: the rest was conjured up
From tragic fictions or true history,
Remembrances and dim admonishments.
The horse is taught his manage, and no star
Of wildest course but treads back his own steps;
For the spent hurricane the air provides
As fierce a successor; the tide retreats
But to return out of its hiding-place
In the great deep; all things have second birth;
The earthquake is not satisfied at once.

In 1791 Wordsworth crossed to Paris, ostensibly to learn French; actually, to test himself by history. Louis XVI and Marie Antoinette were not yet guillotined; Wordsworth observed their prison; made friends with Girondin extremists; became perilously involved in The Terror; escaped only when English relatives stopped his funds. Apart from patriotism, indignation and compassion, civil and political turbulence is endlessly attractive in the dynamics of theater. These notes may infer that the verses which they gloss were without pretension to the craft of verse; that I was content with doggerel. Whatever the quality, ambition was schooled by T. S. Eliot's *Choice of Kipling's Verse* (1941) in which he made distinction between "verse" and "poetry"; "political" and "occasional" verse; and/or *Poetry.* For me, Kipling was a far more masterful model than Clough, Tennyson or Browning. For metrical music, sometimes brass, often organ, both as balladeer and hymnist, he stands with Hopkins and Auden as a lord of the

English language. As Auden wrote in his elegy on Yeats (with reference to Claudel and Kipling, later suppressed) time, intolerant of bravery, innocence or physical beauty

Worships language and forgives
Everyone by whom it lives;
Pardons cowardice, conceit,
Lays its honours at their feet.

Time that with this strange excuse
Pardoned Kipling and his views. . . .

I aimed to compose a sequence of narrative verse, hopefully, neither careless nor monotonous, borrowing from common parlance its coarse-grained savor.* Kipling, a non-combatant participant, was nevertheless a "war-poet," having observed at close hand the North Indian frontier, Boer War and World War I. His only son was killed in 1915 at the Battle of Loos. Those who dismiss Kipling as a jingo imperialist ignore his wreath of epitaphs, among which:

If any question why we died,
Tell them, because our fathers lied.

A cartoon by Bill Mauldin in *Stars & Stripes*, May 10, 1944, like many of his, enshrined a general state of mind. One Mauldin-type scruffy GI consoles another slouching disconsolately on his "entrenching tool" (small spade): *"You'll get over it, Joe. Once I wuz gonna write a book exposin' the army after th' war myself."*

I had no wish to "expose" the army. The core of "expose" is: to lay open; to set out (as for inspection). In photography, "exposure" is a subjection of sensitized surfaces to chemical action of actinic rays. In "A Note on War Poetry,"* T. S. Eliot wrote:

War is not a life: it is a situation,
One which may neither be ignored nor accepted,
A problem to be met with ambush and stratagem,
Enveloped or scattered.

The enduring is not a substitute for the transient,
Neither one for the other. But the abstract conception
Of private experience at its greatest intensity
Becoming universal, which we call "poetry,"
May be affirmed in verse.

When I joined the army it was less to help whip Hitler than to witness enough action to be able to write about it; I was no pacifist. Since childhood I'd been crammed with Civil War lore and taught that the man for whom I was named was a greater general than Grant, Sherman or Lee. In one tactical area I remained defeated: I was never in combat, nor fired a weapon in anger or fear. This vexed me, and made me take irresponsible risks. The single piece in this collection involving mortal contest ("4th Armored") came from encountering an Iowa farmer immediately after incidents recorded. Had I been able to recall all he told, I would have written a more harrowing account. As it was, his impact was so formidable that the result is my single unrhymed rhyme. He knocked rhyme out of me; the subject-matter called for force approaching Kipling's Boer War ballads—"Stellenbosch" or "Chant Pagan." My Iowa farmer and others like him framed experience for me shared by Henry James as a fledgling observer, writing of Union recruits at ease, on their way to Gettysburg, Chancellorsville and Cold Harbor.

---

*"The Soldier's Language" by Frederick Elkin (*American Journal of Sociology*, March 1946, p. 414 ff.) is a brilliant analysis of martial profanity and epithet derivation.

*Written at the request of Miss Storm Jameson, to be included in a book entitled *London Calling* (New York, 1942).

To me, already thirty-six, war was largely didactic. I'd had Harvard, spoke French, some German, and held no rank. Since I never sewed my single stripe on a sleeve, since duties were those of courier, driver or interpreter, external signs of authority were not obligatory. A sly fellow with determination could easily pass where disoriented superior officers might be hindered. In volatile areas there was often no occasion to brandish credentials, so one moved freely in restricted zones.

In the craft of war-writing I had two main mentors. Wystan Auden, as I've recorded, proposed Ronald Firbank's "pathetic ironic," his "happiness of despair"; reduction of self-pity; anti-heroics as comic "relief." When I complained I'd never been in combat, and sensed a capital inadequacy, he comforted me: neither had Walt Whitman nor Rudyard Kipling. Marianne Moore also served as monitor. Raw locutions gave her no offense; this seemed odd to some who took her for a frail maiden lady. She was a Christian communicant; her brother a ranking Navy chaplain. She read me without discomfort, objecting only to mentioning suicide of Japanese in "Buddies." This was heartless; some things should not be mentioned.

Many things aren't uttered, through incompetence rather than discretion. More is forgotten. The one writing here is not he who jotted jingles in Normandy, Lorraine or Bavaria. The residue is a product of thirty-five years, dating from 1943, into the present decade. I was pleased that the book was placed on reading lists by the Army, at the start of war in Southeast Asia. A copy was handed General Creighton Abrams. He acknowledged it; I doubt if he had time to read it. Ten pieces have been added to the original collection, together with the notes, which have been edited with corrective expertise by Hoyt Rogers and Harvey Simmonds.

L. K.

Fall In

"big-boys' club": YMCA, Rochester, New York, 1914.

World War I

"Kaiser Wilhelm": Hohenzollern Emperor whose waxed moustachios, withered arm and arrogant bearing provided for the First World War the symbolic presence Hitler had for the Second.

"Karl Schurz" (1829–1906): German-American soldier, statesman and reformer. A revolutionary student at Bonn, he came to the United States, 1852; fought later at Gettysburg and Chattanooga.

"*Brandenburger Tor*": Berlin's triumphal arch by the great neo-classic architect Carl Gotthard Langhans (1732–1808), celebrating Prussian victories.

"*Kronprinzens elite Korps*": the Imperial Heir's personal regiment, the insolence of whose officers anticipated the manners of Hitler's SS (*Schutzstaffel*).

"George Creel" (1876–1953): Colorado journalist, Chairman of President Woodrow Wilson's Committee for Public Information; chief propagandist for the U.S., World War I, acting as censor and inquisitor; inventor of slogans: "Make the world safe for democracy" and "War to end war"; instigator of a series of pamphlets detailing German atrocities in Belgium.

"Karl Muck" (1859–1940): conductor, Boston Symphony (1912–18); believed to have been both the natural son of Richard Wagner and a German spy. On March 25, 1918, arrested as an enemy alien and interned.

"Pershing": General John J. ("Black Jack") Pershing (1860–1948), commanded American Expeditionary Force in Europe, World War I.

"Harris tweed": imported Scottish woolen suiting.

"Kaiser and Clown Prince": At Doorn Castle, the Netherlands, the exiled Hohenzollern sovereigns sawed firewood for daily exercise.

ABC
(Boston)

"Commonwealth Avenue": planned, 1856, as a boulevard emulating the new Paris of Baron Haussmann, it leads from Public Garden to suburbs, its initial blocks divided by an elm-planted mall with statues.

"Arlington, Berkeley, Clarendon": cross-streets with alphabetically listed English names, alternating three and two syllables.

"shell shock": term coined (1915) by Colonel Frederick Mott, English pathologist who claimed exploding ammunition caused minute cerebral hemorrhages in the brain, although many cases of psychological collapse never came within hearing distance of artillery. In World War II called "combat fatigue."

"Over the Top": command to rush out of trenches to engage the enemy; title of best-selling war narrative (1915–16) by British Sergeant Guy Empey.

"Over There" (France): hit song (1917) by George M. Cohan.

"Arras, Bapaume, and Cambrai": murderous Anglo-Canadian-German battles, northern France, World War I (1916–18).

Basic Training
(Fort Belvoir)

"Belvoir!": U.S. Corps of Engineers headquarters and training facility, Northern Virginia. In the early 18th century, the seat of Colonel William Fairfax, father-in-law of Lawrence Washington, half-brother to George.

"Minié ball": conical rifle bullet invented by French Captain C. E. Minié, who in 1852 was awarded twenty thousand pounds by the British Government, adopting its standard use; an innovation in the American Civil War.

"grapeshot": a cluster of small iron balls used as a cannon charge in the Civil War.

"Brady in albums": Mathew Brady (1823–1896), American photographer of battle-fields and soldiers, living and dead.

"Stonewall, Stuart, or Lee": heroic Confederate generals—Thomas Jonathan Jackson (1824–1863), James Ewell Brown Stuart (1833–1864), Robert Edward Lee (1807–1870).

"Canada": Before U.S. declaration of war many citizens enlisted in the Royal Canadian Air Force and flew with Canadians through the Battle of Britain.

"flak": anti-aircraft artillery fire, from German, *Flieger-abwehr-kanone*.

Barracks

"Lysol": lye-solvent, strong commercial disinfectant.

"Name, Serial Number": stamped metal identification disc, worn at all times by military personnel.

Map & Compass

"Jerry": German.

Cadets

"officers": Second Lieutenants, recently graduated from the U.S. Military Academy, West Point, were sent at once to training camps for command experience.

"grey cloistered brother": The traditional cadet uniform color, except for field-exercise, has always been grey. Captain Alden Partridge, Superintendent of the Academy (1815–17), found the indigo dye used until then exhausted by the War of 1812. Rough grey cloth was used for fatigue uniforms from 1814. At first disdained, since it was cloth worn by slave laborers, it also acquired a bad name since it equipped some poorer volunteers who proved cowardly in early fighting. After the Battle of Chippewa River, Canada, when General Winfield Scott was victorious commanding grey-uniformed troops, the color was accepted.

"Bailey Bridge": designed by Sir Donald Coleman Bailey for rapid assembly; composed of interchangeable latticed panels of electrically welded high tensile steel, coupled into girders with alloy steel pins and laid double, triple or superposed to suit span or load. Lighter than similar American ones, it could replace destroyed structures in a few hours.

Top Kick

"Top Kick": First Sergeant, highest ranking non-commissioned officer. (Warrant Officers are in a special category.) First Sergeants, in charge of a unit of enlisted men, serve as buffer between commissioned officers and enlisted personnel.

"The Book": *Articles of War* and/or *Infantry Drill Regulations*. Official rules and guidelines for military behavior and operations.

"civil hospital": Enlisted men (and even officers) were supposed to use regulation army medical facilities, where records could be kept. There was a superstition that civilian hospitals were more efficient.

"(*Later, for him*)": ritual threat, promising delayed but ultimate retaliation.

4F

"4F": classification under which draftees were found inacceptable for physical or psychological reasons; commonly, for presumed or vaunted homosexuality.

"Lucemachine": corporation founded by Henry Luce and Briton Hadden in 1923, publishing *Time*, *Life*, *Fortune*, etc.

"*This Great Picture*": *Life* featured double-page spreads of photographs snapped under combat conditions which frequently rendered them illegible, whatever their authenticity. Little of the enormous camera coverage of the war was as memorable as the "primitive" plates of the American Civil War.

"[W.] Eugene Smith" (1918–1978): American investigative photographer. His pictures of early U.S. Marine action in the Pacific are among the greatest visual records of the war. See *W. Eugene Smith*, a monograph; Aperture, 1969.

"the Head": naval slang for latrine, from its location over the bowsprit or ship's head in 19th-century sailing ships.

Gloria

"CID": Criminal Investigation Division.

Syko

"Sex shun 8": Section VIII, clause under which personnel could be discharged for psychiatric causes, not necessarily dishonorably; possibly "for the good of the Service." Here, it is imagined that a disturbed soldier, confined in a closed hospital ward, has gained use of a typewriter.

Spec. No.

"Spec. No.": Specialization Number by which draftees were classed according to prior skills. Assignment was often random, causing gloom and/or mirth.

Obstacle Course

"Obstacle Course": Final training exercise before shipment overseas. Combat conditions were simulated, sometimes with live ammunition under which personnel were obliged to crawl.

Fixer
(Washington)

"Lynn": depressed industrial town north of Boston.

"Old State-Navy-and-War": monumental 19th-century granite office-building, adjoining the White House, formerly used by State, War and Navy Departments; now, Presidential Executive Offices.

"Joseph Smith" (1805–1844), "Brigham Young" (1801–1877): co-founders of The Church of Jesus Christ of Latter-Day Saints (Mormon).

"Cumorah Hill": near Manchester, Ontario County, New York; site of discovery of golden plates of *The Book of Mormon*, the sect's bible, buried by the Angel Moroni, published 1829.

"Apostles": Latter-Day Saints (Mormons).

"Gentiles": other than Mormons.

"Quoth Kit Marlow": Christopher Marlowe (1564–1593).

> . . . *I could tell ye*
> *How smooth his brest was, and how white his bellie,*
> *And whose immortal fingers did imprint*
> *That heavenly path with many a curious dint*
> *That runs along his back, but my rude pen*
> *Can hardly blazon forth the loves of men,*
> *Much less of powerful gods. . . .*
>> Hero and Leander
>> First Sestyad, lines 65–71

Next of Kin

"Next of Kin": In case of death, compassionate orders ruled public notification withheld until persons indicated by the soldier on entering the service were informed.

Buddies
For Charles Shannon

"Rabaul": New Britain Island, Bismarck Archipelago; an important Australian base with a fine harbor, captured by the Japanese early, 1942. A powerful air-base dominating New Guinea-New Britain-Solomons, site of sanguinary U.S. Marine action, late 1943.

"O'Donnell's": Washington, D.C., seafood restaurant, the decor of which simulates a clipper-ship's cabin.

P.O.E.
(New York City)

"P.O.E.": Port of Embarkation. Operated by Army Transportation Corps. Located at Boston, New York, Hampton Roads (Va.), Charleston (S.C.), New Orleans, Los Angeles, San Francisco, and Seattle; more than seven million troops, civilians and prisoners passed through from Pearl Harbor to VJ-Day.

"This Is It": oft-repeated phrase, applying to all situations awkward, unpleasing or dangerous. During World War I, equivalents were "C'est la Guerre" and "Good Night Nurse!"

Convoy

"BBCeed": British Broadcasting Corporation.

"Negro troops": Segregation of black personnel was virtually complete in all invasion preliminaries and operations. Only toward the end of the war were black soldiers permitted to engage in much beyond support functions.

As the conflict which was to become World War II approached, Negroes asked with increasing frequency for the opportunity that they believed rightfully theirs in the first place: the opportunity to participate in the defense of their country in the same manner and on the same basis and in the same services as other Americans.

Ulysses Lee and others
The Employment of Negro Troops, Office of the Chief of Military History, Washington, D.C., 1966. Also see *The Invisible Soldier: The Experience of the Black Soldier, World War II*, edited by Mary Penick Motley, 1975.

Troop Train
(Greenock, Scotland, to Shrivenham, Berkshire)

"V signs": The British Broadcasting Corporation employed Victor de Laveleye, a Belgian refugee, who asked listeners to scrawl the letter "V" in public places to stiffen resistance. In July 1941 "Colonel Britton" (Douglas Ritchie) of the BBC opened a seven-language campaign, bidding the Allied world tap out the Morse Code sign for "V": dot dot dot-dash; and proposed the first two fingers for what became Churchill's hand-sign. The first four notes of Beethoven's Fifth Symphony became the sound signal. Dr. Paul Joseph Goebbels, Nazi Propaganda Minister, tried to appropriate the V sign for "Viktoria" (German, victory).

"CO": Commanding Officer.

Pub
(Castle Eaton)

"Pub": Public House, saloon-bar, licensed to sell alcoholic beverages; also serving as informal neighborhood social club.

"released Eyetalian prisoners": Italian prisoners of war, of modest military capacity, were released to work on agricultural projects, replacing British soldiers, many of whom were fighting in Italy. It was not unusual to spot men of common origin from Brooklyn and Bergamo, sharing drinks and cigarettes, while local Britons took a dim view of the fraternization.

"Doubled wartime's": In order to benefit from more daylight, clocks were shifted not one, but two hours ahead.

Tea

(Shrivenham)

"Bayeux to Bangalore": British military operations from Normandy to India.

Two million American soldiers were stationed in Great Britain during World War II. *The G.I.'s: The Americans in Britain, 1942–1945*, by Norman Longmate (London, 1975), is a brilliant chronicle of a complex situation.

Evensong

In Anglican Observance there is, among Evening Prayers, a *Collect for Aid against Perils*: "Lighten our darkness, we beseech thee, O Lord; and by thy great mercy defend us from all perils and dangers of this night. . . ."

"a tower": parish church, Shrivenham, near Swindon, Berkshire.

Engineer

"Kodakchromatic": an early instant-color-film camera with an unstable spectrum of tints.

Riverscape

"Spenser's marriage rhyme": "Prothalamion, or a Spousall Verse made by Edmund Spenser in Honour of the Double Mariage of the two Honorable and vertuous ladies, etc., etc." (1595). Its refrain is: "Sweete *Themmes* runne softly, till I end my Song."

"GI's": The twin letters G and I were usually taken to be abbreviation for "Government (or General) Issue," but actually originated with Quartermaster Corps supply clerks' reference for "Galvanized Iron"—as for garbage cans. Universal adaptation came to mean: individual soldier (noun); Army-issued object, or whatever fulfilled Army regulations (adjective); "GI that floor" (verb); strictness in accord with regulations (adverb).

"Spitfires": an eight-gun fighter-plane, first flown 1936, which became legendary in the Battle of Britain. Twenty-four variants were developed; in production until 1947, some twenty thousand were made and flown.

"Mustangs": American P51, single-seat fighter, operational from 1942. When Air Marshall Hermann Göring saw the first Mustangs escorting day-bombers to Berlin, it was said he knew the war was lost. Still used until 1977, the Mustang was designed and built in 117 days. Reaching the United Kingdom by October 1941, it destroyed more than two hundred flying-bombs over England.

Tudoresque

(Manchester)

"James Agee" (1909–1955): poet, novelist, film-writer. *Permit Me Voyage* (1934) contains his sonnets; these are collected with other verse in paperback. See *Remembering James Agee*, edited by David Madden (Louisiana State University Press, 1974), and *The Restless Journey of James Agee*, by Geneviève Moreau (New York, 1977). Agee was a graduate of Phillips Exeter Academy and of Harvard College (1932).

"Kohinoor and India's Star": famed gems; the Koh-i-noor, a gigantic oriental diamond, was presented to Queen Victoria by the East India Company in 1850 and is among the Crown Jewels.

"*Hound & Horn*": literary quarterly founded by Harvard undergraduates, 1927. It printed James Agee's first considerable poem, "Anne Garner" (Spring 1928), largely written when Agee was still at Exeter.

"A quote from Ezra Pound": "'Tis the white stag, Fame, we're a-hunting, / Bid the world's hounds come to horn!" (From *Personae*, 1909). Pound (1885–1972) came to call the magazine "Bitch and Bugle."

"Theodore Spencer" (1902–1949): critic, poet, professor of English literature, Harvard and Cambridge Universities. Annual lectures by distinguished writers honor his memory.

"Eliot": Thomas Stearns Eliot (1888–1965), Harvard '11; poet, dramatist, critic, editor; prime literary influence over progressive undergraduates, 1925–1935. *Hound & Horn* was modeled on his *Criterion*.

"Widener's shelves": Harry Elkins Widener's family erected this great library in memory of a young Philadelphia book-collector lost on the S. S. *Titanic*, 1913. In the Twenties, as now, the stacks were open for undergraduate browsing.

"Tintagel's drear hotel": the King Arthur Castle Hotel, set on cliffs over the coast, adjacent to a traditional site for the legendary court of the Knights of the Round Table. In the lounge was a massive disc in the style of William Morris' medieval handicraft.

"Debrett's": *Guide to the Peerage, Baronetage and Knightage of the United Kingdom.*

"Wells": English gothic cathedral of the Decorated style; central tower finished 1321. Four vast "strainer" arches prop up its great tower, which immediately started to slip.

"Bloomsbury": London district, adjacent to the British Museum, famed for its concentration of writers, artists, critics, and philosophers, 1910–1940, including Leonard and Virginia Woolf, Lytton Strachey, Maynard Keynes, Clive Bell, Duncan Grant, E. M. Forster, Roger Fry, and many others.

"Lydia Lopokova" (1891–1981): ballerina soubrette of the original Diaghilev Ballets Russes; later the wife of Lord Keynes (1883–1946).

"George the Fifth": A service of national thanksgiving was celebrated at Saint Paul's Cathedral in June, 1929, after recovery of the King from serious illness.

"ole U.K.": United Kingdom; England, Scotland, Wales, and Northern Ireland.

"PX": Post Exchange; supply stores for U.S. Army personnel.

"[Sir Walter] Raleigh" (c. 1552–1618), "Rupert Brooke" (1887–1915): archetype English poet-adventurers.

"[Sir] John Gielgud" (1904–   ): grandnephew of Ellen Terry; the leading Shakespearian actor of his epoch; knighted 1953 for his services to English theater.

"Jack Barrymore" (1882–1942): on 16 December 1922 appeared in *Hamlet*, designed by Robert Edmond Jones; greatest American Shakespearian performance since Edwin Booth's.

"Edwin Booth" (1833–1893): son of eminent actor Junius Brutus, brother of John Wilkes who shot Lincoln; greatest American Shakespearian of the 19th century and first to gain European recognition.

"Sir Henry Irving" (1838–1905): dominated the London stage c. 1870–1905. His *Hamlet* (1874) as a compassionate rather than vacillating prince was developed over three decades. Knighted 1895, the first actor to be so honored.

"[Sir] Johnston Forbes-Robertson" (1853–1937): trained as a painter, turned to acting with Irving and Ellen Terry; produced *Hamlet*, 1897; knighted 1913; then retired.

"*England, what thou wert, thou art*": from "The Vigil," by Sir Henry Newbolt (1862–1938):

> . . . *So shalt thou when morning comes*
>   *Rise to conquer or to fall,*
> *Joyful hear the rolling drums,*
>   *Joyful hear the trumpets call.*
> *Then let Memory tell thy heart;*
>   "*England! what thou wert, thou art!*
>   *Gird thee with thine ancient might,*
>   *Forth! and God defend the Right!*

Boy Scout
(Southampton)

"Southern England": Censorship forbade use of specific place-names. This location was assigned to areas including London, south to the English Channel.

Bobby
For Frederick Maddox

"Bobby": policeman, deriving from Sir *Robert* Peel (1788–1850), legal reformer, statesman, who organized Irish police system c. 1815, copied by England and other countries.

"Buzz bomb": the V-I. In German FZG76, *Fernzeilgerät* (Long-range Target Apparatus) *76*. Also known as doodlebug, flying-bomb and buzz bomb. Hitler's "secret" weapon, used from 1944 in retaliation for the bombing of Germany.

"Limey cop": In order to prevent scurvy, British ships in the 19th century provided lime juice for sailors. "Cop" derives from short, large-headed copper nails on uniform police boots.

"*Gott strafe England!*" (God Punish England!): World War II recapitulation of World War I "Hymn of Hate."

Junior

"He was in peril": On crossings from Southampton to the Norman coast, loud-speakers kept blaring "You Are Now In Peril," which seemed redundant.

Black Joe
(Utah-Rhino Beach)

Black soldiers of World War II showed more courage just surviving, as well as fighting back by all means possible, in southern and in northern camps, than young people today can possibly imagine. Hell, we fought the "man," the system and the Axis powers.

The infantry can't go a damn place without quartermasters and engineers, which a lot of people seem to forget.
   Lieutenant Lacy Wilson, 364th Infantry Regiment. From *The Invisible Soldier*, edited by Mary Penick Motley, 1975, page 61

Bed Check
(Castilly)

"ack-ack": British term for anti-aircraft (AA) fire, deriving from World War I phonetic alphabet, in which letter *A* was *ACK*.

"Bed-Check Charlie": "Bed-check" was a spot roll-call. German reconnaissance planes appeared at nightfall.

Vet
(Pointe du Hoe)

A hundred-foot-high sheer cliff west of Omaha Beach, believed to be an important German gun position, but on D-Day (June 6, 1944), U.S. Rangers scaled the cliff to find the Nazis fled, their guns left a short distance inland.

Ants
(Valognes)

The Germans had various rockets, from the A-4 (also known as V-2), developed by Wernher von Braun and Dornberger, to A-4B, a winged glider which never saw service. *Wasserfall* was a radio-controlled supersonic anti-aircraft missile, capable of destroying planes at 65,000 feet at 550 miles per hour. Its design was based on the A-4. Trials were made but development stopped, 1945. Albert Speer (1905–1981), Hitler's Superintendent of War Production, said the Nazis abandoned attempts at nuclear weaponry in 1942. However, rumor of "secret" weapons persisted until 1945, inevitably reaching Allied Intelligence. In 1939, Hitler in Danzig hinted at death-rays, bacterial bombs, etc.

Lucky Pierre
(Valognes)

"Lucky Pierre": eponymous hero of ancient anecdote, concerning a youth enjoyed between father/mother; man/woman; girl/boy.

"KP's": Kitchen Police, scullions. KP: a duty whose revolving schedule was detested, despite its more or less democratic observance among lower non-commissioned personnel.

"Rehabilitation Corps": units intended to aid the French recover from hostilities; not always welcomed, since the Americans caused more material damage than the Germans.

La Grange
(Valognes)

"Klim": milk spelled backwards; powdered substitute; water added, tasted like wet flannel.

Red Cross
(Isigny)

"Lake Forest": affluent Chicago suburb.

"Jack O'Diamonds, Water Boy": Southern U.S. chain-gang prisoners' work-song; the men called for water from a boy with pail and dipper. The singers Roland Hayes and Paul Robeson sang this in concert during the Twenties and Thirties.

AWOL
(Brix-St. Joseph)

"AWOL": Absent WithOut Leave. Conscious desertion from a duty-post. A serious crime in combat-zones, no longer punished by the firing squad.

"Lucky Conqueror": unit telephone exchange, Third U.S. Army, Cotentin Peninsula, August, 1944. General George Patton's Headquarters was coded as "Lucky Forward."

Chimbly
(Isigny-Carentan)

Ballad essayed in Americanized style of William McConagall (1830–1896), Scottish handloom weaver from Dundee. The first stanza from his "Battle of El-Teb" follows:

Ye sons of Great Britain, I think no shame
To write in praise of brave Colonel Graham!
Whose name will be handed down to posterity
                              without any stigma,
Because, at the battle of El-Teb, he defeated
                              Osman Digma.

"Cherbug": Cherbourg.

"KN": Caen.

"Isigny . . . Carentan": Isigny, town at the base of Cotentin Peninsula, captured by U.S. 29th Division, night of June 9–10, 1944. Carentan, Norman town, five miles inland between Utah and Omaha Beaches, taken June 12, 1944, by 101st Airborne after five days' bloody fighting.

Inter-Service
(Carentan)

"S.O.P.": Standard Operating Procedure.

"Ike's plan": "Ike," nickname for General Dwight David Eisenhower (1890–1969), gained at West Point (Class of 1915). His "plan":

In the matter of command, it can be said here that all relationships between American and British forces were smooth and effective. Because of certain fundamental national differences in methods of military supply and administration, it was early agreed that no unit lower than a corps of one nationality would be placed under command of the other nationality except where unavoidable military necessity made this imperative.
Eisenhower's Own Story of the War, 1946, page 8

"snafu": Situation Normal, All Fucked Up.

"Common Sense": Title of pamphlet by Thomas Paine (1737–1809), published Philadelphia, 9 January 1776, inaugurating open movement for independence of American colonies from the British Crown.

"Tea Party": dumping of tea into Boston Harbor, 16 December 1773, by citizens disguised as Indians protesting "taxation without representation."

"1812": war between Britain and the United States (in which the White House was burned), ending in the Battle of New Orleans, January 1815.

"[Wilfred] Owen" (1893–1918): the most acclaimed poet-martyr of World War I.

"David Jones" (1895–1974): author of In Parenthesis and The Anathemata, important lyrical narratives of the Anglo-Welsh in France.

"[Siegfried] Sassoon" (1886–1967): author of Counter Attack and Memoirs of an Infantry Officer.

Château
(St. Côme du Mont)

"bocage": Fr., copse, grove. Dense margin of tree and bush fencing Norman and Breton roads and fields, connected by trench and tunnel, used by the Germans as hindrance against American tanks and infantry.

"Marivauxdage": Pierre Carlet de Chamblain de Marivaux (1688–1763), playwright, novelist; inventor of stylized theatrical gallantry, characterized by wit, irony and cerebral passion. His plays, among which are La Surprise de l'Amour (1722) and Les Fausses Confidences (1737), remain in classic French repertory.

"La fille de Minos et de Pasiphaë": a line from Phèdre (1677; Act I, Scene I) by the classic dramatist Jean Racine (1639–1699), offered students as perfection of sound and sense in French prosody. Alludes to the parents of Phaedra: her father, Minos, so just he became a judge of the dead in Hades; her mother,

Pasiphaë, enamored of a bull who sired the Minotaur. The father embodies reason, the mother passion; Phaedra, their daughter, is torn between the inborn forces of compassion and lust in her love for Hippolytus. Inference suggests the rape of Europa by Jupiter in his guise as a bull.

Air Strike
(St. Jean de Daye)

On the morning of 25 July [1944] an area 5 miles long and 1 mile wide to the west of St.-Lô was blasted by 1,495 heavy bombers of the Eighth Air Force and 388 aircraft of AEAF dropping over 4,700 tons of bombs. . . . The total of AEAF sorties for this day was 4,979.
     Eisenhower's Own Story of the War, page 65

Massive carpet-bombing was scheduled for 24 July; bad weather intervened. Not all Eighth Air Force planes had word the raid was cancelled, with tragic results. Some B17s hit advanced American infantry units; a large ammunition dump was bombed.

"St. Lô": Norman fortress-town on the River Vire. At the moment of invasion, June 1944, an important German headquarters, and major communications center.

Ville Lumière
(Paris)

Since the invention of electric street-illumination Paris has been known as the City of Light. It fell to the combined forces of General LeClercq's Free French Army and the Americans, 25 August 1944.

Within the city, the police went on strike and defied the German authorities when the latter laid siege to the Prefecture of Police on the Ile-de-la-Cité on 19 August. The traditional barricades appeared in the streets, the resistance movement came into the open, and for over a week a strange, skirmishing battle was fought through the city. . . . For the honor of being the first Allied troops to reenter Paris, the French 2nd

Armored Division was brought up from the Argentan sector where it had formed part of the Third Army spearhead. . . .
Eisenhower's Own Story of the War, page 49

"V-Mail": miniaturized stationery form for air delivery between Theatres of Operations and the U.S.

Hijack
(Châlons-sur-Marne, 19 September 1944)

The Third Army's advance involved herculean tasks in the matter of supply. At the Moselle enemy resistance had stiffened and the problem of supply became increasingly acute, to the extent that General Patton's forces were partially immobilized and physically incapable of mounting assaults on a large scale or of continuing a pursuit had the opportunity offered.
Eisenhower's Own Story of the War, pages 65–66

Shortage of gasoline, partly diverted to aid Montgomery's advance into Holland (Arnhem— "Operation Market Garden"), brought Patton up short. Halted in Lorraine, he faced a long hard battle through the coming winter. He claimed later that had he had gasoline in September he could have been in Berlin by October! In the film Patton (1970), with George C. Scott's riveting impersonation, the incident described shows the General directing traffic; such was not the fact.

Patton
(Lépine-Ste. Menehould)

Metrical scheme: "John Brown's Body"; "Battle Hymn of the Republic." "Mine eyes have seen the glory of the coming of the Lord. . . ."

General George Smith Patton, Jr. (1885–1945); West Point, 1909. He chose the cavalry, served with Pershing in Mexico; a member of his staff in France, World War I; an innovative tank commander, seriously wounded in the Meuse-Argonne offensive. Between wars, tanks were assigned as infantry support; Patton reverted to horse cavalry.

Prone to political tactlessness, a man of psychological complexity, he finally commanded Third U.S. Army, which, under him, took more prisoners, covering more terrain, than any force in our history. Persistent rumors exist that General Patton was assassinated to prevent him from antagonizing the Russians by precipitately turning his attention to Berlin.

"Bulfinch's golden dome": Charles Bulfinch (1763–1844), architect of the Massachusetts State House, Beacon Hill; gilded, it became a famous landmark, and supposedly could be seen from ships approaching port.

"Stars & Stripes": army newspaper, originally serving soldiers of World War I. Revived, London, 1942, when President Franklin D. Roosevelt wished to forestall the Chicago Tribune from publishing independently for the military global sectors. Its liberalism and pro-GI policy caused some brass to fancy it had been commandeered by a "pro-communist cell." It violated regulations, ridiculed command decisions, made awkward comparisons between U.S. and German weapons. A formal investigation of its attitude was cancelled due to the end of the war.

"SHAEF": Supreme Headquarters, Allied Expeditionary Force. General Eisenhower commanded from the Trianon Palace Hotel, Versailles; later, a forward echelon moved to Reims.

"Trier" (Trèves): Ancient Romano-German town which Hitler proposed to restore as a thousand-year-old monument of historic architecture. It fell to Third U.S. Army, 5 March 1945.

"Military governor, Bavaria's shattered state":
Next, I had my final brush with George Patton's impulsiveness. It was an example of a strong-minded man's tendency to oversimplify history. . . . Patton, for reasons known only to himself . . . suggested that the Nazis were just another political party, like the Republicans and Democrats.
Dwight D. Eisenhower
At Ease: Stories I Tell to Friends, 1967, pages 307–8

"Nancy . . . Metz":

On the Third Army's front Nancy had fallen 15 September [1944], but Metz, strongly defended by its outer ring of forts, was to remain in enemy hands until our offensive ultimately reduced it on 22 November.
  Eisenhower's Own Story of the War, page 71

Spy
(Nancy)

"G2": Military Intelligence Division.

Rank
(Toul)

"MI [M2]": light weapon influenced by the sub-machine-gun, calculated to alleviate the average uninstructed GI's problems with pistols. A gas-actuated blowback weapon roughly similar to the M-I rifle.

Guts
(Nancy)

"Thionville": market-town on the River Moselle between Esch and Metz.

Vaudeville
For Lew Christensen

"Echternach": town in the Grand Duchy of Luxemburg, on the River Sûre, close to the German border. A religious center, site of a famous dancing-procession, and known for a great Gospels manuscript.

Trip Ticket
(Esch)

"Jeeps": small, four-wheeled personnel or utility vehicles, carrying five passengers or eight hundred pounds; used for light reconnaissance, some carried stretchers and/or light machine-guns. The name derived from "G.P." or general-purpose, but was also connected with "Eugene the Jeep," a wonder-working character in "Thimble Theater" ("Popeye"), a comic-strip. Designed and built by the Willys Company, Toledo, Ohio; first tested December 1940.

"trip ticket": report required to be filed after each use of motor-pool vehicle. Loss of "bullet-proof" windshields was a serious fault; non-shatter glass was impossible to replace at this time. Loss removed vehicles from service.

DP's
(Meaux)

The incident described is further documented in "Roads to Oz" by Michael B. Shimkin, M.D., presently on the staff of the School of Medicine, University of California, La Jolla (*Perspectives in Biology and Medicine*, Summer 1979, pages 580–81).

"DP's": Displaced Persons; international European refugees.

"*Praschai*": "Farewell"—a familiar Russian folk-song.

Joseph Jones, Jr.
In memory of Pfc. Kevin Cunningham Grahame, Jr.
(Esch)

Tony
For José Martinez

"Special Services officer": charged with entertainment, recreation and maintenance of "morale."

"Joe E. Brown . . . Carmen Miranda": popular American and Brazilian entertainers, late Thirties and early Forties.

"Off Limits": areas restricted from entry by army personnel, often to protect civil properties.

"Pont-à-Mousson": market-town and educational center. Charles, Duc de Guise, founded its Jesuit University, 1572. Badly damaged, World War II, it has since been well restored.

"Begin Their Beguine": "Begin the Beguine," hit song by Cole Porter from *Jubilee* (1935), supposedly inspired by native music on the isle of Alor, Dutch East Indies, and transmuted into "Brazilian" rhythms.

"his Union": AGMA, American Guild of Musical Artists, with jurisdiction also over dancers.

Big Deal
(Maxeville)

"FFI": Forces Françaises de l'Intérieur, clandestine French resistance organization given this name February 1944, but operating through the Nazi occupation; after the Allied invasion, attached to its armies.

"Nancy": capital, Grand Duchy of Bar and Lorraine, last province to enter the French Union; disputed (with Alsace) after the Franco-Prussian War (1870–1871).

"Jean Lamour" (1698–1771): artist in forged and gilded iron, whose masterpiece is the grill of the Place Stanislas, made for the exiled Polish Prince Stanislas Lesczynski, father-in-law of Louis XV.

"Georges du Mesnil de la Tour" (1593–1652): painter, master of candle-light chiaroscuro.

"[Jacques] Callot" (1592–1635): master print-maker, whose depictions of war on a miniature scale anticipate Goya.

"Bar-le-Duc . . . delicious dessert": cream-cheese and fresh currants.

"Battle of the Bulge": on the morning of 16 December 1944 the 5th, 6th and 7th German armies, comprising twenty-five divisions, struck six unsuspecting American divisions in the Ardennes Forest of southern Belgium. Heroic American resistance saved two road junctions—St. Vith and Bastogne. These held, and reinforcements from Holland and Lorraine stopped the Germans short of the River Meuse, near Dinant, 26 December. Grounded by bad weather until then, the Allied Air Forces became operational.

"McAuliffe": Brigadier General Anthony C. McAuliffe (1898–1975), West Point, 1919. On 22 December he was offered "an honorable surrender" by the Nazis for his "battered bastards of Bastogne." His reply was reported as "Nuts!"; there were other versions.

KP
(Maxeville)

"Tec 3": Technical Sergeant, Third Class; grade above Corporal, World War II.

"compassionate leave": granted in cases of emergency family problems.

G2
(Thionville)

"K-rations": field-rations, first developed for airborne troops, consisting of a day's food in three cardboard containers—protein, biscuits, candy or fruit-bar, chewing-gum, and cigarettes. Not gourmet quality but prized by civilian populations.

Comité des Forges
(Joigny)

"[La] Comité des Forges": controlled by an international arms cartel; although formally dissolved in 1940, Schneider-Creuzot factories were not seriously damaged in either world war.

On se bat autour du bassin de Briey . . . mais c'est dans la presse. . . . Il paraît que la Comité des Forges fait pression sur la censure.

Fighting around the reservoir of Briey . . . but it's in the papers. . . . It seems that the Comité des Forges exerts pressure over censorship.
  Paul Morand
  Journal d'un Attaché d'Ambassade (1916–17),
  Paris, 1963, page 154

Load
(Luxemburg City)

"railroad gun": such could be continually moved; camouflaged, almost impossible to spot by day; damage done was more psychological than material.

Réveillon
(Nancy)

"Réveillon": midnight repast; *Réveillon de la Saint-Sylvestre:* New Year's Eve celebration. From *réveiller,* to awake or arouse.

Charlie Boy
(Mainz)

"*Wehrmacht*": Ger., armed might; hence Army.

"*Führer Prinzip*" (*Führerprinzip*): Ger., leadership principal; Hitler's philosophical basis of hypnotic control by which he became Chancellor, January 1933.

"*Auf Wiedersehen*": Ger., until we see (one another) again; farewell, so long.

Das Schloss
(Bamberg)

"Schloss Voss": Pommersfelden, seat of the Prince Bishops Mainz-Bamberg; magnificent baroque palace, built by the Elector Lothar Franz von Schönborn; architects Johann Dientzenhofer and Johann Lukas von Hildebrandt (the stairwell),

from 1711 to 1718. The Elector Archbishop said of its cost: "Building is madness, but everyone wants his own hat."

"*Gräfin*": Ger., Countess.

"Bach's Goldberg Variations": Johann Gottlieb Goldberg (1727–1756), keyboard virtuoso; one of J.S. Bach's most gifted executants, had him compose this series to relieve an insomniac count.

Festspielhaus
(Bayreuth)

Festival opera-house designed and built for Richard Wagner's music-dramas. The first complete *Ring of the Nibelungs* was performed there in 1876.

"*Deutschland über Alles*": "Germany Over All." Pre-World War I Prussian imperialist hymn. ["The German has no sense of equality; only of status." Harold Nicolson, BBC broadcast, 14 September 1939.] The text is an adaptation of a patriotic poem by Walther von der Vogelweide; the tune, written by Haydn in 1797 for the Austrian emperor and still used in Austria, also appears in Haydn's *Kaiserquartett.*

"USO": United Service Organization, created February 4, 1941, to provide services and amenities for localities where civilian facilities were strained. Later, the unified efforts of many religious and social organizations extended the work overseas, hopefully offering a "home away from home."

"Minnesinging": *Minnesang,* love-song; genre of medieval lyric, narrative, religious, and political verse embodied in Walther von der Vogelweide (c. 1170–c. 1230). 15th and 16th century *Meistersinger* looked to him as master.

"Beckmesser": comic villain of Wagner's music-drama *Die Meistersinger von Nürnberg* (1868), who stole the hero's competition prize-song.

Bath
(Erlangen)

"Nudes in wet armor": "The Battle of Naked Men," engraving by Antonio Pollaiuolo (c. 1466); contest cartoons for Leonardo da Vinci's "Battle of Anghiari" (1504–5); Michelangelo's "Battle of Cascina" (1504).

4th Armored
(Wolfratshausen)

"SS bastids": *Schutzstaffel* (Protection Detachments), elite security guards, organized by Hitler, 1925, as protection for Nazi Party meetings; later headed by Heinrich Himmler. By 1939, the SS numbered over 240,000, feared and detested by civilian populations.

"That Colonel Abrams": Creighton W. Abrams (1914–1974), Commander, 37th Tank Battalion, which broke the German siege of Bastogne. Then a lieutenant colonel, he was promoted to general; at his death, U.S. Army Chief of Staff.

"panzer fists": *Panzerfaust*, cant name for German *Faustpatrone*. Hand-launched anti-tank weapon, projectile with tubular tail and four small tail fins. Its effective range was about 33 yards.

"Hitler youth": *Hitlerjugend*, legions of adolescents; toward the end of the war they were recruited or volunteered to augment failing Nazi armies.

The SS and the armored divisions were for the most part made up of fanatical Nazis whose faith in the cause they served could be shaken by little else than annihilation; yet the time was soon to come when even their commanders, realizing the fruitlessness of further struggle, would surrender their units rather than see their men slaughtered to no purpose.
Eisenhower's Own Story of the War, page 96

P.O.W.
(Kempten)

"P.O.W.": Prisoner of War. At war's end, there were some 4,000,000 prisoners. 1.7 million Allied prisoners were in Germany (including 90,000 Americans). The Japanese held 145,000 (including 15,000 Americans). Axis prisoners (exclusive of those held by the Russians) were some 1,070,000, although accurate figures cannot be obtained.

Siegfriedslage
For James Stern
(Tegernsee)

"*Siegfriedslage*": forest-camp of Siegfried, Wagner's tenor-hero of *The Ring of the Nibelungs*.

"High Headquarters": Third U.S. Army.

"Cagney Irishry": James Cagney (1899–1986), American film actor, notable for dynamic impersonation of gangsters and virtuoso character roles.

"stimulated Major, V.I.P.": person with status simulating army rank; a citizen on special commission, but not actually in the Army. V.I.P.: Very Important Person; any ranking troublesome or officious visitor.

"Helmet Liner": plastic (hard-hat) shell worn inside steel helmets, but without these in non-combat zones. All but criminal offense to be found not wearing one, Patton's Headquarters, Munich, June 1945.

"Pastor Wiemöller": Martin Niemöller (1892–1984), Lutheran minister, submarine-commander World War I; won highest German honor, "*Pour le Mérite.*" An early opponent of Hitler, preached against the Nazis openly from his pulpit; arrested, 1937; confined in concentration camps until liberated, 1945.

"Dunstan Morden": Wystan Auden (1907–1973), with simulated rank of major, served in Europe from February 1945 in U.S. Strategic Bombing

Survey. This was a civilian-military body organized November 1944 to study effects of bombing on Germany, in preparation for final attack on Japan, and to determine post-war defense. Reports on European and Pacific areas were published in two series, 316 titles. Auden told a reporter from *Time* magazine, 1963–("but not for attribution")–it was all "a colossal boondoggle." See "The Speer Interrogation: Last Days of the Third Reich" by John Kenneth Galbraith (*Atlantic Monthly*, July 1979, pages 50–57) for a detailed account of the purposes and operations of the Strategic Bombing Survey, including names and services of personnel.

"Hate which 'no man can ever estimate.'"

> . . . *True, love finally is great,*
> *Greater than all; but large the hate,*
> *Far larger than Man can ever estimate.*
> > W. H. Auden and Christopher Isherwood
> > *The Ascent of F6, 1936*

"Organized hatred. *That* is unity." From "Lines on the Death of Bismarck" by John Jay Chapman (1862–1933). Auden included this poem in his and Norman Holmes Pearson's *Poets of the English Language*, Volume V, pages 593–95. Chapman was a brilliant, eccentric critic, biographer and poet. The poem is a splendid statement of factors linking two world wars.

"'Poetry', he said, "s not in the pity.'"

> *This book is not about heroes. English Poetry is not yet fit to speak of them. . . . My subject is War. . . . The Poetry is in the pity.*
> > Wilfred Owen
> > Preface to *Poems*, 1918
> > See *War Poems and Others*, edited, with an introduction and notes, by Dominic Hibberd, London, 1973

"It's in the words": the poet Stéphane Mallarmé (1842–1898), to the painter Edgar Degas (1834–1917), in answer to the latter's request for criticism on his own sonnets, for which he said he had "plenty of *ideas*."

"Ronald Firbank": Arthur Annesley Ronald Firbank (1886–1926), novelist and playwright. *The Flower Beneath the Foot* (1923) is in part a *roman à clef* with frivolously acid vignettes derived from King George, Queen Mary, Vita Sackville-West, the Hon. Evan Morgan, and others. In *A Certain World*, W. H. Auden's "commonplace book" (1970), several entries from Firbank are included, characteristic of his frantic, preposterous, miniature anti-heroics.

Kristallnacht
For Astrid Zydower

On the night of 10 November 1938 there was organized general devastation of Jewish property throughout Germany, marked by massive heaps of shattered window-glass, following the assassination of Ernst vom Rath, third secretary of the German Embassy in Paris. His assassin was Hersh Grynszpan, a seventeen-year-old Polish student whose parents had been made landless and stateless by Richard Heydrich, Chief of the SS in Central Europe at this time.

"Heinrich Heine" (1797–1856): lyric poet and master of German prose. From a family of rich Hamburg merchants, he protested against contemporary Germany, exiling himself to Paris. Many of his poems are set by composers of *Lieder*, German art-songs.

"*Dichter*": Ger., poet.

"*Still ist die Nacht*": "Calm is the night. . . ."

"*Ruhen die Gassen*": "Quiet in the streets. . . ."

"*Mädchen mit dem röten Mündchen*": "Lass with the rosy lips. . . ."

"*Nach Frankreich zogen zwei Grenadier*": "Back towards France slogged two grenadiers. . . ." (from Napoleon's disastrous Russian campaign).

"Because of Quakers good": British religious organizations took the responsibility for sponsoring children of Nazi victims.

"Auschwitz, Belsen, Dachau": Auschwitz (Polish Oświęcim), near Cracow; from 1941, main extermination center for Jews, Poles, Slavs, and gypsies —some 2,000,000 between 1932 and 1944. Bergen-Belsen on Lüneberg Heath, intended to house 8,000 prisoners; by March 1944, held 42,000; in April 1945 the British liberated some 60,000 in a raging typhus epidemic. Dachau, the "model" camp, founded 1933 by Heinrich Himmler as training-school for SS camp administrators; site of the most terrible human "experiments."

"When Heine lay dying. . . .": of a long, terrible disease.

"*métier*": Fr., trade, profession, business.

Kinderlied
(Munich)

"*Nichts gut*. . . .": "It ain't good. It's all shot? How much would your sister cost?"

"M.P.'s": Military Police.

Scraps

"*IN DEM WOHNZIMMER*. . . .": "In his sitting-room lay the mayor and his wife shot in their heads, in a great pool of blood."

"*DIE ÜBERGABE*. . . .": "No question of surrender. The camp is to be immediately evacuated. No prisoner will be permitted to come into the hands of the enemy alive."

"*ARBEIT MACHT FREI*": "Work Sets You Free."

Arts & Monuments
In memory of SS Hauptmann Hermann Bunjes (Trier-Salzkammergut)

For accounts of discovery and recovery of looted art-treasure destined for Hitler's proposed museum (honoring his mother) in Linz, Austria,

see official U.S. *Report of the American Commission for the Protection and Salvage of Artistic and Historic Monuments in War Areas* (U.S. Government Printing Office, Washington, D.C.), pages 106, 154, 159; *The Art Stealers* by Milton Esterow (New York, 1973), pages 98–109; *The Rape of Art* by David Roxan and Ken Wanstall (New York, 1964), pages 154–72.

"*Kaugummi*": chewing-gum.

"[Professor A.] Kingsley Porter" (1883–1933): author of *The Pilgrimage Road to Campostella* and other studies of Romanesque and medieval art.

"flaming Volsung gods": early Teutonic epic deities (*Völsunga Saga*). Hitler foresaw his cataclysmic end in the Berlin Bunker in terms of Wagnerian immolation.

"Salzkammergut": Workers in saltmines knew their future livelihood depended on the mineral resources of their mountains, and defused explosive charges which also would have destroyed stored art-objects.

"Van Eyck's Ghent altar piece": "The Adoration of the Lamb of God" (c. 1432) by Hubert and Jan van Eyck, painted for the church of St. Bavon, Ghent; one of the prime achievements of Western painting. On many oak panels it depicts Christ in Judgment, attended by the Virgin and Saint John, contemplated by Adam and Eve; below, The Lamb of God, shedding His Blood, surrounded by angels, apostles, prophets, martyrs, knights, and hermits.

"Count Czernin's veristic Vermeer": One of the greatest of Jan Vermeer's paintings, it shows the artist in his studio, painting a model clad as Fame. In the Czernin Palace before the war, it is now in the Kunsthistorisches Museum, Vienna.

Michelangelo's "Mother and Child": executed (c. 1506) for the Moscheron family of Bruges, shows a young Virgin and naked Jesus, seven or eight years old, surrounded by superbly carved draperies.

"Napoleon": He systematically looted Italian art to replenish the Louvre and other French museums. After Waterloo, much was restored, notably the four horses of San Marco; lesser works are still found in Paris and the provinces.

Threesome

"GHQ": General Headquarters.

"GI Bill": government legislation enacting system of grants-in-aid toward veterans' education.

Dear John
(Starnberg)

"Dear John": cant term for missives from GI wives, explaining change of heart due to absence of soldier-husbands.

"sky-pilot fairy": cant term for aircorps chaplain used in films more than in the Service.

Hymn
In memory of George Stout
(Ubique)

"Front and center": Command for soldiers to present themselves, center front-line of a parade formation.

"Painter of sorts": Eisenhower, Churchill and Hitler were amateur painters.

"Colonel Charles Codman" (1893–1956): aide-de-camp to General Patton, his comfort, buffer.

"Colonel Geoffrey [Fairbank] Webb" (1898–1970): Cambridge University architectural historian; appointed Architectural Advisor to War Office, November 1943, on the recommendation of Sir Leonard Wooley; in 1944 advisor to SHAEF in all matters concerning Monuments, Fine Arts & Archives. General Patton arbitrarily forbade officers of other Allied armies from intruding into his area, causing conflict with personnel holding orders from Supreme Headquarters.

"Hutch Huchthausen": Captain Walter J. Huchthausen (1910–1945), killed in action, 16 April 1945.

"Sheldon Keck" (1910–   ): eminent conservationist of paintings; taught and worked at Harvard, Brooklyn, Cooperstown, New York.

"[Corporal, later] Lieutenant John [D.] Skilton" (1911–   ): saved the great primitive stone Calvary at Plougastel-Daoulas, Brittany, damaged by shell-fire August 1944. A year later, responsible for salvaging the magnificent Tiepolo frescoes over Treppenhaus and Kaisersaal, Würzburg Residenz. In recognition, in June 1976, he was honored with the Freedom of the City.

"Langdon Warner" (1881–1955): Professor, Far Eastern Art, Harvard. Post-war Japanese historians credit him with saving the temple cities of Kyoto and Nara from fire-bombing through his influence with President Roosevelt, to whom he was connected by marriage. His honored ashes are enclosed within the Horyu-ji monastery, one of the holiest sites in Japan.

"George [L.] Stout" (1901–1978): USNR (1917–19; 1942–46); Head of Conservation Laboratories, Harvard University; Director, Worcester [Massachusetts] Art Museum; Director, Isabella Stewart Gardner Museum, Boston. Editor, *Technical Studies in the Field of Fine Arts*; author, *The Care of Pictures* (1948, republished 1975).

"bridge-blown Rhine": The most formidable water-barrier in Western Europe, presumably even stronger than the "Siegfried Line" man-made defenses, was crossed 7 March 1945 when U.S. 9th Armored Division captured the Ludendorf railway-bridge at Remagen, which the Nazis had failed to destroy.

"*gaijin*": Japanese, alien, foreigner; post-war, specifically American.

Göring

(Veldenstein)

"[Hermann] Göring" (1893–1946): Second only to Hitler, his power faded after 1942; but at the end he persisted as Nazi spokesman. A brilliant aviator, World War I, he became hypnotized by Hitler. Badly wounded in the Munich *Putsch*, November 1923, he became addicted to morphine. He planned the destruction of the Jews, spoliation of Russia, organization of the Luftwaffe; looting of European art. Principal defendant in the Nuremburg trials, he managed to commit suicide.

Franziska Göring was his father's second wife. She became the mistress of Ritter von Eppenstein, family-doctor, wealthy long-standing friend. Partly Jewish, he offered one of his castles, Schloss Veldenstein, to the impoverished Görings. Von Eppenstein, despite his Jewish taint, was considered a foster-parent by Hermann, whose own father drank and died early.

"*Tod, Teufel, Ritter*": Albrecht Dürer's great engraving (1513) of Death, Devil and a Knight. It was appropriated by Hitler's SS as a metaphorical ensign, identifying the elite Nazi crusader who proceeds to victory despite death and evil.

"*Dritte Reich's* Number Two": Göring was slated to succeed Hitler, in case of his death. On 23 April 1945 he was dismissed by Hitler for his offer to take over command. He surrendered May 8 to Americans who were so impressed by their capture they incurred the wrath of General Eisenhower.

"*Hausfreund*": literally, "house-friend"; the wife's lover in a *ménage à trois*.

"*Tausendjahr Reich*": the Germano-Austrian-Czech state, prophesied by Hitler to last a thousand years.

"Uhlans": from Turkish, a lad; commonly, a mounted lancer of Tatar origin, whose sinister black and silver uniform was adopted by crack regiments of the Imperial Prussian Army (including the Death's Head Hussars) up to 1914.

"the Boer": the Anglo-Boer War, South Africa (1899–1902) was the most intense conflict between the Franco-Prussian War of 1870–71 and the outbreak of World War I in 1914.

"*Hoch der Kaiser! Deutschland, hoch!*": abbreviation for "*Hoch lebe der Kaiser!*" "Long live the Emperor!"; enthusiastically shouted precedent in Hohenzollern days for "*Heil Hitler!*"

"*Sachlichkeit*": Ger., efficiency, tidiness, economy.

"*Ehrenhall*": Ger., mansion. Göring improved on the early models of the Eppenstein castles, building "Carinhall," an enormous hunting-lodge on an estate of 100,000 acres north of Berlin. Built at public expense, it was dedicated to the memory of his first wife.

The Chosen

(Hungen)

The records, sacred books, library, and plate of the oldest and richest Dutch synagogues were stored in a church and barn, Hungen, Bavaria.

Truce

(Altaussee)

"so many murdered, maimed or missed": An estimate made by C. Hartley Grattan (*Harper's Magazine*, April 1949), based on then-available records, gave the dollar cost for World War II as 350 billions; troops killed in battle (U.S. alone) 256,330. Total global cost four trillions; forty million soldiers and civilians killed or wounded.

"a deathless beldam": "For I saw with my own eyes the Sibyl hanging in a jar at Cumae, and when the acolytes said, 'Sibyl, what do you wish?' she replied, 'I wish to die!'" (*Satyricon*, Petronius,

Chapter 48). Sibyl, anciently a wise-woman or prophetess; the archetype Sibyl had been granted eternal life by Apollo, but not eternal youth. Her body withered, and was housed dried, in a bottle.

Arrived at Cumae, when you view the flood
Of black Avernus, and the sounding wood,
The mad prophetic Sibyl you shall find,
Dark in a cave, and on a rock reclined.
She sings the fates, and in her frantic fits,
The notes and names, inscribed, to leaves commits.
   Aeneid, Book III, lines 561–66
   Dryden's translation

"windage of what next big wars": After 11 November 1918 the economist Maynard Keynes wrote the novelist D. H. Lawrence: "Whatever may develop neither side can start the war up again." Lawrence answered: "I suppose you think the war is over and that we shall go back to the kind of world you lived in before. But the war isn't over. The hate and evil is greater now than ever. Very soon the war will break out again."

Here Lies

In memory of Lieutenant [J. G.] Harry Dunham; Staff Sergeant Caleb Milne; Lieutenant Frederick Paine, USNR

GI Bill

In memory of F. O. Matthiessen

The Servicemen's Readjustment Act, Public Law 346, 78th Congress, was signed by President Franklin D. Roosevelt, 22 June 1944. It supported educational benefits to returning soldiers, hoping to prevent future unemployment, and enabled segments of the population previously deprived to gain skills and information.

Memorial

In memory of Flight Captain Saunders [Smudge] Draper, RCAF

Metrical scheme imitated from "The Blessed Virgin Compared to the Air We Breathe," by Gerard Manley Hopkins, S.J.

   . . . Yea, mark you this:
It does no prejudice.
The glass-blue days are those
When every colour glows,
Each shape and shadow shows.
Blue be it: this blue heaven
The seven or seven times seven
Hued sunbeam will transmit
Perfect, not alter it. . . .

Private Poet

by W. H. Auden

A note on the first edition of *Rhymes of a Pfc*. 1964:

Lincoln Kirstein has long been the name of an impresario, the promoter of *Hound & Horn*, the Director of a Ballet Company who, by giving George Balanchine the opportunity to exercise his genius, has done as much as anyone alive for the cause of Classical Ballet. An impresario is, by definition, someone who does not himself "create"; should he, by any chance, produce a work of his own, one assumes that it must be the trifle of a dilettante, unworthy of serious attention.

During a war, day after day, night after night, we read and hear of little else but war, and our anxiety to learn what is really happening is exacerbated by our knowledge that what we are being told is, at best, but half of the truth, couched, furthermore, in the nauseating clichés of journalese. Consequently, when peace comes, one of the greatest blessings it brings is freedom from war-news, and the last thing we feel like reading is a war book. It is now, however, over nineteen years since V-J Day, time enough, surely, for us to have gotten over our feelings of satiety. As for Mr. Kirstein the impresario, I can only implore the reader to forget his existence and approach these poems as if they were anonymous.

Despite all changes in values, interests, sensibility, the basic assumptions governing the treatment of warfare in poetry remained pretty well unchanged from Homer's time down until the Napoleonic Wars. These assumptions may be summarized as follows. 1) The Warrior is a Hero, that is to say, a numinous being. 2) War is pre-eminently the sphere of public deeds of heroism by individual persons; in no other sphere can a man so clearly disclose to others who he is. 3) Since his deeds are public, the warrior himself does not have to relate them. That duty falls to the professional poet who, as the legend of Homer's blindness indicates, is not himself a combatant. 4) The poet's job is to take the known story and sing of it in a style worthy of its greatness, that is to say, in a "high" style.

It was not until the eighteenth century that, under the influence of the Enlightenment, men began to question the numinous nobility of the Warrior, and, then, the scale of the Napoleonic Wars, involving huge armies and the whole continent of Europe, made it impossible to think of war in terms of individuals and choice. Stendhal, and Tolstoy after him, depict war as an irrational form of human behavior to which men are driven by forces quite outside their conscious control, and a battle as an unholy mess in which nothing happens as the commanders on either side intend. Irrational behavior cannot be sung of in a high style; the notes it calls for are the macabre, the ironic, the comic; and it cannot be truthfully described except by an eye-witness. Since 1800, no poet has been able to "sing" of war, and war poems written by civilians from a safe distance, like "The Charge of the Light Brigade" have been worthless. At the beginning of World War I, for a generation which had never experienced it, war was still felt to be glamorous, but by 1916, it was known to be, not merely irrational, but an obscene inexcusable nightmare.

It must be admitted, I think, that the Second World War has produced, so far at any rate, less literature of outstanding merit, whether in verse or prose, than the First. For this I can see three possible reasons. The more mechanized warfare becomes, the fewer the number of soldiers directly engaged in combat compared to the number engaged in services behind the firing-line; fewer, that is, are directly confronted by the "naked face" of war. Then, remembering the reckless waste of human lives in the First, the military authorities in the Second were determined to save as many lives as possible and to assign the individual soldier to a post which matched his character and talents. As a result, a draftee with the education and sensibility required to become a writer was very unlikely to find himself among the combat troops; most probably he would end up as a Tec Sergeant with a desk job. (Luckily for us, Mr. Kirstein had the misfortune to have a black mark against him in the records—I have never understood exactly what it was, except that it was something political—and on that account never rose above the rank of Pfc.) Lastly, the emotional attitude of an Englishman or an American to the Second World War was more complicated. In 1914 the nations of Europe had blundered into a war none of them wanted and without the faintest notion of what a modern war would be like. Whatever their politicians and generals might think, by 1916 no common soldier on either side could see a reason why they should be fighting each other. Consequently, what Wilfred Owen called "The pity of war, the pity war distilled," was a simple emotion of compassion for one's fellow sufferers in the common nightmare, which made no distinction between friend and foe. In 1939, on the other hand, it was obvious that the German Reich had fallen into the hands of very wicked men who offered the rest of Europe only the alternative of war or capitulation. The compassion which an English or American soldier might feel for his German fellow-sufferer was complicated by his conviction that the latter was suffering in an evil cause. It would have been impossible to write such a poem as Owen's "Strange Meeting."

The problem for a poet in writing about modern war is that, while he can only deal with events of which he has first-hand knowledge—invention, however imaginative, is bound to be fake—his poems must somehow transcend mere journalistic reportage. In a work of art, the single event must be seen as an element in a universally significant pattern:

the area of the pattern actually illuminated by the artist's vision is always, of course, more or less limited, but one is aware of its extending beyond what we see far into time and space.

For any American, this raises special difficulties. Until 1922, when immigration quotas were imposed, the United States was the New World, and to leave the Old for it expressed a decision to make a complete break with the past and begin history afresh. In trying to envision the present *sub specie aeternitate*, it is natural for a poet of the Old World to make use of whatever mythical and historical past is closest to him, as David Jones made use of Celtic Mythology in his great war book *In Parenthesis*. An American cannot. For Mr. Kirstein, History began in 1848 when his German-Jewish grandparents emigrated from the Rhineland: even had they been Aryan, he could not have used German mythological material, the *Niebelungen Lied* for example, without being false to them and to himself. For any American, the mythical war is the Civil War.

Yet my civil war's nearer than that war over the blue:
  World War II,
Which means zero to me save for drab facts which
                  inspire me to fear;
    I'm absurdly quite here
Trying hard to pretend our crack halfback lieutenant,
                  Bill Beady Eye,
Risks a charge under raking cross fire to let fly
    Carbines and a thin cheer.

At the same time, for all American intellectuals, the Old World had a fascination, an exotic cultural glamour. (Had. The States are no longer new, Europe no longer cultured.) For some it was France, for others, like Mr. Kirstein, England.

    Often Hamlet was Jim;
We got drunk on Shakespeare's iambics and Britain's
                  dynastic rainbow.
    I most remember him
Flipping the pages of portraits vignetted for the
                  London News—

The First War's English dead,
Glorious young men all, each a university graduate.
Fate haloed every head,
All officers, baron or baronet, not one a mere private;
History was alive.

Lacking a common mythological past, every American artist has, in weaving his pattern, to make use of a personal mythology which means that, in order to make this intelligible to others, he has to provide many more autobiographical facts than a European would need to. Pfc. Lincoln Kirstein is, as he tells us, a member of three minorities. (To a western European, the term *minority* has no emotional significance.) Firstly he is a Jew in a society which was, and still is, more anti-Semitic than it cares to admit. Secondly, his parents were assimilated enough and rich enough to send him to Exeter and Harvard, institutions almost exclusively Wasp; he has never known either the ghetto home life of New York Jews or the heterogeneous society of a State High School and University. Lastly, he is an intellectual aesthete who in childhood was, or believed himself to be, a sissy (again a term with no real European equivalent): consequently, his Lame Shadow, half worshipped, half despised, is a gentile inarticulate warrior-athlete. In peace time, relations between people of different educational backgrounds and cultural tastes are impossible or artificial; in war the only compensation for its discomforts and horrors is that such relations become possible, for in war there is only one significant social-psychological division, the one between officers and enlisted men. Mr. Kirstein relates his experiences in a roughly chronological order. He undergoes Basic Training in the States; for himself and his fellow draftees, the war still seems pretty remote, but mothers and wives are already beginning to receive regretful telegrams. He is shipped over to England, where he is billeted in a Manchester suburb and finds himself assigned to the Third Army. More training for the Invasion, the prospect of which looms steadily more menacing. He crosses the Channel twenty days after D Day, and is in the real terrifying thing. Though he never himself fires a shot, he is in close contact with combat troops, he comes under shell-fire, and he gets wounded, even if only in a jeep accident. With the Third Army, commanded by General Patton, whom he greatly admires, he enters Germany where he makes his one big contribution to the war effort. By a fantastic stroke of luck, he learns where the bulk of the art treasures looted by the Germans from all over Europe have been hidden.

His principal literary influences are, I should guess, Browning, Hardy, and Kipling. From the first he learns how to write a dramatic monologue, from Hardy and Kipling a fondness for complicated stanzas, which he handles with great virtuosity. How effective, for example, is the rhyming and the sudden lack of rhyme in the following:

We woke up early one morning. My! what a gorgeous
day!
We'd crossed Germany's borders to capture a German
May;
Strawberries-in-wine was the weather. All out-
doors smelled of fresh heather,
And my puffy captain had a lousy toothache.

The characters he meets and the stories he has to tell are of all kinds. Some are comic, like the Major who builds himself a fireplace out of liberated bricks which turn out to be made of dynamite. Others are ghastly, like the drunken Captain who kills an innocent civilian but, when it comes to his Court-Martial:

The charge was not murder, mayhem, mischief
malicious,
Yet something worse, and this they brought out time
and again:
Clearly criminal and caddishly vicious
Was his: Drinking With Enlisted Men.

Others, again, are concerned with sex, depicting it as the grubby activity which in wartime it usually is.

From Kipling, too, I think, he got the idea of trying to let his G. I.'s speak in their own low–very low–

style, and in this he is brilliantly successful as Kipling was not: Kipling's Tommies speak stage Cockney. Not being a born American and, therefore, not quite trusting my own conviction that Mr. Kirstein had gotten the speech right, I have tried the poems out on a number of people born and bred in the States, and they have all confirmed it. Again, as a born Englishman, I am astounded at his success. In England, during the nineteenth century, it was possible for writers like Barnes and Hardy, who were brought up in the country and lived all their lives there, to reproduce accurately their local rustic dialect, but no English writer who has had the equivalent of Mr. Kirstein's education—Winchester and New College, let us say—can ever hope to imitate the speech of another class.

That Mr. Kirstein should succeed is a credit, I think, not only to his ear, but to American culture; whatever its faults, it is at least not bedeviled by accent-consciousness. Not only can Mr. Kirstein reproduce "low" American speech; he also catches the subtle variations of vocabulary and intonation within it which distinguish one kind of character from another. Here are three examples.

I thought: Gloria, If Ize in some Christless spot

Who'd I turn to? Fred, natch. So the Least poor I could
do—
try and help Himmm. Hotel room in Norfolk with
Whooo
> *but a marine guard. Get the Picture? I had to get*
> *permission from his commandant before they'd let*
me Innn. They left the door Open so they could listen
and
needn't Buggg it. Now I begin to Understand
> *it's a Court-Martial offenssse; but—they better*
Be Sure
> *and Prove it. Just get us a good lawyer, but your*
Sainted Mother now found that Some people are just
Viiile.

Program formally opens as Fatso (tenor M.C.)
> *Brays "Rose Marie,"*
Shoots two lousy flat jokes. A fruity trombone introduces
> *La Tony,*
Who grabs at her cue. Dialogue goes
Sorta like this: "Hey you gotta fulla bag there, Rose
> *Marie sweetheart; what's" (rolling her eyes)*
> > *"you got in it?"*
> *"Just like you, sista: it's fulla shit."*
(Groans.) Now: the chorus. In tutus, six boys:
Indescribable noise.

We had 75's, 88's, 101's, evry fuckin gun you kin
think of
In hills back of this town, listenin fer one shot.
They hear this one shot.
Christ: we start to fire, just at roof level:
One, two, three.
Then we hit a leetle lower, a leetle lower—an lower.
Special, we pick out any tall tower, like a church
steeple.
One, two, three.
Man, was this cute! Like a typewriter:
One, two,
Three.

I shall not pretend that Mr. Kirstein's poetry is without faults. Any reader will notice passages which are clumsy, or prolix, or overloaded with adjectives, or too defiantly unfashionable. I cannot believe, however, that any poet, no matter how accomplished, will read these poems without admiration and envy. As a picture of the late war, *Rhymes of a Pfc.* is by far the most convincing, moving, and impressive book I have come across.